Egyptian
Arabic

A ROUGH GUIDE
PHRASEBOOK

Compiled
by Lexus

D1444482

Credits

Compiled by Lexus with Ahmed M. A. Abdel-Hady

Lexus Series Editor: Sally Davies
Rough Guides Phrasebook Editor: Jonathan Buckley
Rough Guides Series Editor: Mark Ellingham

This first edition published in 1998 by Rough Guides Ltd, 1 Mercer Street, London WC2H 9QJ.

Distributed by the Penguin Group.

Penguin Books Ltd, 27 Wrights Lane, London W8 5TZ
Penguin Books USA Inc., 375 Hudson Street, New York 10014, USA
Penguin Books Australia Ltd, 487 Maroondah Highway, PO Box 257, Ringwood, Victoria 3134, Australia
Penguin Books Canada Ltd, Alcorn Avenue, Toronto, Ontario, Canada M4V 1E4
Penguin Books (NZ) Ltd, 182–190 Wairau Road, Auckland 10, New Zealand

Typeset in Rough Serif and Rough Sans to an original design by Henry Iles. Printed by Cox & Wyman Ltd, Reading.

British Library Cataloguing in Publication Data
A catalogue for this book is available from the British Library.

ISBN 1-85828-319-1

CONTENTS

HELP US GET IT RIGHT

Lexus and Rough Guides have made great efforts to be accurate and
informative in this Rough Guide Egyptian Arabic phrasebook. However,
if you feel we have overlooked a useful word or phrase, or have any
other comments to make about the book, please let us know. All
contributors will be acknowledged and the best letters will be
rewarded with a free Rough Guide phrasebook of your choice. Please
write to 'Egyptian Arabic Phrasebook Update', at either Mercer Street
(London) or Hudson Street (New York) – for full address see opposite.
Alternatively you can email us at mail@roughguides.co.uk

Online information about Rough Guides can be found at our website
www.roughguides.com

INTRODUCTION

The Rough Guide Egyptian Arabic phrasebook is a highly practical introduction to the contemporary language. Laid out in clear A-Z style, it uses key-word referencing to lead you straight to the words and phrases you want – so if you need to book a room, just look up 'room'. The Rough Guide gets straight to the point in every situation, in bars and shops, on trains and buses, and in hotels and banks.

The first part of the Rough Guide is a section called **The Basics**, which sets out the fundamental rules of the language and its pronunciation, with plenty of practical examples. You'll also find here other essentials like numbers, dates, telling the time and basic phrases.

Forming the heart of the guide, the **English-Arabic** section gives easy-to-use transliterations of the Arabic words plus the text in Arabic script, so that if the pronunciation proves too tricky, you can simply indicate what you want to say. To get you involved quickly in two-way communication, the Rough Guide also includes dialogues featuring typical responses on key topics – such as renting a room and asking directions. Feature boxes fill you in on cultural pitfalls as well as the simple mechanics of how to make a phone call, what to do in an emergency, where to change money, and more. Throughout this section, cross-references enable you to pinpoint key facts and phrases, while asterisked words indicate where further information can be found in The Basics.

The **Arabic-English** section is in two parts: a dictionary, arranged phonetically, of all the words and phrases you're likely to hear (starting with a section of slang and colloquialisms); then a compilation, arranged by subject, of all the signs, labels, instructions and other basic words you might come across in print or in public places.

Finally the Rough Guide rounds off with an extensive **Menu Reader**. Consisting of food and drink sections arranged by subject (each starting with a list of essential terms), it's indispensable whether you're eating out, stopping for a quick drink, or browsing through a local food market.

رحلة سعيدة!

reHla saAeeda!

have a good trip!

The Basics

PRONUNCIATION

Throughout this book, Arabic words have been transliterated into romanized form so that they can be read as though they were English bearing in mind the notes on pronunciation given below:

Vowels

a	as in **at**	ī	sounds like **eye** or like the **ai** in Th**ai**
ā	longer **a** as in c**ar**		
ay	as in s**ay**	o	as in h**ot**
e	as in b**ed**	ō	**oa** as in m**oan**
ee	as in s**ee**	ow	as in n**ow**
i	as in b**it**		

Consonants

h	is always pronounced, except in the following combinations: gh, kh, sh and th	J	like the **s** in lei**s**ure
		kh	like the **ch** in the Scottish word lo**ch**
j	as in **j**am	r	strongly rolled **r**
		s	as in mi**ss**

When double consonants such as **bb** or **mm** occur, both letters should be pronounced.

Capitals D, S, T and Z are like d, s, t and z only more heavily pronounced.

Special Sounds

A	**aargh** sound, said from the throat, a heavy forced **a**
gh	like a French **r**
H	an emphatic **h**, said from the back of the throat
Q	similar to an emphatic pronunciation of 'cu' as in **cut**, said from the back of the throat
'	a glottal stop, similar to that heard in regional forms of English when the letter 't' is not pronounced; for example, 'wa'er' for 'water'.

Q and ' represent the same letter in Egyptian Arabic, known as the 'qaf'; however, when represented by Q, it is more strongly pronounced.

Letters given in bold type indicate the part of the word to be stressed.

ABBREVIATIONS

adj	adjective	m	masculine
f	feminine	pl	plural
lit	literally	sing	singular

ARABIC AND THE ARABIC ALPHABET

Classical Arabic, the universal written language of the entire Arabic-speaking world, is rarely spoken. Colloquial Arabic is the spoken language and its grammar, pronunciation and vocabulary vary between countries. The colloquial Arabic used in this book is Egyptian.

Arabic is written from right to left. Each letter of the alphabet has up to four different forms: one where it stands alone, one at the beginning of a word, one in the middle of a word and one when it is the final letter. The alphabet as listed below consists almost entirely of consonants; Arabic words do not contain written short vowels (although the long vowels are written). Words consist of a string of consonants and the Arabic speaker knows from experience how the vowels must be added in speech to make sense. Sometimes, therefore the same written word can often be pronounced in more than one way, but usually only one version makes sense in a particular context.

Isolated	Initial	Medial	Final	Pronounced
أ	ا ، أ	ا	ا	a
ب	بـ	ـبـ	ـب	b
ت	تـ	ـتـ	ـت	t
ث	ثـ	ـثـ	ـث	th
ج	جـ	ـجـ	ـج	g

Isolated	Initial	Medial	Final	Pronounced
ح	حـ	ـحـ	ـح	H
خ	خـ	ـخـ	ـخ	kh
د			ـد	d
ذ			ـذ	th
ر			ـر	r
ز			ـز	z
س	سـ	ـسـ	ـس	s
ش	شـ	ـشـ	ـش	sh
ص	صـ	ـصـ	ـص	S
ض	ضـ	ـضـ	ـض	D
ط	طـ	ـطـ	ـط	T
ظ	ظـ	ـظـ	ـظ	Z
ع	عـ	ـعـ	ـع	A
غ	غـ	ـغـ	ـغ	gh
ف	فـ	ـفـ	ـف	f
ق	قـ	ـقـ	ـق	Q or '
ك	كـ	ـكـ	ـك	k
ل	لـ	ـلـ	ـل	l
م	مـ	ـمـ	ـم	m
ن	نـ	ـنـ	ـن	n
ة	هـ	ـهـ	ـة ه	h
و			ـو	w
ى	يـ	ـيـ	ـى	y

NOUNS

Gender

All Arabic nouns have one of two genders – masculine or feminine. Most nouns ending in **-a** are feminine:

m**a**ktaba	library
ahwa	coffee; café
gars**o**na	waitress

Some nouns that do not end in **-a** are feminine:

bint	girl
omm	mother
shams	sun
floos	money

The names of many countries, cities and parts of the body are feminine:

ma**s**r	Egypt
aswãn	Aswan
T**a**nTa	Tanta
rãs	head
rigl	leg
eed	hand

Feminine nouns that do not end in **-a** and are not obviously feminine are marked (f) in the English-Arabic section of this book.

Some masculine nouns end in **-a**; these are also indicated in the English-Arabic section:

howa	air (m)

All other nouns that do not end in **-a** or fall into the above categories can be assumed to be masculine.

Construct Form

Some rules require the final **-a** of a feminine noun to be replaced by **-it** when two nouns are used together. This is known as the construct form:

tarab**a**yza	table
akl	food

    tarab**a**yzit el akl
    the food table

t**a**zkara	ticket
T**ī**yãra	plane

    t**a**zkarit el Tīyãra
    the plane ticket

The construct form is also used to form the plural of some words (see opposite); it is also used with possessive suffixes (see page 12).

Plurals of Nouns

There are three types of plural in Arabic. The dual, the standard and the collective plural.

Dual Plural

This is used when referring to two of anything. It is formed by adding a suffix to the singular form of the noun.

To form the dual plural for masculine nouns and feminine nouns that do not end in **-a**, add **-ayn** to the noun:

mat-Haf	museum
mat-Hafayn	two museums

aTr	train
aTrayn	two trains

To form the dual plural for feminine nouns ending in **-a**, remove the final **-a** and add **-tayn**:

ezaza	bottle
ezaztayn	two bottles

madrasa	school
madrastayn	two schools

Aarabayya	car
Aarabaytayn	two cars

For some nouns, the dual plural is formed by adding **-ayn** to the construct form:

sha'a	flat
sha'itayn	two flats

gizma	shoe
gizmitayn	two shoes

Standard Plural

To form this, add **-een** to masculine nouns:

farrān	baker
farraneen	bakers

Add **-t** to feminine nouns and change the final **a** to **ā**:

magalla	magazine
magallāt	magazines

Collective Plural

This plural is used to describe a whole class or group of items and it mostly occurs with fruit and vegetables collectively and generally. The collective plural of fruit and vegetables is more widely used than the singular or standard plural. If you need to refer to a singular item, you can do so by adding **-a** to the collective form:

toffāH (pl)	apples
toffāHa (sing)	an apple
khayār	cucumbers
khayāra	a cucumber

The singular and standard plural forms of these types of noun are only used if it is necessary to specify the number of items:

	collective plural
mishmish	apricots
	singular
mishmisha	an apricot
	standard plural
talat mishmishāt	three apricots

Further examples of the collective form are:

bayD	eggs	shaAr	hair
samak	fish	shagar	trees

Irregular Plurals

Many Arabic nouns have irregular plurals. Here is a list of the most common ones:

singular		plural	
shanTa	bag	shonaT	bags
'bank'	bank	bnook	banks
sireer	bed	saráyer	beds
Hizām	belt	Hizima	belts
kitāb	book	kotob	books
walad	boy	welād	boys
akh	brother	ekhwāt	brothers
gamal	camel	gimāl	camels
korsee	chair	karāsee	chairs
sigāra	cigarette	sagāyer	cigarettes
sitāra	curtain	satāyer	curtains
yōm	day	īyām	days
sāHib	friend	soHāb	friends
bint	girl	banāt	girls
fondo'	hotel	fanādi'	hotels
bayt	house	byoot	houses
moftāH	key	mafāteeH	keys
gowāb	letter	gowabāt	letters
rāgil	man	riggāla	men
de'ee'a	minute	da'āye'	minutes
shahr	month	shihoor	months
gāmiA	mosque	gawāmiA	mosques
mat-Haf	museum	matāHif	museums
ism	name	asāmee	names
maktab	office	makātib	offices
Taba'	plate	aTba'	plates
ōDa	room	ewaD	rooms
TābeA	stamp	TawābeA	stamps
shāriA	street	shawāriA	streets
Tālib	student	Talaba	students
tazkara	ticket	tazākir	tickets
madeena	town	modon	towns

| aTr | train | 'oTora | trains |
| isbooA | week | asābeeA | weeks |

ARTICLES

The definite article (the) is **el**:

magalla   magazine   el magalla   the magazine

When the noun begins with **d, D, n, r, s, S, sh, t, T, z** or **Z**, the **l** is omitted from **el** and the initial consonant of the noun is lengthened. This change is optional for the letters **g** and **k**.

Some examples of nouns where **el** is assimilated:

| SobH | morning | eS-SobH | the morning |
| Taboor | queue | eT-Taboor | the queue |

The form of **el** also changes when it is used with some prepositions:

bee (by) + el = **bil**
  bil gow   by air

fee (in; per) + el = **fil**
  fil baHr   in the sea
  fil maya   per cent
  fil ezāza   per bottle

lee (to) + el = **lil**
  lil maTār   to the airport
  lil fondo'   to the hotel
  lil o'sor   to Luxor

Aala (on) + el = **Aalal**
  Aalal blāj   on the beach
  Aalal korsee   on the chair

There is no indefinite article in Arabic. For example:

fondo' can mean 'hotel' or 'a hotel'

magalla can mean 'magazine' or 'a magazine'

ADJECTIVES

Adjectives come after the noun they describe and agree with the noun in gender and number. The masculine form of the adjective is given in the English-Arabic and Arabic-English sections of this book. The feminine of adjectives is formed by adding **-a** to the masculine:

masculine	feminine	
beAeed	beAeeda	far
kebeer	kebeera	big

el mat-Haf beАeed	el gamАa beАeeda
the museum is far	the university is far
bayt kebeer	sha'a kebeera
a big house	a big apartment

Adjectives ending in **-ee** (for example, adjectives of nationality), change as shown below for the feminine:

masculine	feminine	
amrekānee	amrekanaya	American
Аarabee	Аarabaya	Arab
ostrālee	ostralaya	Australian
kanadee	kanadaya	Canadian
maSree	maSraya	Egyptian
ingleezee	ingleezaya	English

If you use **awee** (very) with an adjective then this always follows the adjective it refers to:

el aTr sareeА awee	the train is very quick

If the definite article is used then it must be repeated in front of the adjective(s) that refer to the noun:

el maHatta er-ra'eesaya	the main station
el mat-Haf el Qowmee	the national museum
el gizma es-sōda	the black shoes

Plural Adjectives

If a plural noun refers to people then the plural form of the adjective must be used. To form this, add **-een** to the singular adjective:

sing	plural	
momtāz	momtāzeen	excellent
Tabbākheen momtāzeen		excellent chefs

If a plural noun refers to inanimate objects, the feminine singular form of the adjective must be used (irrespective of the gender of the noun):

feminine	byoot kebeera	big houses

masculine	otobeesāt sareeʌa	fast buses

A dual plural noun should always be followed by a plural adjective, for example:

a'lamayn kobār	two large pens

Irregular Plural Adjectives

Many plural adjectives are irregular. Here is a list of the most common ones:

singular	plural	
gameel	gomāl	beautiful
rekhees	rokhās	cheap
neDeef	noDāf	clean
aleel	olāl	few
kebeer	kobār	large
adeem	odām	old (objects, buildings etc)
aHmar	Homr	red
soghīyar	soghār	small
shedeed	shodād	strong

Comparatives and Superlatives

The comparative (more expensive, bigger etc) and superlative (best, biggest etc) forms of the adjective are the same in Arabic. They do not change according to either gender or number.

Some common comparatives and superlatives are as follows:

adjective		comparative/superlative
weHesh	bad	awHash	worse/worst
gameel	beautiful	agmal	more/most beautiful
kebeer	big	akbar	bigger/biggest
rekhees	cheap	arkhaS	cheaper/cheapest
ghālee	expensive	aghla	more/most expensive
beʌeed	far	abʌad	further/furthest
kwayis	good	aHsan	better/best
keteer	many	aktar	more/most
Helw	nice; pretty	aHla	nicer/nicest; prettier/prettiest
soghīyar	small	aSghar	smaller/smallest

shemm**ā**ma **a**kbar   a bigger melon
el shemm**ā**ma el **a**kbar   the bigger/biggest melon

To compare two things, use the comparative form of the adjective and **min** (than):

abʌad min   further than

aswān **a**bʌad min **a**syooт
Aswan is further (away) than Asiut

DEMONSTRATIVES

Demonstrative pronouns and adjectives are as follows:

da   this (one); that (one)
       (m sing)
dee   this (one); that (one)
       (f sing); these; those
       (referring to objects or animals)
dōl   these; those (referring to
       people)

Demonstratives agree in number and gender with the noun they refer to. The word order when using demonstratives is:

el + noun + demonstrative
    adjective

el **ga**mal da   this/that camel
el ez**ā**za dee   this/that bottle

es-sow**ā**'een dōl
these/those drivers

es-sett**a**t dōl
these/those women

el н**ī**wanāt dee
these/those animals

When the gender of a demonstrative is uncertain, then either **dee** or **da** may be used:

dee/da **a**нsan
that's better

momkin **a**khod dee/da?
can I have that one?

POSSESSIVES

Possessive adjectives are not separate words in Arabic; they are in the form of suffixes that are added to the noun to indicate the possessive. They are added either to a masculine noun or to the construct form of a feminine noun (see page 6).

The possessive suffixes are:

-ee	my	-ha	her
-ak	your (m sing)	-na	our
-ik	your (f sing)	-koo	your (pl)
-oo	his	-hom	their

alamee	my pen
tazkartak	your ticket (said to a man)
tazkartik	your ticket (said to a woman)
Aarabayyitna	our car
bayt-hom	their house

Possession can also be expressed using **btãA** (of). There are different forms of **btãA**, depending on whether the object possessed is masculine or feminine. These forms are also used to express the possessive pronoun (mine, yours etc):

m object	f object	
btãAee	**btaAtee**	my; mine
btãAak	**btaAtak**	your; yours (to a man)
btãAik	**btaAtik**	your; yours (to a woman)
btãAoo	**btaAtoo**	his
btaAha	**btaAit-ha**	her; hers
btaAna	**btaAitna**	our; ours
btaakoo	**btaAitkoo**	your; yours (pl)
btaAhom	**btaAit-hom**	their; theirs

The word order is: definite article + noun + **btãA**

el **gizma btaAtee**	my shoe; the shoe is mine
el **korsee btaAee**	my chair; the chair is mine
dee btaAtee! (f)	that/this is mine!
el **kitãb btãAee**	my book; the book is mine
el **bayt btãAee**	my house; the house is mine

btãA should only be used for objects and animals, not when referring to people. For example, to say 'my father' you must use the suffix form of the possessive on page 12. **btãA** should always be used with any word that originates from a foreign language:

el **forsha btaAtee**	my toothbrush

PRONOUNS

Subject Pronouns

Subject pronouns are as follows:

ana	I	**ha**yya	she; it
inta	you (m sing)	**eH**na	we
inti	you (f sing)	**in**too	you (pl)
howa	he; it	**hom**ma	they

In Arabic, subject pronouns may be omitted when the form of
the verb makes it obvious who the subject of the sentence is.
ana (I) is most likely to be omitted:

kat**a**bt	I wrote

Direct and Indirect Object Pronouns

Direct object (me, you etc) or indirect object (to me, to you etc)
personal pronouns in Arabic are in the form of suffixes that are
added to the verb:

direct object		indirect object	
-ee	me	-nee	to me
-ak	you (m sing)	-lak	to you (m sing)
-ik	you (f sing)	-lik	to you (f sing)
-oo	him; it	-loo	to him; to it
-ha	her; it	-lha	to her; to it
-na	us	-lina	to us
-koo	you (pl)	-likoo	to you (pl)
-hom	them	-lihom	to them

sallimt Aa**lay**hom
I greeted them

ba**Heb**boo/ba**Heb**baha (m/f)
I like it

Hadd**ee**lak/Hadd**ee**lik el
wa**H**da be**kham**sa gen**eeh**
(to man/woman)
I'll give it to you for five
pounds

When a sentence contains
both direct and indirect object
pronouns, the word order is
the same as in English:

verb + direct object +
indirect object

ed**dee**hanee! give it to me!

Pronouns and Prepositions

Pronoun suffixes are often added to prepositions. The suffixes vary depending on whether the preposition ends in a consonant or a vowel:

Aalashān	for	maΛa	with
Aalashā-nee	for me	maΛā-ya	with me
Aalashān-ak	for you (m sing)	maΛā-k	with you (m sing)
Aalashān-ik	for you (f sing)	maΛā-ik	with you (f sing)
Aalashān-oo	for him	maΛā-h	with him
Aalashan-ha	for her	maΛā-ha	with her
Aalashan-na	for us	maΛā-na	with us
Aalashan-koo	for you (pl)	maΛā-koo	with you (pl)
Aalashan-hom	for them	maΛā-hom	with them

The same endings can be used with these words:

min	from
zay	like
Aala	on; against

da min-noo that's from him

hayya Taweela **zay**ik
she's tall like you

da Aalashanhom?
is that for them?

'OF'

Phrases such as 'the name of the street' are expressed as follows:

noun (possessed) + el +
noun (possessor)

ism esh-shariAa
the name of the street

Ainwān el mat-Haf
the address of the museum

raQam el otobees
the number of the bus

Feminine nouns that are possessed are in the construct form (see page 6):

shanTit el bint
the girl's bag

To make the phrase indefinite, omit the definite article:

Hettit Aaysh
a piece of bread

maHaTTit otobees
a bus stop

VERBS

Basic Verb Forms

There is no infinitive (to do, to buy etc) in Arabic. Instead, the basic form of the verb (the root) is the perfect tense of the third person masculine singular. This form is shown in the first column in the table of Arabic verbs below.

Where in English sentences you would use an infinitive, in Arabic, both verbs must agree with the subject of the sentence:

> Aīzeen nakol
> we want to eat

The table shows the basic form of the verb (third person masculine singular, perfect tense) and the first person singular of the two Arabic tenses (see pages 17–18):

third person sing, perfect	first person sing, imperfect	first person sing, perfect	
sa'al	as'al	sa'alt	ask
kan		kont	be*
edir	a'dar	edirt	be able to
bada'	abda'	bada't	begin
gab	ageeb	gibt	bring
ishtara	ashteree	ishtarayt	buy
ga	'āgee	gayt	come*
sharab	ashrab	sharabt	drink
kal	'ākol	kalt	eat
edda	addee	iddayt	give
rāH	arooH	roHt	go*
	Aandee		have*
Aaraf	aAraf	Aaraft	know
Hab	aHebb	Habbayt	like; love
boss	aboSS	baSSayt	look
Aamal	aAmil	Aamalt	make; do
HaT	aHoT	HaTayt	put
'āl	a'ool	olt	say; tell
shāf	ashoof	shoft	see
nām	anām	nimt	sleep

itkallim	atkallim	kallimt	speak
khad	ākhod	khat	take
fakkar	afakkar	fakkart	think
fehim	afham	fehimt	understand*
mishee	imshee	mishayt	walk; go away
Aāz	Aayiz	Aozt	want*
ishtaghal	ashtaghal	ishtaghalt	work

* see pages 19–21

Tenses

There are only two true tenses of the verb in Arabic: the imperfect (indicates incomplete action in the present or the future) and the perfect (indicates completed action in the past). Whether the present or future is meant, is indicated by the different prefixes added to the imperfect verb form.

Imperfect Tense

The imperfect tense is formed by adding prefixes and suffixes to the verb stem. To obtain the verb stem, remove the initial **a-** from the first person singular imperfect form in the table opposite:

ashrab (I drink) gives the stem **-shrab**

The basic conjugation is obtained by adding the following prefixes and suffixes to the stem. If you want to form a present tense verb you also have to add the prefix **bi-**.

verb stem **-shrab**
prefix/suffix

a-	**a**shrab	I drink
ti-	**ti**shrab	you drink (m sing)
ti-...-ee	**ti**shrab**ee**	you drink (f sing)
yi-	**yi**shrab	he drinks
ti-	**ti**shrab	she drinks
ni-	**ni**shrab	we drink
ti-...-oo	**ti**shrab**oo**	you drink (pl)
yi-...-oo	**yi**shrab**oo**	they drink

TIME

You will find that sometimes the first vowel of the verb is pronounced or transliterated as **e** or **i** in different verbs, depending on the actual sound of the word.

Present Usage

The imperfect conjugation is used for the equivalent of the present tense. The prefix **bi-** is added to the forms of the imperfect tense to indicate that the action is taking place in the present:

verb stem **-shrab**

b**a**shrab	I drink
b**i**t**i**shrab	you drink (m sing)
b**i**t**i**shrabee	you drink (f sing)
b**a**y**e**shrab	he drinks
b**i**t**i**shrab	she drinks
b**i**n**i**shrab	we drink

b**i**t**i**shraboo	you drink (pl)
b**a**y**e**shraboo	they drink

Future Usage

To indicate that an action will take place in the future, use the imperfect conjugation as on page 17 and modify it as follows, adding the prefix **Ha-**:

verb stem **-shrab**

Hashrab	I will drink
Hat**i**shrab	you will drink (m sing)
Hat**i**shrabee	you will drink (f sing)
Hishrab	he will drink
Hat**i**shrab	she will drink
Hanishrab	we will drink
Hat**i**shraboo	you will drink (pl)
Hishraboo	they will drink

Perfect Tense

The perfect tense is used to indicate completed action in the past. It is the equivalent of the simple past and the perfect tense in English. Therefore, '**ana kallimtoo**' translates as 'I spoke to him' or 'I have spoken to him' depending on the context.

The perfect tense is formed by adding suffixes to the third person masculine singular form.

Most verbs follow the pattern of the perfect conjugation below:

verb stem **katab-**
suffix

-t	kat**a**bt	I wrote, I have written
-t	kat**a**bt	you wrote, you have written (m sing)
-tee	kat**a**btee	you wrote, you have written (f sing)

	katab	he wrote, he has written
-it	**ka**tabit	she wrote, she has written
-na	ka**tab**na	we wrote, we have written
-too	katab**too**	you wrote, you have written (pl)
-oo	kata**boo**	they wrote, you have written

Exceptions are the verbs 'give', 'like' and 'put'. For these, re-move **-ayt** from the forms in the perfect column on pages 16–17 to obtain the verb stem and then add the following suffixes:

verb stem **idd-**
suffix

-ayt	idd**ayt**	I gave, I have given
-ayt	idd**ayt**	you gave, you have given (m sing)
-aytee	idd**aytee**	you gave, you have given (f sing)
	idda	he gave, he has given
-it	**idd**it	she gave, she has given
-ayna	idd**ayna**	we gave, we have given
-aytoo	idd**aytoo**	you gave, you have given (pl)
-oo	**idd**oo	they gave, they have given

'To Be'

There is no present tense of the verb 'to be' in Arabic:

agaztak **i**mta? (to man)
when is your vacation?
lit: vacation your (suffix) when

ana min iskinder**a**ya
I'm from Alexandria
lit: I from Alexandria

el **ma**t-Haf el **ma**sree kebeer
the Egyptian Museum is big
lit: the museum the Egyptian big

kit**ā**bak da?
is this your book?
lit: book your (suffix) this

In the past tense the verb 'to be' is as follows:

ana kont	I was
inta kont	you were (m sing)
inti **k**ontee	you were (f sing)
howa kan	he was; it was
hayya k**ā**nit	she was; it was
e**H**na **k**onna	we were
intoo **k**ontoo	you were (pl)
homma ka**noo**	they were

| kanoo fayn homma? | where were they? |
| kānit fayn? | where was it? |

Negatives are formed in the standard way (see page 22):

| inti makonteesh | you weren't |
| homma makanoosh | they weren't |

Note the following:

fee	there is; there are
mafeesh	there isn't; there aren't
kan fee	there was; there were
makansh fee	there wasn't; there weren't

'To Have'

The preposition **Aand** is used with the possessive suffixes to form the present tense of 'to have':

Aandee	I have
Aandak	you have (m sing)
Aandik	you have (f sing)
Aandoo	he has
Aandaha	she has
Aandina	we have
Aandokoo	you have (pl)
Aandohom	they have

The future tense of 'to have' is formed by adding the word **Hīkoon** before the present tense forms:

| Hīkoon Aandee | I will have |
| Hīkoon Aandak | you will have etc |

The past tense of 'to have' is formed by adding the word **kan** before the present tense forms:

| kan Aandee | I had |
| kan Aandak | you had etc |

'To Want'

The equivalent of the present tense of 'to want' (for all singular conjugations) is Aayiz (if the subject is masculine) and Aiza (if the subject is feminine). Aizeen is used for all plural forms.

Negatives are formed by adding **mish**:

mish Aayiz ahwa   I don't want coffee

The past tense of 'to want' is as follows:

kont Aayiz	I wanted (m)
kont Aiza	I wanted (f)
kont Aayiz	you wanted (m sing)
kontee Aiza	you wanted (f sing)
kan Aayiz	he wanted
kanit Aiza	she wanted
konna Aizeen	we wanted
kontoo Aizeen	you wanted (pl)
kanoo Aizeen	they wanted

The negative is:

makontish Aayiz	I didn't want (m)
makontish Aiza	I didn't want (f)
makontish Aayiz	you didn't want (m sing)
makonteesh Aiza	you didn't want (f sing)
makanshee Aayiz	he didn't want
makanitshee Aiza	she didn't want
makonnash Aizeen	we didn't want
makontoosh Aizeen	you didn't want (pl)
makanoosh Aizeen	they didn't want

'To Come', 'To Go', 'To Understand'

The following are often used as alternatives to the usual present tense:

	come	go	understand
all m sing forms	gī	rīeH	fāhim
all f sing forms	gīya	rīHa	fahma
all plural forms	gīyeen	rīHeen	fahmeen

For example:

ana rīeH   I'm going
inti fahma?   do you understand?

To make these negative, add the word **mish** before the verbal form:

ana mish rīeH   I'm not going

Negatives

To form the negative, add the **ma-** to the beginning of the verb and **-sh** to the end:

bashrab   I drink
mabashrabsh   I don't drink
Aamalt   I did
maAamaltish   I haven't
               done

Another way of making a verb negative is to place the word **mish** before the verb:

ana māshee   I am going
mish māshee   I am not going

There are a few verbs which must take the **mish** form of the negative. For example, 'to want' and the alternative of the present tense mentioned above i.e. 'to go', 'to come' and 'to understand'.

mish rīeH   I am not going
mish fāhim   I don't under-
               stand
mish gīya   I am not coming

Imperative

To form an imperative, take the second person singular or plural of the imperfect tense and remove the initial **t-**:

ishrab!   drink up!

Some other useful imperatives are:

o'Aod!   sit down!
warrehālee   show it to me
estanna hena   stay here
imshee!   go away!
o'af!   stop!
taAala hena!   come here!

To form the negative imperative take the second person singular or plural of the verb in the imperfect tense and add **ma-** at the beginning and **-sh** at the end:

matroHsh!   don't go!
matestannash   don't wait
matbossish   don't look

QUESTIONS

To change a statement into a question, use the same intonation at the end as you would in English:

> da toHfa
> it's an antique

> da toHfa?
> it's an antique?

Interrogatives

fayn?	where?	lay?	why?
imta?	when?	izzay?	how?

Interrogatives usually come at the end of a question. They are sometimes used at the beginning of a sentence for special emphasis:

> el mat-Haf fayn?
> OR fayn el mat-Haf?
> where is the museum?

DATES

In business, Egypt uses the Western calendar; for Islamic holidays and festivals, legal and state affairs the lunar calendar is used (see public holidays pages 153–4).

Use the numbers on pages 25–6 to form dates. For the first of the month, the ordinal can also be used. The word order for dates is:

> day + month + year

Thus:

8 February 1998
tamania fibrīyer alf we tisAomaya tamania we tisAeen
lit: eight February thousand and nine hundred eight and ninety

5 September
khamsa sebtambir

27 December 1998
sabAa we Aishreen disambir alf we tosAomaya tamania we tisAeen

DAYS

Monday	yōm el itnayn	يوم الإثنين
Tuesday	yōm et-talāt	يوم الثّلاث
Wednesday	yōm el arbaA	يوم الأربع
Thursday	yōm el khamees	يوم الخميس
Friday	yōm el gomAa	يوم الجمعة
Saturday	yōm es-sabt	يوم السبت
Sunday	yōm el Had	يوم الحدّ

MONTHS

January	yanāyer	يناير
February	fībrīyer	فبراير
March	māris	مارس
April	ibreel	إبريل
May	māyo	مايو
June	yonyo	يونيو
July	yolyo	يوليو
August	aghosTos	أغسطس
September	sebtamber	سبتمبر
October	oktōbar	أكتوبر
November	novamber	نوفمبر
December	disamber	ديسمبر

TIME

what time is it? es-sāAa kam?
(it's) one o'clock es-sāAa waHda
(it's) two o'clock es-sāAa itnayn
at one o'clock es-sāAa waHda
at two o'clock es-sāAa itnayn

five past one es-sāAa waHda
  we khamsa
ten past two es-sāAa itnayn
  we Aashara
quarter past one es-sāAa
  waHda we robA
quarter past two es-sāAa itnayn

we robA
half past two es-sāAa itnayn
 we nos
half past ten es-sāAa Aashara
 we nos
twenty to one waHda illa tilt
twenty to ten Aashara illa tilt
quarter to one waHda illa robA
quarter to two itnayn illa robA
am es-SobH
pm (in the afternoon) baAd eD-
 Dohr
 (in the evening) bil layl
2am es-sāAa itnayn es-SobH
2pm es-sāAa itnayn
6am es-sāAa sitta es-SobH
6pm es-sāAa sitta bil layl
10am es-sāAa Aashara es-SobH
10pm es-sāAa Aashara bil layl
noon eD-Dohr
midnight nos el layl
hour sāAa
minute de'ee'a
second sanya
two minutes de'i'tayn
quarter of an hour robA sāAa
half an hour nos sāAa
three quarters of an hour talat
 erbaA sāAa

NUMBERS

For numbers above ten
(except multiples of ten), **we**
(and) is used. Thus, 31 is
wāHid we talateen (literally
one and thirty), 27 is sabAa we
Aishreen (literally seven and
twenty) and so on.

0	Sifr	•
1	wāHid (m), waHda (f)	١
2	itnayn	٢
3	talāta	٣
4	arbaAa	٤
5	khamsa	٥
6	sitta	٦
7	sabAa	٧
8	tamania	٨
9	tisAa	٩
10	Aashara	١٠
11	Hidāshar	١١
12	itnāshar	١٢
13	talattāshar	١٣
14	arbaAtāshar	١٤
15	khamastāshar	١٥
16	sittāshar	١٦
17	sabaAtāshar	١٧
18	tamantāshar	١٨
19	tisaAtāshar	١٩
20	Aishreen	٢٠
21	wāHid we Aishreen	٢١
22	itnayn we Aishreen	٢٢
30	talateen	٣٠
31	wāHid we talateen	٣١
32	itnayn we talateen	٣٢
40	arbiAeen	٤٠

41	wāHid we arbiAeen	٤١
50	khamseen	٥٠
51	wāHid we khamseen	٥١
60	sitteen	٦٠
70	sabAeen	٧٠
80	tamaneen	٨٠
90	tisAeen	٩٠
100	maya	١٠٠
101	maya we wāHid	١٠١
102	maya witnayn	١٠٢
103	maya we talāta	١٠٣
104	maya we arbaAa	١٠٤
105	maya we khamsa	١٠٥
200	mitayn	٢٠٠

300	toltomaya	٣٠٠
400	robAomaya	٤٠٠
500	khomsomaya	٥٠٠
600	sittoomaya	٦٠٠
700	sobAomaya	٧٠٠
800	tomnomaya	٨٠٠
900	tisAomaya	٩٠٠
1,000	alf	١٠٠٠
2,000	alfayn	٢٠٠٠
3,000	talat talāf	٣٠٠٠
10,000	Aashar talāf	١٠٠٠٠
50,000	khamseen alf	٥٠٠٠٠
1,000,000	milyōn	١٠٠٠٠٠٠

Ordinals

	masculine	feminine	masculine	feminine
1st	el owil	el oola	الأوّل	الأُولى
2nd	et-tānee	et-tania	التاني	التانية
3rd	et-tālit	et-talta	التالت	التالتة
4th	er-rābiA	er-rabAa	الرابع	الرابعة
5th	el khāmis	el khamsa	الخامس	الخامسة
6th	es-sāddis	es-sadsa	السادس	السادسة
7th	es-sābiA	es-sabAa	السابع	السابعة
8th	et-tāmin	et-tamna	التامن	التامنة
9th	et-tāsiA	et-tassAa	التاسع	التاسعة
10th	el Aāshir	el Aashra	العاشر	العاشرة

BASIC PHRASES

yes īwa
أيوه

no la'
لأ

OK kwayis
كويس

hello ahlan
أهلاً

(answer on phone) aloo
ألو

good morning sabāH el khayr
صباح الخير

good evening masā' el khayr
مساء الخير

good night masā' el khayr
مساء الخير

goodbye maAassalāma
مع السلامة

see you! netlā'a baAdayn!
نتلاقى بعدين!

see you later ashoofak
baAdayn
أشوفك بعدين

please (to man/woman) low
samaHt/samaHtee
لو سمحت/سمحتى

yes, please īwa, low samaHt/
samaHtee
أيوه لو سمحت/سمحتى

could you please …? momkin
… low samaHt/samaHtee?
ممكن …لو سمحت/
سمحتى؟

please don't ma … low
samaHt/samaHtee
ما …لو سمحت/
سمحتى

thanks, thank you shokran
شكراً

thank you very much shokran
giddan
شكراً جدّاً

no thanks la' motshakkir
لأ متشكر

don't mention it el Aafw
العفو

how do you do? (to man/woman)
Aāmil/Aāmla ay?
عامل/عاملة إيه؟

how are you? (to man/woman) izzayak/izzayik?

إزَّيك / إزَّيك؟

fine, thanks, and you? (to man/woman) bekhayr, shokran, winta/winti?

بخير، شكراً، وإنتَ/ وإنتِ؟

pleased to meet you tsharrafna

تشرّفنا

excuse me (to get past: to man/woman) low samaHt/samaHtee

لو سمحت/سمحتى

(to get attention) min faDlak

من فضلك

(to say sorry: said by man/woman) ana āsif/āsfa

أنا آسف/آسفة

I'm sorry (said by man/woman) ana āsif/āsfa

أنا آسف/آسفة

sorry?/pardon (me)? afanddim?

أفنّدم؟

I see (I understand) īwa

أيوه

I don't understand mish fāhim

مش فاهم

speak: do you speak English? (to man/woman) betikkallim/betikkallimee ingleezee?

بتتكلّم/بتتكلّمى إنجليزى؟

I don't speak ... ana mabakkallimsh ...

أنا مابتكلّمش ...

could you repeat that? momkin teAeed/teAeedee tanee?

ممكن تعيد/تعيدى تانى؟

CONVERSION TABLES

1 centimetre = 0.39 inches	1 inch = 2.54 cm

1 metre = 39.37 inches = 1.09 yards

1 foot = 30.48 cm

1 yard = 0.91 m

1 kilometre = 0.62 miles = 5/8 mile

1 mile = 1.61 km

km	1	2	3	4	5	10	20	30	40	50	100
miles	0.6	1.2	1.9	2.5	3.1	6.2	12.4	18.6	24.8	31.0	62.1

miles	1	2	3	4	5	10	20	30	40	50	100
km	1.6	3.2	4.8	6.4	8.0	16.1	32.2	48.3	64.4	80.5	161

1 gram = 0.035 ounces

g	100	250	500
oz	3.5	8.75	17.5

1 kilo = 1000 g = 2.2 pounds
1 oz = 28.35 g
1 lb = 0.45 kg

kg	0.5	1	2	3	4	5	6	7	8	9	10
lb	1.1	2.2	4.4	6.6	8.8	11.0	13.2	15.4	17.6	19.8	22.0

kg	20	30	40	50	60	70	80	90	100
lb	44	66	88	110	132	154	176	198	220

lb	0.5	1	2	3	4	5	6	7	8	9	10	20
kg	0.2	0.5	0.9	1.4	1.8	2.3	2.7	3.2	3.6	4.1	4.5	9.0

1 litre = 1.75 UK pints / 2.13 US pints

1 UK pint = 0.57 l	1 UK gallon = 4.55 l
1 US pint = 0.47 l	1 US gallon = 3.79 l

centigrade / Celsius

$C = (F - 32) \times 5/9$

C	-5	0	5	10	15	18	20	25	30	36.8	38
F	23	32	41	50	59	65	68	77	86	98.4	100.4

Fahrenheit

$F = (C \times 9/5) + 32$

F	23	32	40	50	60	65	70	80	85	98.4	101
C	-5	0	4	10	16	18	21	27	29	36.8	38.3

English-Arabic

A

a, an*

about: about 20 Hawālee
Aishreen

حوالي ٢٠

it's about 5 o'clock Hawālee
es-saAa khamsa

حوالي الساعة ٥

a film about Egypt 'film' Aan
maSr

فيلم عن مصر

above foo'

فوق

abroad (go) lil khāreg

للخارج

(live) fil khāreg

في الخارج

absorbent cotton oTn Tebbee

قطن طبي

accept mwāfi'

موافق

accident Hadsa

حادثة

there's been an accident kan
fee Hadsa

كان في حادثة

accommodation sakan

سكن

see room and hotel

accurate maZbooT

مظبوط

ache wagaA

وجع

my back aches Dahree
wageAni

ظهري واجعني

across: across the road Aabr
esh-shariA

عبر الشارع

address Ainwān

عنوان

what's your address? (to man/
woman) Ainwānak/Ainwānik
ay?

عنوانك/عنوانِك ايه؟

The words for street (shāriA),
road (Taree') and square
(medān) always precede the
name in Arabic addresses.
Whole blocks may often share a
single number, which may be in
Arabic or English. The number
also precedes the words street,
avenue etc. Foreigners may
write addresses in romanized
Arabic as follows:

Adil Ameen
8 Abedoos Street
Shobra
1121
Cairo – Egypt

address book kitāb Aanaween

كتاب عناوين

admission charge rasm

eddokhool

رسم الدخول

adult (man/woman) bāligh/

balgha

بالغ / بالغة

advance: in advance

mo'addam

مقدّم

aeroplane Tīyāra

طيارة

after baAd

بعد

after you (to man/woman)

baAdak/baAdik

بعدك / بعدك

after lunch baAd el-ghada

بعد الغدا

afternoon baAd eD-Dohr

بعد الظهر

in the afternoon feD-Dohraya

فى الظهرية

this afternoon eD-Dohraya

الظهرية

aftershave kolonya baAd el

Helā'a

كولونيا بعد الحلاقة

aftersun cream kraym shams

كريم شمس

afterwards baAdayn

بعدين

again marra tania

مرّة تانية

against Did

ضد

age Aomr

عمر

ago: a week ago min isbooA

من اسبوع

an hour ago min sāAa

من ساعة

agree: I agree ana mwāfi'

انا موافق

AIDS eedz

ايدز

air howa

هوا

by air beT-Tīyāra

بالطيارة

air-conditioning takyeef howa

تكييف هوا

airmail: by airmail bil bareed

eg-gowee

بالبريد الجوّى

airmail envelope zarf bareed

gowee

ظرف بريد جوّى

airplane Tīyāra

طيارة

airport maTār

مطار

to the airport, please lil maTār, low samaHt

للمطار، لو سمحت

airport bus otobees el maTār

اوتوبيس المطار

airport tax Dareebit el maTār

ضريبة المطار

aisle seat korsee Aala elmamar

كرسي على الممر

alabaster rokhām

رخام

alarm clock minabbeh

منبه

alcohol koHol

كحول

Alcohol can be obtained in most parts of Egypt, but the range of outlets is limited. In the Western Desert oases or Middle Egypt, its sale is severely restricted or entirely prohibited. As a rule of thumb, hotels or Greek restaurants are the places to try. When you do manage to locate a drink, bear in mind that the hot dry climate makes for dehydration, and agonising hangovers can easily result from overindulgence. Public →

drunkenness is totally unacceptable in Egypt.
see **beer**, **wine** and **café**

alcoholic koHolee

كحولي

Alexandria iskinderaya

اسكندرية

Algeria eggazā'ir

الجزاير

Algerian* gazīree

جزايري

all kol

كل

all of it koloo

كله

all of them kolohom

كلهم

that's all, thanks bas keda, shokran

بس كده، شكرا

Allah Allāh

الله

praise be to Allah el Hamdo lillāh

الحمد لله

allergic: I'm allergic to ... ana Aandee Hasasaya min ...

انا عندى حساسية من...

alligator timsāH

تمساح

allowed: is it allowed? da
masmooH?

دا مسموح؟

all right kwayis

كويس

I'm all right (said by man/woman)

ana kwayis/kwayisa

انا كويس/كويسة

are you all right? (to man) inta
kwayis?

انت كويس؟

(to woman) inti kwayisa?

انتي كويسة؟

almond lōz

لوز

almost ta'reeban

تقريبا

alone waHeed

وحيد

already khalās

خلاص

also kamān

كمان

although berrāghm min

بالرغم من

altogether kolohom

كلهم

always dīman

دايما

am*

am: at 7am es-sāAa sabAa es-

SobH

الساعة سبعة الصبح

at 1am es-sāAa waHda
es-SobH

الساعة واحدة الصبح

amazing (surprising) mish
maA'ool

مش معقول

(very good) momtāz

ممتاز

ambulance isAāf

اسعاف

call an ambulance! eTlob el
isAāf!

اطلب الاسعاف!

Dial 211 for the ambulance
service.

America amreeka

امريكا

American* amrekānee

امريكاني

I'm American (said by man/
woman) ana amrekānee/
amrekanaya

أنا امريكاني
/امريكانية

among bayn

بين

amp: a 13-amp fuse

talat**t**ashar amb**ee**r 'fuse'

١٣ امبير فيوز

ancient ad**ee**m

قديم

and wa

و

angry zaAl**ā**n

زعلان

animal H**ī**yaw**ā**n

حيوان

ankle kaAb

كعب

annoy: this man's annoying
me er-r**ā**gil da miDaye'nee

الراجل دا مضايقني

annoying mozAig

مزعج

another tanee

تانى

can we have another room?
momkin n**ā**khod **ō**Da tania?

ممكن ناخد اوضة تانية؟

another beer, please (to man/
woman) momkin b**ee**ra tania,
low samaHt/samaHtee?

ممكن بيرة تانية، لو
سمحت/سمحتي؟

antibiotics moD**ā**d H**ī**yowee

مضاد حيوي

antihistamine dowa

lelHas**ā**saya (m)

دوا للحساسية

antique: is it an antique? da
toHfa?

دا تحفة؟

antique shop maHal toHaf

محل تحف

antiquities toHaf

تحف

antiseptic bing lilgrooH

بنج للجروح

any: have you got any bread? (to
man/woman) Aandak/Aandik
Aaysh?

عندك/عندك عيش؟

do you have any ...? (to man/
woman) fee Aandak/
Aandik ... kh**ā**lis?

فى عندك/عندك ... خالص؟

sorry, I don't have any (said by
man/woman) **ā**sif/**ā**sfa,
maAandeesh kh**ā**lis

آسف/أسفة ما عنديش خالص

anybody aī Had

أىّ حد

does anybody speak English?
fee aī Had bayetkallim

inglayzi?

فى أىّ حد بيتكلم
إنجليزى؟

there wasn't anybody there
makansh fee aī Had hināk

ماكانش فى أىّ حد هناك

anything aī Hāga

أىّ حاجة

•••••• DIALOGUES ••••••

anything else? aī Hāga tania?
nothing else, thanks mafeesh aī
Hāga tania, shokran
would you like anything to drink?
(to man) teHib teshrab aī Hāga?
(to woman) teHib-bee teshrabee
aī Hāga?
I don't want anything, thanks (said
by man/woman) ana mish Aayiz/
Aīza aī Hāga, shokran

apart from monfaSil

منفصل

apartment sha'a

شقة

appetizer fateH lil shahaya

فاتح للشهية

apple toffāHa

تفّاحة

appointment maAād

معاد

•••••• DIALOGUE ••••••

good morning, how can I help you?
SabāH elkhayr, momkin
asaAdak?
I'd like to make an appointment
(said by man/woman) ana Aayiz/
Aīza aHgiz maAād
what time would you like? (to man)
imta teHeb teHgiz elmaAād?
(to woman) imta teHebbee
teHgizee elmaAād?
three o'clock es-sāAa talāta
I'm afraid that's not possible
lil'asaf mish momkin
is four o'clock all right? (to man)
teHeb teHgiz es-sāAa arbaAa
(to woman) teHebbee teHgizee
es-sāAa arbaAa?
yes, that will be fine īwa, da
maAād kwayis
the name was ...? el esm
howa ...?

apricot mishmish

مشمش

April ibreel

أبريل

Arab* Aarabee

عربى

the Arabs el Aarab

العرب

Arabic (language) logha

Aarabaya

لغة عربية

archeology asār

اثار

are*

area manTe'a

منطقة

arm drāA

ذراع

arrange: will you arrange it for
us? (to man/woman) momkin
terattibha/terattibiha lena?

ممكن ترتبها/ ترتيبها لنا؟

arrival wesool

وصول

arrive wasal

وصل

when do we arrive?
HanewSal imta?

حنوصل إمتى؟

has my fax arrived yet? waSal
faksi walla lessa?

وصل فاكسي وللا لسة؟

we arrived today waSalna en-
naharda

وصلنا النهار دا

art fann

فن

art gallery Sālit AarD el finoon

صالة عرض الفنون

as: as big as kebeer zaī

كبير زي

as soon as possible be'sraA
wa't

بأسرع وقت

ashore Aash-shaT

على الشط

ashtray Tafīya

طقاية

ask Talab

طلب

I didn't ask for this
maTalabtish da

ما طلبتش دا

could you ask him to ...? (to
man) momkin tis'aloo ye-...?

ممكن تسأله يـ ... ؟

(to woman) momkin tis'alha
te-...?

ممكن تسألها تـ ... ؟

asleep: she's asleep hayya
nīma

هيّ نائمة

aspirin asbreen

أسبرين

asthma rabw

ربو

Aswan aswān

أسوان

at: at the hotel Aand el fondo'

عند الفندق

at the station Aand el

maHaTTa

عند المحطة

at six o'clock es-sāAa sitta

الساعة ستة

at Ahmed's Aand aHmad

عند أحمد

ATM el 'bank' esh-shakhSee

البنك الشخصي

August aghosTos

أغسطس

aunt (mother's sister) khāla

خالة

(father's sister) Aamma

عمّة

Australia ostralya

أُستراليا

Australian* ostralee

أُسترالى

I'm Australian (said by man/
woman) ana ostrālee/
ostralaya

أنا أُسترالى/أُسترالية

autumn khareef

خريف

in the autumn fil khareef

فى الخريف

avenue Taree'

طريق

awake: is he awake? howa

sāHee?

هوّ صاحى؟

is she awake? hayya SaHīa?

هىّ صاحية؟

away: is it far away? howa da
beAeed?

هوّ دا بعيد؟

awful faZeeA

فظيع

B

baby 'baby'

بيبى

baby food akl aTfāl

أكل أطفال

baby's bottle ezāzit reDāAa

قزازة رضاعة

baby-sitter dāda

دادة

back (of body) Dahr

ضهر

(back part) Teez

طيز

at the back fil ākher

فى الآخر

can I have my money back?
momkin araggaA floosee?

ممكن أرجّع فلوسى؟

come back ragaA

رجع

go back rāH

راح

backache wagaA feD-Dahr

وجع فى الظهر

bad weHesh, mish kwayis

وحش ،مش كويس

a bad headache

SodāA shedeed

صداع شديد

badly weHesh, mish kwayis

وحش ،مش كويس

bag shanTa

شنطة

(carrier bag) kees

كيس

baggage shonaT

شُنط

baggage checkroom maktab

amanāt

مكتب أمانات

baggage claim akhd el HaQā'ib

أخذ الحقائب

bakery (for bread) forn

فرن

(for cakes) makhbaz

مخبز

balcony (of house) balakōna

بلكونة

a room with a balcony ōDa

bebalakōna

أوضة بيلكونة

ball kōra

كورة

ballpoint pen 'alam gāf

قلم جاف

banana mōza

موزة

band (musical) fer'a

فرقة

bandage robāT shāsh

رباط شاش

Bandaid® blastar

بلاستر

bank (money) 'bank'

بنك

Opening hours are generally Monday to Thursday 8.30am–2.30pm, plus an evening shift (5–8pm in winter, 6–9pm in summer); some banks also open similar hours on Saturday and from 10am to noon on Sunday. Most foreign banks open Mon–Thurs 8.30am–1pm, and sometimes on Sunday. For arriving visitors, the banks at Cairo airport and the border crossings from Israel are open 24 hours daily, and those at ports open whenever a ship docks. In addition, 5-star hotels have a 24-hour banking and money changing service. →

Commission is not generally charged on straight exchanges, but there might be a small stamp duty. Rather than going through the hassle of re-exchanging Egyptian pounds, it's better to spend it all before leaving.

Forex bureaux (the generic term for private exchanges) are largely confined to Cairo, Alexandria and the Canal Cities. As a rule of thumb, Forex offer the best rates for cash, but may not take traveller's cheques; the transaction is also faster than in banks. If you're carrying American Express or Thomas Cook traveller's cheques – or cash – it's often quicker to do business at their local branches.

bank account Hisāb fil 'bank'
حساب فى البنك
bar bār
بار
see beer and café
barber's Salōn Hilā'a
صالون حلاقة
bargaining mosowma
مساومة

•••••• DIALOGUE ••••••
how much are they? bekam da?
ten pounds each el wāHid beAashara geneeh
that's too expensive da ghālee awee
how about five pounds? khalleena bekamsa geneeh?
I'll let you have it for eight pounds Haddihālak bitamanya geneeh
can you reduce it a bit more? (to man/woman) momkin tenazzil/ tenazzilee es-seAr shwaya kamān?
OK, it's a deal Tayib, khalās Hashtreeha

Bargaining is standard practice in markets, but it's not the custom to bargain in large Western-style shops or supermarkets.

When bargaining, start by offering half the suggested price; the seller might then suggest you pay two-thirds. If the seller won't reduce the price after being asked twice, then it's polite not to insist any further and you should accept the price or decide not to buy.

basket (for storage) afaS
قفص

(in shop) **sabat**

سبت

bath banyo

بانيو

can I have a bath? **momkin**
ākhod Hammām?

ممكن آخذ حمام؟

bathroom Hammām

حمام

with a private bathroom
beHammām khās

بحمام خاص

bath towel fooTit Hammām

فوطة حمام

bathtub HōD

حوض

battery baTTaraya

بطاريّة

bay khaleeg

خليج

bazaar soo'

سوق

be*

beach blāj

بلاج

on the beach **Aalal blāj**

على البلاج

see **dress** and **women**

beach mat Haseerit blāj

حصيرة بلاج

beach umbrella shamsayit blāj

شمسية بلاج

beads kharaz

خرز

beans fool

فول

(dried) **lobyā**

لوبيا

green beans **fāsolya**

فاصوليا

beard da'n (f)

ذقن

beautiful gameel

جميل

because Aalashān

علشان

because of ... **bisabab e-...**

بسبب ال ...

bed sireer

سرير

I'm going to bed now **ana**
dākhil anam dilwa'tee

أنا داخل أنام دلوقتى

bed and breakfast nōm wefTār

نوم وفطار

see **hotel**

Bedouin badawee

بدوى

bedroom Hogrit nōm

حجرة نوم

beef betelloo

بتلو

beer beera

بيرة

two beers, please (to man/
woman) ezaztayn beera, low
samaHt/samaHtee

قزازتين بيرة، لوسمحت/
سمحتى

Beer is the most widely available
form of alcohol in Egypt. The
main beer brewed under licence
is Stella – a light lager in half-
litre bottles. Stella Export, with
a blue rather than yellow label,
is pricier and comes in smaller
bottles. Marzen, a dark bock
beer, appears briefly in the
spring; Aswali is a dark beer
produced in Aswan. Imported
beer, which is the most expensive, only appears in bars,
expensive hotels and restaurants. There is also Birrel, a
non-alcoholic beer.

before abl

قبل

beggar shaHāt

شحات

begin bada'

بدا

when does it begin? bitebda'

imta?

بتبدأ إمتى؟

beginner (man/woman) mobtadi'/
mobtadi'a

مبتدئ/ مبتدئة

beginning: at the beginning fil
bedāya

فى البداية

behind wara

ورا

behind me warāya

ورايا

belly-dancer ra'āsa

رقاصة

belly-dancing ra's shar'ee

رقص شرقى

below taHt

تحت

belt Hizām

حزام

bend (in road) malaf

ملف

berth (on ship) sireer

سرير

beside: beside the ... gamb e-...

جنب ال ...

best aHsan

أحسن

better aHsan

أحسن

are you feeling better? (to man)

inta kwayis?

إنت كويس؟

(to woman) inti kwayisa?

إنتى كويسة؟

between bayn

بين

beyond abAad min

أبعد من

bicycle Aagala

عجلة

big kebeer

كبير

too big kebeer awee

كبير قوى

it's not big enough Soghiyar
awee

صغير قوى

bikini bikeenee

بيكينى

bill fatoora

فاتورة

(US: banknote) wara'

ورق

could I have the bill, please?

(to man/woman) momkin el
fatoora, low samaHt/
samaHtee?

ممكن الفاتورة، لو
سمحت/سمحتى؟

see tipping

bin zibāla

زبالة

bird Tayr

طير

birthday Aeed milād

عيد ميلاد

happy birthday! Aeed milād
saAeed!

عيد ميلاد سعيد!

biscuit baskōt

بسكوت

bit: a little bit Hetta Soghīyara

حتة صغيرة

a big bit Hetta kebeera

حتة كبيرة

a bit of ... Hetta min el ...

حتة من ال ...

a bit expensive ghāliya
shwaya

غالية شوية

bite (by insect) arSa

قرصة

(by animal) AaDDa

عضة

bitter (taste etc) mor

مر

black eswid

أسود

blanket baTTanaya

بطانية

bless you! rabbina yebarek
lak!

ربنا يبارك لك!

blind **a**Ama

أعمى

blinds sat**ā**yer

ستاير

blocked mazd**oo**d

مسدود

blond (adj) **a**sh'ar

أشقر

blood damm

دم

   high blood pressure D**a**ghT

   damm m**o**rtafiA

ضغط دم مرتفع

blouse bl**oo**za

بلوزة

blow-dry seshw**ā**r

سيشوار

blue **a**zra'

أزرق

   blue eyes Aoy**oo**n z**a**r'a

عيون زرقة

boarding house bansy**ō**n

بنسيون

boarding pass biT**a**'it SOA**oo**d

بطاقة صعود

boat m**a**rkib

مركب

   (for passengers) 'launch'

لنش

(Egyptian sailboat) fal**oo**ka

فلوكة

body gism

جسم

boiled egg bayD masl**oo**'

بيض مسلوق

bone A**a**Dm

عضم

bonnet (of car) kabb**oo**t

كبّوت

book (noun) kit**ā**b

كتاب

   (verb) H**a**gaz

حجز

   can I book a seat? m**o**mkin

   aHgiz k**o**rsee?

ممكن أحجز كرسى؟

•••••• DIALOGUE ••••••

I'd like to book a table for two
m**o**mkin **a**Hgiz Tarab**a**yza
litn**a**yn

what time would you like it booked
for? (to man) el s**ā**Aa k**ā**m t**e**Heb
t**e**Hgezh**ā**?

(to woman) el s**ā**Aa k**ā**m t**e**Hebee
t**e**Hgezeeha?

half past seven sabab**a**Aa wen**o**s

that's fine kw**a**yis

and your name? wel esm eeh?

bookshop, bookstore makt**a**ba

مكتبة

boot (footwear) **gizma** boot

جزمة بوت

(of car) **shanTa**

شنطة

border (of country) **Hedood**

حدود

bored: I'm bored (said by man/woman) **ana zah'ān/zah'āna**

أنا زهقان/زهقانة

boring **momil**

ممل

born: I was born in Manchester **ana etwaladt fi 'Manchester'**

أنا إتولدت في مانشستر

borrow (money) **istalaf**

إستلف

(other items) **istaʌār**

إستعار

may I borrow ...? (item) **momkin astaʌeer ...?**

ممكن أستعير...؟

both **litnayn**

الإتنين

bother: sorry to bother you (said by man/woman) **ana āsif/āsfa ʌalāl izāāg**

أنا آسف/أسفة على الإزعاج

bottle **ezāza**

قزازة

a bottle of beer **ezāzit beera**

قزازة بيرة

bottle-opener **fattāHa**

فتاحة

bottom (of person) **Teez**

طيز

at the bottom of the ... (hill, street etc) **ʌand ākhir el ...**

عند آخر ال...

box **sandoo'**

صندوق

box office **shebbāk tazākir**

تذاكر

boy **walad**

ولد

boyfriend **sāHib**

صاحب

bra **sotyāna**

سوتيانا

bracelet **iswera**

إسورة

brains **mokh**

مخ

brakes **farāmil**

فرامل

brandy 'cognac'

كونياك

brass **neHās asfar**

نحاس أصفر

made of brass **min en-neHās**

من النحاس

bread Aaysh

عيش

white bread Aaysh feeno

عيش فينو

brown bread Aaysh beradda

عيش بردّة

wholemeal bread Aaysh
baladee

عيش بلدى

white pitta bread Aaysh
shāmee

عيش شامى

break (verb) kasar

كسر

I've broken the ... kasart el ...

كسرت ال ...

I think I've broken my wrist
aZon innee kasart resghee

أظن إنّى كسرت رسغى

break down AaTal

عطل

I've broken down el Aarabaya
AaTalit

العربية عطلت

breakdown (mechanical) AoTl

عطل

breakdown service khidma
lelAarabayyāt

خدمة للعربيات

breakfast feTār

فطار

The typical breakfast in Egypt
consists of dried broad beans
(fool medammis) cooked in a
variety of ways (for example
with oil, tahini or tomatoes),
falāfel (mashed then fried
broad beans), cheese, boiled
eggs, bread (baguette or flat
bread), jams and omelettes.
Most Egyptians prefer to have
fool medammis and falāfel
for breakfast, but younger
people tend to have cornflakes
or other cereals.

break-in: I've had a break-in
ana baytee itsara'

أنا بيتى إتسرق

breast bezz

بز

breeze nisma

نسمة

bridge (over river) kobree

كوبرى

brief mokhtaSar

مختصر

briefcase shanTa

شنطة

bright (light etc) zāhee

زاهى

bright red aHmar zāhee

أحمر زاهى

brilliant (idea, person) momtāz

ممتاز

bring gāb

جاب

I'll bring it back later ana
Hageebo tāni baAdayn

أنا حاجيبه تانى بعدين

Britain ingiltera

إنجلترا

British ingleezee

إنجليزى

brochure nashra

نشره

broken maksoor

مكسور

brooch brōJ

بروج

broom moknisa

مكنسه

brother akh

أخ

brother-in-law neseeb

نسيب

brown bonnay

بُنّى

bruise waram

ورم

brush (noun) forsha

فرشة

buffet car Aarabayyit el akl

عربية الأكل

buggy (for child) Aarabayyit
aтfāl

عربية أطفال

building mabna

مبنى

bunk sireer

سرير

bureau de change maktab Sarf

مكتب صرف

see bank

burglary Hādis sir'a

حادث سرقة

burn (noun) Haree'a

حريقة

(verb) Hara'

حرق

burnt: this is burnt da maHroo'

دا محروق

burst: a burst pipe masoora
maksoora

ماسورة مكسورة

bus otobees

أوتوبيس

what number bus is it to ...?
otobees nimra kam yerooH
li ...?

أوتوبيس نمرة كام يروح
ل ....؟

when is the next bus to ...?
(when at stop) el otobees ellay

bayrooH le ... gī imta?

الأوتوبيس اللى بيروح
ل ... جاى إمتى؟

(when booking) imta el
otobees el-lee bayrooH
le ... baAdo?

إمتى الأوتوبيس اللى
بيروح بعده؟

what time is the last bus? imta
ākhir otobees?

إمتى آخر أوتوبيس؟

•••••• DIALOGUE ••••••

does this bus go to ...? howa el
otobees da bayrooH le ...?
no, you need a number ... (to man)
la', inta Aayiz otobees nimra ...
(to woman) la', inti Aīza otobees
nimra ...

Inter-city buses are an inexpensive way to travel, and are often preferable to trains. Besides being quicker for short trips along the Nile Valley, buses serve areas beyond the rail network, such as Sinai, the oases, Abu Simbel and Hurghada. On most routes there's a choice between air-conditioned (A/C) buses – which are usually new(ish) and fast – and non-→

A/C ones, generally old and uncomfortable. The former are invariably more expensive, but whether their A/C actually works depends on the bus company and the route.

Though most towns have a single bus depot for all destinations, cities such as Cairo, Alexandria, Port Said and Ismailiya have several terminals. English- or French-speaking staff are fairly common at the larger ones, but rare in the provinces. Timetables (usually posted in Arabic only) change frequently so check the times in person. Hotels in Sinai and the oases, and the tourist offices in Luxor and Aswan can also supply information.

At city terminals, tickets are normally sold from kiosks, up to 24 hours in advance for A/C or long-haul services. In the provinces, tickets may only be available an hour or so before departure, or on the bus itself in the case of through services, which are often standing room only when they arrive. Passengers on A/C services are usually assigned a seat (the number is written in Arabic on your ticket).

business shoghl

شغل

bus station mow'af otobees

موقف أوتوبيس

bus stop maHaTTit otobees

محطة أوتوبيس

busy maJghool

مشغول

I'm busy tomorrow (said by man/
woman) ana maJghool/
maJghoola bokra

أنا مشغول/مشغولة
بكرة

but lākin

لكن

butcher's gazzār

جزّار

butter zebda

زبدة

button zorār

زرار

buy ishtara

إشترى

where can I buy ...? fayn
a'adar ashteree ...?

فين أقدر أشتري...؟

by: by bus bil otobees

بالأوتوبيس

by car bil Aarabayya

بالعربيّة

by the window gamb
esh-shebbāk

جنب الشبّاك

by the sea gamb el baHr

جنب البحر

by Thursday yōm el
khamees

يوم الخميس

bye maAssalāma

مع السلامة

C

cabin (on ship) kabeena

كبينة

café ahwa

قهوة

The most popular Egyptian
drinks are tea, coffee, fruit
juices and familiar brands of
soft drinks. Invitations to drink
tea ('teshrab shī?') are as much
a part of Egyptian life as they are
in Britain.

All these beverages are widely
consumed in traditional coffee
houses or tearooms (ahwa),
which are predominantly male
territory. Foreign women won't
be turned away but may feel
uneasy, especially if unaccom→

panied by a man. For a more relaxed tea or coffee, go to one of the middle-class places (in larger towns), which are often joined to patisseries, and where Egyptian women may be found.

Cairo el Qahira

القاهرة

Old Cairo maSr el adeema

مصر القديمة

cake shop Halawanee

حلوانى

call (verb) nadah

نده

(to phone) ettaSal

إتّصل

what's it called? ismaha ay?

إسمها إيه؟

he/she is called ... ismoh/ ismaha ...

إسمه/إسمها ...

please call the doctor momkin teTlob el doktōr?

ممكن تطلب الدكتور؟

please give me a call at 7.30am tomorrow (to man) low samaHt ittasil bayya bokra el saAa sabAa wenos

لو سمحت إتّصل بى بكرة الساعة ٧,٣٠ الصبح

(to woman) low samaHtee

ittaSilee bayya bokra el saAa sabAa wenos

لو سمحتى إتّصلى بى بكرة الساعة ٧,٣٠ الصبح

please ask him to call me (to man/woman) low samaHt/ samaHtee ool/oolee loh yettasil baya

لوسمحت/سمحتى قول/ قولى له يتّصل بى

call back: I'll call back later (come back) ana HargaA tānee baAdayn

أنا حارجع تانى بعدين

(phone back) ana Hatesil tānee

أنا حاتّصل تانى

call round: I'll call round tomorrow Hāgee bokra

حاجى بكرة

camcorder kamirit tasgeel

كاميرة تسجيل

camel gamal

جمل

camel driver raAee gemāl

راعى جمل

camel racing sibā' gimāl

سباق جمال

camel ride rokoob eg-gimāl

ركوب جمال

how much is a camel ride to ...? bekam rokoob eg-gimal le ...?

بكم ركوب الجمال ل...؟

camel trip reHla beg-gimal

رحلة بالجمال

camera kamira

كاميرة

camera shop maHal kamirāt

محل كاميرات

camp (verb) Aaskar

عسكر

can we camp here? momkin neAaskar hena?

ممكن نعسكر هنا؟

camping gas gaz el-moAaskar

جاز المعسكر

campsite mowQiA el-moAaskar

موقع المعسكر

Most campsites are located on the coast, lack shade and often have few facilities. Rather better are the occasional campsites attached to hotels, which may offer ready-pitched tents with camp beds, plus use of the hotel shower and toilet. As for camping rough, you should always check with the authorities about any coastal site –
→

some beaches are mined, others patrolled by the military. In the oases it's less of a problem, though any land near water will belong to someone, so ask permission.

can (tin) SafeeHa

صفيحة

a can of beer Aelbit beera

علبة بيرة

can*: can you ...? (to man/woman) momkin inta/inti ...?

ممكن إنت/إنتى ...؟

can I have ...? momkin ana ...?

ممكن أنا ...؟

I can't ... ma'adartish ...

ماقدرش ...

Canada 'Canada'

كندا

Canadian* kanadee

كندى

I'm Canadian (said by man/woman) ana kanadee/kanadaya

أنا كندى/كنديّة

canal Qanāl

قناة

cancel lagha

لغى

candies Halawayāt

حلويّات

candle shamAa

شمعة

can-opener fattāHa

فتّاحة

cap (of bottle) ghaTā

غطا

captain (of ship) QobTān

قبطان

car Aarabayya

عربيّة

by car bil Aarabayya

بالعربيّة

card (birthday etc) kart

كارت

here's my (business) card da el kart betaAee

دا الكارت بتاعى

careful HareeS

حريص

be careful! khallee bālak!

خلّى بالك!

caretaker (man/woman) farrāsh/farrāsha

فرّاش/فرّاشة

car ferry maAadayya

معديّة

car park mow'af Aarabayyāt

موقف عربيّات

carpet siggāda

سجّادة

car rental ta'geer Aarabayyāt

تأجير عربيّات

Renting a car pays obvious dividends if you are pushed for time or plan to visit remote sites, but whether you'd want to drive yourself is another matter – it's not much more expensive to hire a car with a driver. Any branch of Misr Travel, and numerous local tour agencies, can fix you up with a car and driver. An alternative is simply to negotiate with local taxi drivers.

carriage (of train) Aarabayyit aTr

عربيّة قطر

carrier bag kees

كيس

carry shāl

شال

carry-cot Hammālit aTfāl

حمّالة أطفال

carton kartōn

كرتون

carving naHt

نحت

carwash ghaseel Aarabayya

غسيل عربيّة

cash (noun) floos

فلوس

(verb) saraf

صرف

will you cash this for me?

momkin tesriflee da?

ممكن تصرف لى دا؟

cash desk kays

كيس

cash dispenser el 'bank' esh-shakhsee

البنك الشخصى

cassette 'cassette'

كاسيت

cassette recorder tazgeel

تسجيل

castle alAa

قلعة

casualty department Qism el Tawāri'

قسم الطوارئ

cat otta

قطة

catacombs saradeeb

سراديب

catch (verb) masak

مسك

where do we catch the bus to ...? minayn nākhod el

otobees le ...?

منين ناخذ الأوتوبيس ل....؟

Catholic katholeeki

كاثوليكى

cave maghāra

مغارة

ceiling sa'f

سقف

cemetery Torab

طرب

(historic, Islamic) madfan

مدفن

centigrade daraga me'awaya

درجة مئويّة

centimetre 'santimetre'

سنتيمتر

central ra'eesee

رئيسى

centre wesT

وسط

how do we get to the city centre? izzay newSal li wesT el balad?

إزّاى نوصل لوسط البلد؟

ceramics khazaf

خزف

cereal Hoboob

حبوب

certainly TabAan

طبعا

certainly not la' TabAan

لأ طبعاً

chair korsee

كرسى

change (noun: money) Sarf

صرف

(verb: money) Saraf

صرف

can I change this for ...?
momkin aghīyar da be ...?

ممكن أغيّر دا ب...؟

I don't have any change
maAayeesh aī fakka

ماعييش فكّة

can you give me change for a
five-pound note? momkin
teddeeni fakkit khamsa
geneeh?

ممكن تدينى فكّة خمسة
جنيه؟

•••••• DIALOGUE ••••••

do we have to change (trains)?
eHna lāzim nighīyar?

yes, change at Luxor/no, it's a direct
train naAam, Hanghīyar fī lo'sor/
la', da aTr sareeA

changed: to get changed
Ha'aghīyar

حاغيّر

charge (noun) taman

تمن

(verb) Hāsib

حاسب

cheap rekhees

رخيص

do you have anything cheaper?
(to man/woman) Aandak/
Aandik aī Hāga arkhaS?

عندك/عندك أىّ
حاجة أرَخص؟

check (verb) kashaf

كشف

check (US: noun) sheek

شيك

(bill) fatoora

فاتورة

could you check the ..., please
(to man/woman) momkin
tekshif/tekshifee Aala ...,
low samaHt/samaHtee

ممكن تكشف/تكشفى
على ... لو سمحت/
سمحتى؟

check book daftar sheekāt

دفتر شيكات

check card kart sheekāt

كارت شيكات

check in: where do we have to
check in? fayn iHna lāzim

nesallim esh-shonaT?

فين إحنا لازم نسلّم الشنط؟

check-in moragaΪt el kowntar

مراجعة الكاونتر

cheek (on face) khad

خد

cheerio! 'bye-bye'!

باى باى!

cheers! (toast) fee SeHHetak!

فى صحّتك!

cheese gibna

جبنة

chemist's agzakhana

اجزاخانة

see pharmacy

cheque sheek

شيك

do you take cheques? (to man/ woman) bitākhod/bitakhdee sheekāt?

بتاخذ /بتاخذى شيكات؟

see traveller's cheque

cheque book daftar sheekāt

دفتر شيكات

cheque card kart sheekāt

كارت شيكات

chess shaTarang

شطرنج

chest sedr

صدر

chewing gum lebān

لبان

chicken frākh

فراخ

child Tefl

طفل

children aTfāl

أطفال

child minder dāda

دادة

children's pool Hammām sibāHa lil aTfāl

حمّام سباحة للأطفال

children's portion naSeeb aTfāl

نصيب أطفال

chilled sa'Aa

سقعة

chin da'n (f)

ذقن

Chinese* seenee

صينى

chips baTāTis maHammara (f)

بطاطس محمّرة

(US) shebsee

شيبسى

chocolate shokalāta

شوكولاتة

milk chocolate shokalāta bil laban

شوكولاتة باللبن

plain chocolate shokalāta

sāda

شوكولاتة سادة

a hot chocolate kakow

كاكاو

cholera 'cholera'

كوليرا

choose ikhtār

إختار

Christian meseeHee

مسيحى

Christmas Aeed milād el meseeH

عيد ميلاد المسيح

Christmas Eve wa'fit Aeed milād el meseeH

وقفة عيد ميلاد المسيح

merry Christmas! Aeed milād saAeed!

عيد ميلاد سعيد!

church kineesa

كنيسة

cigar sigār

سيجار

cigarette sigāra

سيجارة

Almost the entire adult male population of Egypt smokes, and offering cigarettes around is common practice. The most popular brand is Cleopatra.
→

Locally produced versions of Marlboro, Rothmans and Camel have a much higher tar content than their equivalents at home; the genuine article can be found in duty-free shops.

cigarette lighter wallāAet sagāyer

ولاّعة سجاير

cinema 'cinema'

سينما

cinnamon erfa

قرفة

circle Hala'a

حلقة

citadel alAa

قلعة

city madeena

مدينة

city centre wesT el balad

وسط البلد

clean (adj) neDeef

نضيف

can you clean these clothes for me? momkin tenaD-Daf el hodoom dee Aalashānee?

ممكن تنضّف الهدوم دى علشانى؟

cleaning solution (for contact

lenses) maHlool tanDeef

محلول تنظيف

cleansing lotion marham tanDeef

مرهم تنظيف

clear wāDiH

واضح

clever shāTer

شاطر

cliff Hāfit el gabal

حافة الجبل

climbing TolooA

طلوع

clinic Aayāda

عيادة

clock saAet HayT

ساعة حيط

close (verb) āfāl

قفل

• • • • • • DIALOGUE • • • • • •

what time do you close?
imta beti'filo?

we close at 8pm on weekdays and
6pm on Saturdays beni'fil es-sāAa
tamanya ayyām el esbooA wessāAa sitta ayyām es-sabt

do you close for lunch? beti'fil
saAt el ghada?

yes, between 1 and 3.30pm
naAam, min es-sāAa waHda les-
sāAa talāta wenos

closed āfil

قافل

cloth (fabric) omāsh

قماش

(for cleaning etc) Hettit omāsh

حتة قماش

clothes hedoom

هدوم

clothes line Habl ghaseel

حبل غسيل

clothes peg maJbak ghaseel

مشبك غسيل

cloud seHāb

سحاب

cloudy meghīyem

مغيم

clutch debrayāJ

دبرياج

coach (on train) Aarabayyit aTr

عربية قطر

coach trip reHla syaHayya bil otobees

رحلة سياحية بالأوتوبيس

coast sāHil

ساحل

on the coast ala es-sāHil

على الساحل

coat (long coat) balTo

بالطو

(jacket) Jākit

جاكت

coathanger shammāᴀa

شمّاعة

cobra teᴀbān kobra

تعبان كوبرا

cockroach sᴏrsār

صرصار

code (for phoning) kōd

كود

what's the (dialling) code for Alexandria? ᵃay raQam el kōd betāᴀ iskinderaya?

إيه رقم الكود بتاع إسكندرية؟

coffee ahwa

قهوة

two coffees, please (to man/woman) itneen ahwa, low samaHt/samaHtee

إتنين قهوة، لو سمحت/ سمحتى

Coffee is traditionally of the Turkish kind, served in tiny cups or glasses and pre-sugared as customers specify. Most middle-class or tourist establishments also serve European-style instant coffee, made from Nescafé or Misrcafe rather than Turkish coffee, with the option of having it with milk.

→

Some useful terms:

ahwa sāda coffee without sugar

ahwa ᴀar-reeHa slightly sweetened coffee

ahwa maᴢbooᴛa medium-sweet coffee

ahwa zayāda very sweet coffee

ahwa meHowega coffee spiced with cardomom seeds

ahwa bel-laban coffee with milk

coffee house ahwa

قهوة

coin ᴀomla

عملة

Coke® kakoola

كاكولا

cold bard

برد

I'm cold (said by man/woman) ana bardān/bardāna

انا بردان/بردانة

I have a cold ana ᴀandee zokām

أنا عندى زكام

collapse: he's collapsed oghma ᴀalayh

أُغمى عليه

collar yā'a

ياقة

collect akhad

أخذ

I've come to collect ... ana gī akhod ...

أنا جاى آخذ ...

college kollaya

كليّة

colour lōn

لون

do you have this in other colours? (to man/woman) Aandak/Aandik alwān ghayr dee?

عندك/عندِك ألوان غير دى؟

colour film 'film' milowwin

فيلم ملون

comb mishT

مشط

come waSal

وصل

•••••• D I A L O G U E ••••••

where do you come from? (to man/woman) inta/inti minayn?
I come from Edinburgh ana min 'Edinburgh'

come back ragaA

رجع

I'll come back tomorrow ana HargaA bokra

أنا حارجع بكرة

come in ga

جا

comfortable moreeH

مريح

compact disc 'CD'

سي دى

company (business) shirka

شركة

compartment (on train) salōn

صالون

compass boSla

بوصلة

complaint shakwa

شكوى

I have a complaint Aandee shakwa

عندى شكوى

completely tamām

تمام

computer 'computer'

كومبيوتر

concert Hafla moseeQayya

حفلة موسيقيية

conditioner (for hair) monaAim lil shaAr

منعم للشعر

condom Aāzil Tibbee

عازل طبّى

conference mo'tamar

مؤتمر

confirm akkid

أكد

congratulations! mabrook!

مبروك!

connection waSla

وصلة

constipation imsāk

إمساك

consulate Qonsolaya

قنصليّة

contact lenses Aadasāt lasQa

عدسات لاصقة

contraceptive māneA lil Haml

مانع للحمل

convenient molā'im

ملائم

that's not convenient da mish molā'im

دا مش ملائم

cook (verb) Tabakh

طبّاخ

not cooked nī

نى

cooker botagāz

بوتاجاز

cookie baskōt

بسكوت

cool raTeb

رطب

Coptic ebTee

قبطى

Coptic monastery dayr ebTee

دير قبطى

coriander kozbara

كزبرة

cork fīlla

فلّة

corkscrew bareema lifatH el azaīz

بريّمة لفتح القزايز

corner: on the corner Aalal naSya

على الناصية

in the corner fil rokn

فى الركن

cornflakes 'cornflakes'

كورن فلايكس

correct (right) SaH

صح

corridor Tor'a

طرقة

cosmetics mawād tagmeel

مواد تجميل

cost (verb) kallif

كلّف

how much does it cost? bekam?

بكام؟

cot sireer aTfāl

سرير أطفال

cotton oTn

قطن

cotton wool oTn Tebbee

قطن طبّى

couch (sofa) **kanaba**

كنبة

couchette **sireer**

سرير

cough **koHHa**

كحة

cough medicine **dowa koHHa**

دوا كحة

could: could you ...? (to man/ woman) **momkin inta/inti ...?**

ممكن إنت/إنتى ....؟

could I have ...? **momkin ana ākhod ...?**

ممكن أنا آخد ....؟

I couldn't ... **ma'adartish ...**

ماقدرتش ...

country (nation) **balad**

بلد

(countryside) **reef**

ريف

couple (two people) **itnayn**

إتنين

a couple of ... **gōz ...**

جوز ...

courier **morāfiQ sayāHee**

مرافق سياحى

course: of course **TabAan**

طبعا

of course not **la' TabAan**

لأ طبعا

cousin (on mother's side: aunt's

daughter) **bint khala**

بنت خالة

(aunt's son) **ibn khala**

إبن خالة

(uncle's daughter) **bint khāl**

بنت خال

(uncle's son) **ibn khāl**

إبن خال

(on father's side: aunt's daughter) **bint Aamma**

بنت عمة

(aunt's son) **ibn Aamma**

إبن عمة

(uncle's daughter) **bint Aamm**

بنت عم

(uncle's son) **ibn Aamm**

إبن عم

cow **ba'ara**

بقرة

crab **kāborya**

كابوريا

craft shop **maHal kherdawātee**

محل خضرواتى

crash (noun) **Hādsa**

حادثة

I've had a crash **Hasalit lee Hādsa**

حصلت لى حادثة

crazy **magnoon**

مجنون

cream (in cake, lotion) 'cream'

كريم

(colour) **kray**mi

كريمى

creche HaDāna

حضانة

credit card 'credit card'

كريديت كارد

do you take credit cards? (to man/woman) bit**ā**khod/ bitakhdee 'credit card'?

بتاخد / بتاخدى كريديت كارد؟

•••••• DIALOGUE ••••••

can I pay by credit card? momkin adfaʌ bil 'credit card'?

which card do you want to use? (to man) aī 'card' teHebb testakhdim?

(to woman) aī 'card' teHebbee testakhdimee?

Access/Visa

yes, sir naʌam ya ostāz

what's the number? ay el-raQam?

and the expiry date? we ay ākhir miʌad intihā'ō?

Credit cards are accepted at major hotels, top-flight restaurants, some shops and airline offices, but virtually nowhere else. American →

Express, Mastercard and Visa are the likeliest to be accepted. In Cairo, Alexandria, Luxor, Hurghada and a few other main tourist resorts, branches of the Banque Misr have cash machines/ATMs that allow you to withdraw cash using Visa, Mastercard or Cirrus cards.

crime

Pickpockets can be a problem in Cairo, notably in queues and on the crowded buses to the pyramids. To play safe, keep your valuables in a money belt or a pouch under your shirt. Generally, though, casual theft is more of a problem. Campsites, hostels and cheap hotels often have poor security, making it unwise to leave valuables there. At most places, you can deposit them at the reception (always get a receipt for cash).

crisps shebsee®

شيبسى

crockery fokhār

فخار

crossing (by sea) ʌoboor

عبور

crossroads taQāTOA Toro'

تقاطع طرق

crowd nās keteer

ناس كتير

(at sporting event)

motafarregeen

متفرجين

crowded zaHma

زحمة

crown (on tooth) tāg

تاج

cruise Aoboor

عبور

If you're looking for a cruise once in Egypt, shop around and don't necessarily go for the cheapest deal: some boats leave a lot to be desired in terms of hygiene and living conditions, so always try to look round the vessel first. The best deals are available from local agents (or directly from the boats) in Luxor or Aswan.

Feluccas, the lateen-sailed boats used on the Nile since antiquity, still serve as transport along many stretches of the river and are favoured by tourists for sunset cruises.

---

crutches Aokkāz

عكاز

cry (verb) Sarakh

صرخ

cucumber (small) khayār

خيار

(large) fa'oos

فاقوس

cumin kammoon

كمون

cup fongān

فنجان

a cup of ..., please (to man/woman) fongān ..., low samaHt/samaHtee

فنجان ... ، لو سمحت/ سمحتي

cupboard dolāb

دولاب

cure (verb) shafa

شفى

curly akrat

أكرت

current (in water, electric) tīyār

تيّار

curtains satāyer

ستاير

cushion makhadda

مخدة

custom gomrok

جمرك

Customs gamārek

جمارك

Egyptian Customs allows you to bring in 200 cigarettes (or 250g of tobacco) and one litre of alcohol. Though personal effects and cameras are exempt from duty, items such as electronic equipment and video cameras should be declared and listed on the form provided. If you lose them, they will be assumed 'sold' when you come to leave and you will have to pay 100 per cent duty unless you have police documentation of theft. On items with a high resale value (for example laptop computers or video cameras) you may be required to pay a deposit against possible duty charges, which is refundable on departure. If Customs officers insist on impounding goods, get a receipt and contact your consulate.

cut (noun) 'iTAa

قطعة

(verb) aTaA

قطع

I've cut myself ana Aowart

nafsee

أنا عوّرت نفسى

cutlery faD-Dayāt

فضّيات

Cyprus obros

قبرص

D

dad abb, baba

أب، بابا

daily yowmayan

يوميا

damage (verb) kharrab

خرب

damaged kharrabt

خربت

I'm sorry, I've damaged this
(said by man/woman) ana āsif/
āsfa, ana kharrabtahā

أنا آسف/أسفة، أنا
خرّبتها

damn! ellaAna!

اللعنة!

damp (adj) raTeb

رطب

dance (noun) ra's

رقص

(verb) ra'aS

رقص

would you like to dance? (to

woman) teHebee tor'oSee?

تحبى ترقصى؟

dangerous khaTar

خطر

Danish* denmarkee

دنماركى

dark (adj: colour) Dalma

ضلمة

(hair) asmar

أسمر

it's getting dark HatDallim

حتضلم

date*: what's the date today?

et-tareekh ay en-naharda?

التاريخ إيه النهارده؟

let's make a date for next
Monday khalleena nerattib
maAAd layōm letnayn eg-gī

خلينا نرتب معاد ليوم
لتنين الجاى

dates (fruit) balaH

بلح

daughter bint

بنت

daughter-in-law mrāt ibn

مراة إبن

dawn fagr

فجر

at dawn Aand el fagr

عند الفجر

day yōm

يوم

the day after el yōm el-lee
baAdo

اليوم اللى بعده

the day after tomorrow baAd
bokra

بعد بكرة

the day before el yōm el-lee
ablo

اليوم اللى قبله

the day before yesterday owil
embāriH

أول إمبارح

every day kol yōm

كل يوم

all day Tool el yōm

طول اليوم

in two days' time khilāl
yōmayn

خلال يومين

have a nice day! yōm
saAeed!

يوم سعيد !

day trip reHla yōmaya

رحلة يومية

dead mīyit

ميت

deaf **aTrash**

أطرش

deal (business) **SafQa**

صفقة

it's a deal **ettafa'na**

إتفقنا

death **mōt**

موت

decaffeinated coffee **ahwa bedoon kafayn**

قهوة بدون كافين

December **disamber**

ديسمبر

decide **Qar-rar**

قرر

we haven't decided yet **lessa maQar-rarnāsh**

ماقررناش

deck (on ship) **Dahr el markib**

ظهر المركب

deckchair **korsee blāJ**

كرسى بلاج

deep **ghoweeT**

غويط

definitely **TabAan**

طبعا

definitely not **la' TabAan**

لا طبعا

degree (qualification) **shahāda gamiAayya**

شهادة جامعية

dehydrated (person) **mīyit min el AaTash**

ميت من العطش

dehydration **gafāf**

جفاف

delay (noun) **ye'khar**

يأخر

deliberately **bil'asd**

بالقصد

delicacy **nak-ha**

نكهة

delicatessen **ba'āl**

بقال

delicious **lazeez**

لذيذ

deliver **waSSal**

وصّل

delivery (of mail) **towSeel**

توصيل

Denmark **ed-denmark**

الدنمارك

dental floss **khayT lelasnān**

خيط للسنان

dentist **garrāH asnān**

جرّاح أسنان

•••••• DIALOGUE ••••••

it's this one here **dee el-lee hena**

this one? **dee?**

no that one **la' dee**

here **hena**

yes **īwa**

dentures Ta'm asnān

طقم أسنان

deodorant mozeel lereeHt el
Aara'

مزيل لريحة العرق

department Qism

قسم

department store maHal kebeer

محل كبير

departure safar

سفر

departure lounge sālit es-safar

صالة السفر

depend: it depends yimkin

يمكن

it depends on ... yeAtemid
Aala ...

يعتمد على ...

deposit Aarboon

عربون

desert SaHara

صحرا

in the desert fee eS-SaHara

في الصحرا

dessert Helw

حلو

destination maHaTTa

محطة

develop HammaD

حمّض

could you develop these films?
momkin teHammaD el aflām
dee?

yes, certainly īwa, TabAan

when will they be ready? imta
yekhalaSoo?

tomorrow afternoon bokra baAd
eD-Dohr

how much is the four-hour-service?
bekam khidmet arbaA saAāt?

diabetic (noun) mareeD
bes-sokkar

مريض بالسكّر

dial (verb) Darab telefōn

ضرب تليفون

dialling code nimrit el kōd

نمرة الكود

To dial direct, dial 00 for an
international line, then dial the
country code (below), followed
by the number, leaving out the
initial digit of the local code:

Australia 61
Canada 1
Ireland 353
New Zealand 64
UK 44
USA 1

ENGLISH ◆ ARABIC **Di**

diamond mās

ماس

diaper kafoola

كافولة

diarrhoea es-hāl

إسهال

do you have something for diarrhoea? (to man/woman)

Aandak/Aandik Haga lil es-hāl?

عندك/عندك حاجة للإسهال؟

diary mofakkera

مفكرة

didn't* ma Aamaltish

ما عملتش

die māt

مات

diesel deezil

ديزل

diet rayJeem

ريجيم

I'm on a diet ana baAmil rayJeem

أنا باعمل ريجيم

I have to follow a special diet lāzim attabiA rayJeem moAayan

لازم أتّبع ريجيم معيّن

difference ekhtelāf

إختلاف

what's the difference? ay el far'?

إيه الفرق؟

different mokhtalif

مختلف

this one is different da mokhtalif

دا مختلف

a different table Tarabayza tania

ترابيزة تانية

difficult SaAb

صعب

difficulty SoAooba

صعوبة

dinghy markib Soghīyar

مركب صغيّر

dining room ōDit es-sofra

أوضة السفرة

(in hotel) Sālit el akl

صالة الأكل

dinner (evening meal) Aasha

عشا

to have dinner yetAash-sha

يتعشا

direct (adj) mobāshir

مباشر

is there a direct train? fee aTr mobāshir?

فى قطر مباشر؟

direction ettigāh

إتجاه

which direction is it? fee ay
ettigāh?

فى أىّ إتّجاه؟

is it in this direction? fil
ettigāh da?

فى الإتّجاه دا؟

directory enquiries daleel
telefonāt

دليل تليفونات

The number for directory
enquiries is 140; international
directory enquiries is 125.

dirt wasākha

وساخة

dirty mish neDeef

مش نظيف

disabled moAowaQ

معوّق

is there access for the
disabled? fee bab lil
moAowaQeen?

فى باب للمعوّقين؟

disappear ekhtafa

إختفى

it's disappeared ekhtafit

إختفت

disappointed: I was disap-

pointed ana khāb amalee

أنا خاب أملى

disappointing mokhayib lil
amāl

مخيّب للآمال

disaster karsa

كارثة

disco 'disco'

ديسكو

discount takhfeeD

تخفيض

is there a discount? fee
takhfeeD?

فى تخفيض؟

disease maraD

مرض

disgusting mo'rif

مقرف

dish (meal) wagba

وجبة

(bowl) Tab'a

طبق

disk (for computer) desk

ديسك

disposable diapers/nappies
nābee

نابى

distance masāfa

مسافة

in the distance beAeed

بعيد

district manTe'a

منطقة

disturb ezAāg

إزعاج

diving board manaT

منط

divorced (man/woman) meTala'/
meTala'a

مطلق/مطلقة

dizzy: I feel dizzy (said by man/
woman) ana dāyekh/dīkha

أنا دايخ/دايخة

do (verb) Aamal

عمل

what shall we do? HaneAmel
ay?

حنعمل إيه؟

how do you do it? (to man/
woman) beteAmelhā/
beteAmelayhā ezzāi?

بتعملها/بتعمليها إزّاى؟

will you do it for me? (to man/
woman) momkin teAameloo/
teAmelayhā Aalashānee?

ممكن تعمله/تعمليها
علشاني؟

•••••• DIALOGUES ••••••

how do you do? (to man/woman)
izzayak/izzayik?

nice to meet you forSa saAeeda

what do you do? (work: to man/
woman) betishtaghal/

betishtaghalee ay?

I'm a teacher (said by man/woman)
ana modariss/modarissa

and you? (to man/woman) we inta/
inti?

I'm a student (said by man/woman)
ana Tālib/Tāliba

what are you doing this evening?
(to man/woman) HateAmil/
HateAmilee ay el-leelādee?

we're going out for a drink
Hanokhrog neshrab

do you want to join us? (to man/
woman) teHebb/teHebbee teegee
maAāna?

do you want coffee? (to man)
teHebb teshrab ahwa?
(to woman) teHebbee teshrabee
ahwa?

I do, but she doesn't (said by man/
woman) ana Aayiz/Aīza, bas
hayya mish Aīza

doctor (man/woman) doktōr/
doktōra

دكتور/دكتورة

we need a doctor eHna
meHtageen doktōr

إحنا محتاجين دكتور

please call a doctor momkin
teTlob doktōr?

ممكن تطلب دكتور؟

• • • • • • DIALOGUE • • • • • •

where does it hurt? (to man/woman)
fayn byewgaAak/byewgaAik?

right here hena bezzabT

does that hurt now? (to man/
woman) byewgaAak/byewgaAik
delwa'tee?

yes īwa

take this to the pharmacy khod
dee lil agzakhāna

Private doctors are common;
expect to pay about 50 Egyptian
pounds a session, excluding
the price of any drugs you
are prescribed. If you get
seriously ill, private hospitals
are generally preferable to
public sector ones. Those
attached to universities are
usually well equipped and
competent, but small town
hospitals are often inadequate.
Many hospitals (most**a**shfa)
require a deposit of around 200
Egyptian pounds. Normally you
must pay this on admission
and a delayed payment by
your insurance company is not
acceptable. Obviously, it's
advisable to take out health
insurance before you travel.

document mostanad
مستند

dog kalb
كلب

doll Aaroosa leAba
لعبة

domestic flight reHla dākhilaya
رحلة داخلية

donkey Homār
حمار

donkey-drawn cart HanToor
حنطور

don't!* la'!
لا!

don't do that! mateAmelsh
keda!
ماتعملش كده!

door bab
باب

doorman bowwāb
بوّاب

double gōz
جوز

double bed sireer litnayn
سرير لتنين

double room ōDa litnayn
أوضة لتنين

down taHt
تحت

down here hena taHt
هنا تحت

put it down over there

HoTTaha henāk

حُطّها هناك

it's down there on the right

hayya henāk Aala elyemeen

هيّ هناك على اليمين

it's further down the road

hayya oddām shwīya

هيّ قدّام شويّة

downmarket (restaurant etc)

maA'ool

معقول

downstairs ed-dōr et-taHtānee

الدور التحتاني

dozen dasta

دستة

half a dozen noS dasta

نص دستة

drawer dorg

درج

drawing rasm

رسم

dreadful mo'rif

مقرف

dream (noun) Helm

حلم

dress (noun) fostān

فستان

Be aware of the importance of dress: shorts are acceptable only at beach resorts (and for women →

only in private resorts or along the Aqaba coast). In the oases, where attractions include open-air springs and hot pools, it's OK to bathe – but do so in at least a T-shirt and leggings: oasis people are among the most conservative in the country. Shirts (for both sexes) should cover your shoulders. For women particularly, the more modest your dress, the less hassle you will attract: loose opaque clothes that cover all 'immodest' areas (thighs, upper arms, chest), and hide your contours are a big help, and essential if you are travelling alone in rural areas, where long hair should also be covered.

Bear in mind that northern Egypt can be cold and damp in winter, while the desert gets freezing at night, even in the spring and autumn. A warm sweater is invaluable. So, too, are a solid pair of shoes: burst pipes are commonplace, and wandering around muddy streets in sodden sandals is a miserable experience.

dressed: to get dressed labas

لبس

dressing gown rōb
deshambbar

روب ديشامبير

drink (noun: alcoholic) shorb

شرب

(non-alcoholic) mashroob

مشروب

(verb) sharab

شرب

a cold drink Haga sa'Aa

حاجة ساقعة

can I get you a drink? (to man/
woman) teshrab/teshrabee
Hāga?

تشرب / تشربى حاجة؟

what would you like (to drink)?
(to man) teHebb teshrab ay?

تحب تشرب إيه؟

(to woman) teHebbee
teshrabee ay?

تحبى تشربى إيه؟

no thanks, I don't drink la'
shokran, ana mabashrabsh

لأ شكرا، أنا مابشريش

I'll just have a drink of water
ana Hākhod kobbāyit mīya
bas

أنا حاخذ كوبّاية ميّة بس

drinking water mīyit shorb

ميّة شرب

is this drinking water? el mīya
SalHa lesh-shorb?

الميّة صالحة للشرب

drive (verb) sā'

ساق

we drove here gayna bil
Aarabayya

جينا بالعربية

I'll drive you home HawaSalak
lil bayt bil Aarabayya

حوصلك بالعربية

driver (man/woman) sowā'/
sowā'a

سوّاق / سوّاقة

driving
Driving in Egypt is not for the
faint-hearted or inexperienced
motorist. Although driving on
the right is pretty much universal, other rules of the road vary.
Traffic in cities is relentless
and anarchic, with vehicles
weaving between lanes, signal-
ling by horn. Two beeps means
'I'm alongside and about to
overtake.' A single long blast
means 'I can't (won't) stop
and I'm coming through!'. Ex-
tending your hand, fingers
raised and tips together, is
the signal for 'watch out, don't
pass now'; spreading your
→

fingers and flipping them forwards indicates 'go ahead'. Although the car in front usually has right of way, buses and trams always take precedence.

On country roads – including the two-lane east and west bank highways along the Nile Valley – trucks and cars routinely overtake in the face of oncoming traffic. The passing car usually flashes its lights as a warning, but not always. Most roads are bumpy, with deep potholes and all manner of traffic, including donkey carts and camels. Avoid driving after dark, when Egyptians drive without lights, only flashing them to high beam when they see another car approaching. The official speed limit is 90km per hour (100km on the Cairo-Alexandria desert road), but on certain stretches it can be as low as 30km per hour. The minimum age for driving in Egypt is 25 years, the maximum age is 70 years.

driving licence rokhsit sewā'a

رخصة سواقة

drop: just a drop, please (of drink: to man/woman) shwīya soghīyareen, low samaHt/ samaHtee

شويّة صغيّرين، لو سمحت/سمحتى

drug dowa (m)

دوا

drugs (narcotics) mokhaddarāt

مخدّرات

Egypt has strict anti-drugs laws that make hanging or life imprisonment mandatory for convicted smugglers and dealers (which could be interpreted to mean someone caught with a few sachets of the stuff). Mere possession or use merits a severe prison sentence and a heavy fine (plus legal costs). Despite this, bango (marijuana) is still consumed by Egyptians who can afford it, and by tourists in Dahab, Luxor, Aswan, Hurghada and Cairo.

drunk (adj) sakrān

سكران

dry (adj) nāshif

ناشف

(wine) 'dry'

دراى

dry-cleaner tanDeef Aala
en-nāshif

تنضيف على الناشف

due: he was due to arrive
yesterday howa kan
mafrooD yewsal en-naharda

هوّ كان مفروض يوصل
النهار ده

when is the train due? el aTr
gī imta?

القطر جاى إمتى؟

dull (pain) mo'lim

مؤلم

(boring) momil

ممل

dummy (baby's) bazzāza

بزّازة

during fee nafs elwa't

فى نفس الوقت

dust torāb

تراب

dusty metarrab

متربّ

Dutch* holāndee

هولاندى

duty-free (goods) beDāAa Horra

بضاعة حرّة

duty-free shop maHal beDāAa
Horra

محل بضاعة حرّة

duvet leHāf

لحاف

dynasty osra malakaya

أسرة ملكية

dysentery dosentārya

دوسنتاريا

E

each (every) kol

كل

how much are they each?
bekam el waHda?

بكام الواحدة؟

ear widān

ودان

earache: I have earache
widānee wagaAānee

ودانى وجعانى

early badree

بدرى

early in the morning eS-SobH
badree

الصبح بدرى

I called by earlier ana
Aaddayt badree

أنا عدّيت بدرى

earrings Hel'ān

حلقان

earthenware fokhar

فخار

east shar'

شرق

in the east fesh-shar

فى الشرق

Easter Aeed sham el neseem

عيد شم النسيم

eastern shar'ee

شرقى

Eastern Desert eS-SaHara' esh-shar'aya

الصحراء الشرقيّة

easy sahl

سهل

eat kol

كل

we've already eaten, thanks

eHna kalna khalāS, shokran

إحنا أكلنا خلاص، شكرا

eau de toilette kolonia

كولونيا

economy class daraga tania

درجة تانية

egg bayDa

بيضة

Egypt maSr

مصر

Ancient Egypt maSr el faraoonaya

مصر الفرعونيّة

Egyptian maSree

مصرى

either: either ... or ...

ay ... ow ...

أى ... أو ...

either of them ay wāHid feehom

أىّ واحد فيهم

elbow kooA

كوع

electric bil kahraba

بالكهربا

electrical appliances adawāt kahrabā'ayya

أدوات كهربائيّة

electrician kahrabā'ee

كهربائى

electricity kahraba

كهربا

elevator asansayr

أسانسير

The current in Egypt is 220V, 50Hz. North American travellers with appliances designed for 110V should bring a converter. Most sockets are for round-pronged plugs, so you'll need an adaptor. Brief power cuts are quite common.

else: something else Hāga tania

حاجة تانية

somewhere else Hetta tania

حتة تانية

Menu Reader:

Drink

ESSENTIAL TERMS

beer beera

بيرة

bottle ezāza

قزازة

  a bottle of beer ezāzit beera

قزازة بيرة

coffee ahwa

قهوة

cup fongān

فنجان

glass (tumbler) kobbāya

كوبّاية

  (wine glass) kās

كاس

milk laban

لبن

mineral water mīya
maAdanaya

ماء معدنيه

orange juice AaSeer borto'an

عصير برتقال

red wine nebeet aHmar

نبيذ أحمر

soft drink mashroob ghayr
koHollee

غير كوحوليّ

sugar sokkar

سكر

tea (drink) shī

شاي

water mīya

ميّة

white wine nebeet abyaD

نبيت أبيض

wine nebeet

نبيت

a cup of ..., please (to man/
woman) fongān ..., low
samaHt/samaHtee

فنجان...، لو
سمحت/سمحتي

another beer, please (to man/
woman) momkin beera tania,
low samaHt/samaHtee?

ممكن بيرة تانية لو
سمحت/سمحتي؟

ALCOHOLIC DRINKS

زبيب zebeeb an aniseed-flavoured spirit, similar to Greek ouzo

جاز jaz bottle; brandy

عمر الخيام omar khīam a dry red wine

'كرو دى بطليموس 'Cru des Ptolémées' a dry white wine

بيرة beera beer

ستيلا بيرة beera stella® lager

نبيت أحمر nebeet aHmar red wine

وردى wardee rosé wine

روبيس دى إجبت roobis 'd'Egypt' a rosé wine

أحمر aHmar® a type of brandy

معتق meAatta'® a type of brandy

فين yin® a type of brandy

نبيت أبيض nebeet abyaD white wine

نبيت nebeet wine

COFFEE, TEA ETC

قهوة ahwa coffee, Turkish coffee

قهوة كابوتشينو ahwa 'cappuccino' cappuccino

قهوة محوجة ahwa meHowega coffee spiced with cardamom seeds

قهوة باللبن ahwa bel laban coffee with milk

قهوة سادة ahwa sāda coffee without sugar

قهوة إسبريسو ahwa 'espresso' espresso

قهوة مظبوطة ahwa mazbooTa medium-sweet coffee

قهوة فرنساوى ahwa fransawi Nescafé; filter coffee

قهوة عالريحة ahwa Aar-reeHa slightly sweetened coffee

قهوة زيادة ahwa zayāda very sweet coffee

شاى shī tea

شاى باللبن shī bel laban tea with milk

ينسون yansoon aniseed tea

قرفة erfa cinnamon tea

حلبة Helba fenugreek tea

كركديه karkaday hibiscus flower tea

شاى متلج shī metaleg iced tea

شاى بالنعناع shī ben neAnāA mint tea

سادة **sāda** without sugar

كاكاو **kakow** hot chocolate

سحلب **saHlab** hot drink made from ground rice and cornflour with milk, sugar and nuts

FRUIT JUICES AND OTHER SOFT DRINKS

عصير موز **AaSeer mōz** banana milk shake

سبورت كولا 'Sport Cola®' brand of cola

بركة **baraka**® brand of mineral water

سيوة **Siwa**® brand of mineral water

عصير جزر **AaSeer gazar** carrot juice

كاكولا **kakoola**® Coca Cola®

خروب **kharroob** cold carob-flavoured drink

عصير فواكه **AaSeer fowākih** fruit juice

عصير جريب فروت **AaSeer graybfroot** grapefruit juice

عصير جوافة **AaSeer gowafa** guava juice

عصير لمون **AaSeer lamoon** lemonade (made with real lemon juice)

عرقسوس **Aer'soos** liquorice water

عصير منجة **AaSeer manga** mango juice

لبن **laban** milk

مية معدنية **mīya maAadanaya** mineral water

كوكتيل 'cocktail' mixed fruit juices

كندا دراي 'Canada dry'® fizzy drink in a variety of flavours

تيم **teem** ® orange drink

عصير برتقال **AaSeer borto'ān** orange juice

سڤن أب '7 Up'® 7-Up®

عصير فراولة **AaSeer farowla** strawberry juice

عصير قصب **AaSeer 'asab** sugar cane juice

بيبسي 'Pepsi'® Pepsi®

صودا **sōda** soda water

مشروب بيرل **mashroob birl** spring water

عناب **Aennab** tamarind and hibiscus drink

تمر هندى **tamr hindee** tamarind juice with water

مية **mīya** water

Stay in touch with us!

ROUGH*NEWS* **is Rough Guides' free newsletter. In three issues a year we give you news, travel issues, music reviews, readers' letters and the latest dispatches from authors on the road.**

I would like to receive ROUGH*NEWS*: please put me on your free mailing list.

NAME . . . .

ADDRESS . . . .

Please clip or photocopy and send to: Rough Guides, 1 Mercer Street, London WC2H 9QJ, England

or Rough Guides, 375 Hudson Street, New York, NY 10014, USA.

Wherever you're headed, **Rough Guides** tell you what's happening – the history, the people, the politics, the best beaches, nightlife and entertainment on your budget

GUIDES
100 destinations worldwide
...to Zimbabwe.

¿Qué pasa?

WHAT'S HAPPENING?
A ROUGH GUIDES SERIES –
ROUGH GUIDES PHRASEBOOKS

Rough Guide Phrasebooks represent a complete shakeup of the phrasebook format. Handy and pocket sized, they work like a dictionary to get you straight to the point. With clear guidelines on pronunciation, dialogues for typical situations, and tips on cultural issues, they'll have you speaking the language quicker than any other phrasebook.

Czech, French, German, Greek, Hindi & Urdu, Italian, Indonesian, Mandarin Chinese, Mexican Spanish, Polish, Portuguese, Russian, Spanish, Thai, Turkish, Vietnamese
Further titles coming soon...

would you like anything else? (to
man/woman) teHeb/teHebbee aī
shay' tānee?

no, nothing else, thanks la', bas
keda, shokran

embassy safāra

سفارة

emergency Tawāri'

طوارئ

this is an emergency! dee
Hālit Tawāri'!

دى حالة طوارئ!

emergency exit bab eT-Tawāri'

باب الطوارئ

empty fāDee

فاضى

end (noun) nehāya

نهاية

at the end of the street fee
ākhr eT-Taree'

فى اخر الطريق

when does it end? betekhlas
imta?

بتخلص إمتى؟

engaged (toilet, telephone)
maJghool

مشغول

(to be married: man/woman)
khāTeb/makhTooba

خاطب/مخطوبة

engine (car) motōr

موتور

England ingiltera

إنجلترا

English ingleezee

إنجليزى

I'm English (said by man/woman)
ana ingleezee/ingleezaya

أنا إنجليزى/إنجليزية

do you speak English? (to man/
woman) betitkallim/
betitkallimee ingleezee?

بتتكلّم/ بتتكلمى
إنجليزى؟

enjoy: enjoy oneself istamtaA

إستمتع

•••••• DIALOGUE ••••••

how did you like the film? (to man/
woman) Aagabak/Aagabik el
'film'?

I enjoyed it very much, did you
enjoy it? Aagabnee geddan,
istamtaAt beeh?

enjoyable momteA

مُتع

enlargement (of photo) takbeer

تكبير

enormous Dakhm

ضخم

enough kifāya

كفاية

there's not enough mish kifāya

مش كفاية

it's not big enough mish kebeer kifāya

مش كبير كفاية

that's enough da kifāya

دا كفاية

entrance madkhal

مدخل

envelope zarf

ظرف

epileptic mosāb bil saraA

مصاب بالصرع

equipment moAiddāt

معدّات

error ghalaT

غلط

especially khosooSan

خصوصا

essential asāsee

أساسى

it is essential that ... da Darooree en ...

دا ضرورى ان ...

Eurocheque esh sheek el orobbee

الشيك الأوروبى

Eurocheque card kart esh sheek el orobbee

كارت الشيك الأوروبى

Europe orobba

أوروبا

European orobbee

أوروبى

even Hatta

حتّى

even if ... Hatta low ...

حتّى لو ...

evening mesa

مساء

this evening ellaylādee

الليلة دى

in the evening bil layl

بالليل

evening meal Aasha

عشا

eventually akheeran

آخيرا

ever abadan

أبدا

•••••• DIALOGUE ••••••

have you ever been to the Egyptian Museum? (to man) Aomrak roHt lil mat-Haf el-maSree?

(to woman) Aomrik roHtee lil mat-Haf elmaSree?

yes, I was there two years ago

īwa, roHt henāk min sanatayn

every kol

كل

every day kol yōm

كل يوم

everyone kol wāHid

كل واحد

everything kol Hāga

كل حاجة

everywhere kol Hetta

كل حتة

exactly! beZZabT!

بالظبط!

exam imtaHān

إمتحان

example mesāl

مثال

for example masalan

مثلاً

excellent momtāz

ممتاز

except maAada

ماعدا

excess baggage Aafsh zayid

عفش زايد

exchange rate seAr et-taHweel

سعر التحويل

exciting (day, holiday) gameel

جميل

(film) moseer

مشير

excursion reHla oSīyara

رحلة قصيرة

excuse me (to get past: to man/
woman) low samaHt/
samaHtee

لو سمحت/سمحتي

(to get attention) min faDlak

من فضلك

(to say sorry: said by man/woman)

ana āsif/āsfa

أنا آسف/آسفة

exhaust (pipe) eJ-Jakmān

الجاكمان

exhausted (tired) mayit min
et-taAab

ميّت من التعب

exhibition maAraD

معرض

exit khoroog

خروج

where's the nearest exit? fayn
a'rab bab?

فين أقرب باب؟

expect towaQQaA

توقع

expensive ghālee

غالى

experienced khabeer

خبير

explain **waDDaH**

وضّح

can you explain that? (to man/woman) **momkin tewaDDaH/ tewaDDaHee da?**

ممكن توضّح/توضّحى دا؟

express (mail) **mestaAgil**

مستعجل

(train) **magaree**

مجرى

extension (telephone) **taHweela**

تحويلة

extension 221, please (to man/ woman) **taHweela maytayn wāHid weAeshreen, low samaHt/samaHtee**

تحويلة ٢٢١ لو سمحت/ سمحتى

extension lead **meHowil**

محول

extra: can we have an extra one? **momkin nākhod wāHid zayāda?**

ممكن ناخذ واحد زيادة؟

do you charge extra for that? **Had-daffaAanee aktar Aashān da?**

حتدفعنا أكتر علشان دا؟

extraordinary **ghayr Aādee**

غير عادى

extremely **giddan**

جداً

eye **Aayn** (f)

عين

will you keep an eye on my suitcase for me? (to man/woman) **momkin tekhallee bālak/ balik min shanTetee?**

ممكن تخللي بالك/ بالك من شنطتى؟

eye drops **aTra lil Aayn**

قطرة للعين

eyeglasses **naDDāra**

نضّارة

F

face **wish**

وش

factory **maSnaA**

مصنع

Fahrenheit **Fahrenhayt**

فهرنهايت

faint (verb) **oghma Aalayh**

أغمى عليه

she's fainted **oghma Aalayha**

أغمى عليها

I feel faint (said by man/woman) **ana Hasis/Has-sa ennee Hayoghma Aalaya**

أنا حاسس/حاسّة إنّى حايغمى على

fair (funfair) **moolid**

مولد

(trade) **maAraD**

معرض

(adj) **AarD**

عرض

fairly **belHa'**

بالحق

fake (noun) **ta'leed**

تقليد

fall (verb) **we'eA**

وقع

she's had a fall **hayya we'Ait**

هيّ وقعت

fall **khareef**

خريف

in the fall **fil khareef**

فى الخريف

false **mozayaf**

مزيّف

family **Aayla**

عيلة

famous **mash-hoor**

مشهور

fan (electrical, hand-held)

marwaHa

مروحة

(sports: man/woman) **moshaggeA/**

moshaggeAa

مشجع / مشجعة

fantastic **modhish**

مدهش

far **beAeed**

بعيد

•••••• DIALOGUE ••••••

is it far from here? **howa beAeed**
min hena?

no, not very far **la', mish beAeed**
awee

well how far? **Hawālee ad ay?**

it's about 20 kilometres **Hawālee**
Aeshreen kelomitr

fare **ogra**

أجرة

farm **mazraAa**

مزرعة

fashionable **ākher mōDa**

آخر موضة

fast **sareeA**

سريع

fat (person) **tekheen**

تخين

(on meat) **simeen**

سمين

father **abb**

أب

father-in-law **Hama**

حما

faucet **Hanafaya**

حنفيّة

fault **zamb**

ذنب

sorry, it was my fault (said by

man/woman) āsif/āsfa, da kan
zambee ana

آسف/أسفة، دا كان ذنبى
أنا

it's not my fault mosh zambee
ana

مش ذنبى أنا

faulty fee Aayb

فى عيب

favourite mofaDDal

مفضّل

fax (noun) 'fax'

فاكس

(verb) fakas

فكس

Most hotels with three or more
stars have fax machines,
making fax the best way to
reserve a room from abroad.
Faxes can be sent from (and
received at) certain telephone
offices in the main cities; you
can also have them sent to
American Express offices, who'll
hold them like client mail but
won't notify the recipient.

fax machine gihāz 'fax'

جهاز فاكس

February fibrīyer

فبراير

feel: I feel hot (said by man/woman)
ana Harrān/Harrāna

أنا حرّان/حرّانة

I feel unwell (said by man/
woman) ana taAbān/taAbāna

أنا تعبان/تعبانة

I feel like going for a walk (said
by man/woman) ana Aayiz/Aīza
atmasha

أنا عايز/عايزة أتمشّى

how are you feeling? (to man/
woman) izzay SeHetak/
SeHetik?

إزّاى صحّتك/صحّتك؟

I'm feeling much better (said by
man/woman) ana Hāsis/Has-sa
bitaHasson

نا حاسس/حاسّة بتحسّن

fence soor

سور

fender (US) ekseDām

إكسضام

ferry meAaddaya

معدّية

Local ferries cross the Nile and
the Suez at various points. They
are generally cheap, battered
and crowded. There are also
smarter tourist ferries between
Luxor and the West Bank, but

→

it's more fun to use the ordinary boats.

Long-distance services are confined to the Red Sea and the Gulf of Aqaba, where the old slow boats have largely been superseded by the Flying Cat, a deluxe high-speed catamaran that zips over from Hurghada to Sharm el-Sheik once a day in under two hours. The fare isn't much more than that charged by the last of the old boats (which take over five hours), and is worth it to avoid the long overland journey via Suez. The Flying Cat also runs to the Jordanian port of Aqaba, and takes diving groups to various destinations.

festival mahragān

مهرجان

Moolids are the equivalent of medieval European saints' fairs: their ostensible aim is to obtain blessing (baraka) from the saint, but the social and cultural dimensions are equally important. Moolids are an opportunity for people to escape their hard-working lives in several →

days of festivities, and for friends and families from different villages to meet. The largest events draw crowds of over a million, with people running stalls and rides, and music blaring into the small hours. Smaller, rural moolids tend to be heavier on the practical devotion, with people bringing their children or livestock for blessing, or the sick to be cured.

fetch gāb

جاب

I'll fetch him Hageeboh

حاجيبه

will you come and fetch me later? momkin tegee takhodnee baAdayn?

ممكن تيجى تاخدنى بعدين؟

feverish maHmoom

محموم

few: (a) few shwīya

شويّة

a few days baAd shwīyet ayyām

بعد شويّة أيّام

fiancé khaTeeb

خطيب

fiancée khaTeeba

خطيبة

field magāl

مجال

fight (noun) khinā'a

خناقة

figs teen

تين

fill in mala

ملى

do I have to fill this in? howa ana lāzim amla dee?

هوّ أنا لازم أملى دى؟

fill up mala

ملى

fill it up, please imlāha, low samaHt

إملاها، لو سمحت

filling (in sandwich, in tooth) Hashw

حشو

film 'film'

فيلم

•••••• DIALOGUE ••••••

do you have this kind of film? (to man/woman) Aandak/Aandik 'film' min en-nooA da?

yes, how many exposures? (to man/woman) īwa, Aayiz/Aīza kām? 36 sitta wetalateen

film processing taHmeeD aflām

تحميض أفلام

filthy wesikh

وسخ

find (verb) la'a

لأ

I can't find it mosh la'eeh

مش لقيه

I've found it la'aytoh

لقيته

find out iktashaf

إكتشف

could you find out for me? (to man/woman) momkin teshoof/ teshoofee le?

ممكن تشوف/تشوفى لى؟

fine (weather) kwayis

كويّس

(punishment) gharāma

غرامة

•••••• DIALOGUES ••••••

how are you? (to man/woman) izzayak/izzayik?

I'm fine, thanks (said by man/woman) ana kwayis/kwayisa, shokran

is that OK? da kwayis?

that's fine, thanks da kwayis, shokran

finger sobaA

صبع

finish (verb) khalaS

خلاص

I haven't finished yet lessa
makhal-lastish

لسة ماخلصتش

when does it finish?
betekhal-las imta?

بتخلّص إمتى؟

fire (in hearth) nār (f)

نار

(campfire) nār el mokhayam

نار المخيّم

(blaze) lahab

لهب

fire! Haree'a!

حريقة

can we light a fire here?
momkin newallaA nār hena?

ممكن نولّع نار هنا؟

it's on fire mewallaAa

مولّعة

fire alarm garas inzār

جرس إنذار

fire brigade el maTāfee

المطافئ

The number for the fire brigade
is 125.

---

fire escape makhrag Haree'

مخرج حريق

fire extinguisher Taffīyet Haree'

طفّاية حريق

first awwil (m)/olā (f)

أوّل/أولى

I was first (said by man/woman)
ana kont el awwil/olā

أنا كنت الأوّل/الأولى

at first awwalan

أوّلا

the first time el marra el olā

المرة الأولى

first on the left el awwal Aala
eedak esh-shemāl

الأوّل على إيدك الشمال

first aid isAāf awwalee

إسعاف أوّلى

first-aid kit shanTit isAāf
awwalee

شنطة إسعاف أوّلى

first-class (travel etc) daraga olā

درجة أولى

first floor ed-dōr el awwil

الدور الأوّل

(US) ed-dōr el arDee

الدور الأرضى

first name esm

إسم

fish (noun) samak

سمك

fishing sayd samak

صيد سمك

fishing boat markib sayd

مركب صيد

fishing village Qaryit sayd
samak

قرية صيد سمك

fishmonger's bayyāA samak

بيّاع سمك

fit (attack) azma

أزمّة

fit: it doesn't fit me mish
monāsib laya

مش مناسب لى

fitting room ōDit taghyeer
malābis

أوضة تغيير ملابس

fix (arrange) rattib

رتّب

can you fix this? (repair)
momkin tessallaH da?

ممكن تصلح دا؟

fizzy fowwār

فوّار

flag Aalam

علم

flannel fooTit wish

فوطة وش

flash (for camera) 'flash'

فلاش

flat (noun: apartment) sha'-a

شقّة

(adj) mosaTTaH

مسطح

I've got a flat tyre el kowetsh
nayim

الكاوتش نايم

flavour TaAm

طعم

flea barghoot

برغوت

flight reHla gowaya

رحلة جوّية

flight number raQam er-riHla

رقم الرحلة

flippers zaAānif

زعانف

flood fīaDān

فيضان

floor (of room) arD (f)

أرض

(storey) dōr

دور

on the floor Aalal arD

على الأرض

florist maHal zohoor

محل زهور

flour de'ee'

دقيق

flower warda

وردة

flu infelwanza

إنفلونزا

fluent: he speaks fluent Arabic

howa bayetkallim Aarabee

kwayis awee

هوّ بيتكلّم عربى كويس قوى

fly (noun) dibbāna

دبّانة

(verb) Tar

طار

fly spray bakhākhit dibbān

بخّاخة دبّان

fog shaboora

شابورة

foggy: it's foggy eg-gow

shaboora

الجوّ شابورة

folk dancing ra'S shaAbee

رقص شعبى

folk music moseeQa shaAbaya

موسيقى شعبيّة

(in Upper Egypt) moseeQa

SeAeedee

موسيقى صعيدى

follow tebeA

تبع

follow me emshee warāya

إمشى ورايا

food akl

اكل

food poisoning tasammom

تسمم

food shop/store maHal beʼāla

محل بقالة

foot (of person) rigl

رجل

(measurement) adam

قدم

on foot Aala er-riglayn

على الرجلين

football (game) kōrit Qadam

كورة قدم

(ball) kōra

كورة

football match motsh kōra

ماتش كورة

for: do you have something

for ...? (headache/diarrhoea etc: to

man/woman) Aandak/Aandik

Haga le ...?

عندَك/عندِك حاجة

ل...؟

•••••• DIALOGUES ••••••

who's the molokhayya for?

lemeen el molokhayya?

that's for me dee Aalashānee

and this one? wedee?

that's for her dee Alashānha

where do I get the bus for Giza?

minayn ākhod el otobees el-lee

bayrooh eg-geeza?

the bus for Giza leaves from Rameses Street otobees eg-geeza bayeTlaA min shāriA ramsees

how long have you been here? kam ba'ālak hena?

I've been here for two days, how about you? (to man/woman) ba'ālee hena yōmayn, winta/winti?

I've been here for a week ba'ālee hena esbooA

forehead oora
قورة

foreign agnabee
أجنبى

foreigner (man/woman) agnabee/agnabaya
أجنبى/أجنبية

forest ghāba
غابة

forget nasa
نسى

I forget, I've forgotten nasayt
نسيت

fork shōka
شوكة

(in road) tafreeAa
تفريعة

form (document) namoozag
نموذج

formal rasmee
رسمى

fortnight isboAayn
إسبوعين

fortress alAa
قلعة

fortunately leHosn el HaZ
لحسن الحظ

forward: could you forward my mail? momkin tebaAt/tebaAtee gowabātee Aalal Ainwān eg-gedeed?
ممكن تبعت/تبعتى جواباتى على العنوان الجديد؟

forwarding address el Ainwān eg-gedeed
العنوان الجديد

fountain (ornamental) nafoora
نافورة

(for drinking) Hanafaya
حنفيّة

foyer sāla
صالة

fracture (noun) sha'
شق

France faransa
فرنسا

free (no charge) bebalāsh
ببلاش

is it free (of charge)? da

bebalāsh?

دا ببلاش؟

freeway eT-Taree' es-sareeA

الطريق السريع

freezer frayzar

فريزر

French faransāwee

فرنساوى

French fries baTaTes meHammara

بطاطس محمّرة

frequent AalaTool

على طول

how frequent is the bus to Ma'adee? kam otobees bayrooH el maAādee?

كم أوتوبيس بيروح المعادى؟

fresh Tāza

طازة

fresh orange juice AaSeer borto'an Tāza

عصير برتقان طازة

Friday el gomAa

الجمعة

fridge tallāga

تلاجة

fried ma'lee

مقلى

fried egg bayDa ma'laya

بيضة مقليّة

friend (male/female) SaHib/SaHba

صاحب/صاحبة

friendly Hebbee

حِبّى

from min

من

when does the next train from Alexandria arrive? imta yewSal el aTr el gī min iskinderaya?

إمتى يوصل القطر الجاى من إسكندريّة؟

from Monday to Friday min el etnayn lil gomAa

من الإتنين للجمعة

from next Thursday min el khamees el gī

من الخميس الجاى

•••••• DIALOGUE ••••••

where are you from? (to man) inta minayn?

(to woman) inti minayn

I'm from Slough ana min 'Slough'

front wag-ha

واجهة

in front oddām

قدّام

in front of the hotel oddām el fondo'

قدّام الفندق

at the front fil mo'addima

فى المقدّمة

fruit fawākih

فواكه

fruit juice AaSeer fawākih

عصير فواكه

full malyān

مليان

it's full of … malyana be …

مليانة

I'm full (said by man/woman) ana shabAān/shabAāna

أنا شبعان/ شبعانة

full board iqāma kamla

إقامة كاملة

funeral ganāza

جنازة

funny (strange) ghareeb

غريب

(amusing) mosallee

مسلّى

furniture asās

أساس

further abAad

أبعد

it's further down the road hayya oddām shwīya

هىّ قدّام شويّة

•••••• DIALOGUE ••••••

how much further is it to Shubra?
fāDil kam keelo Aala shobra?
about five kilometres Hawālee
khamsa keelo

future mosta'bal

مستقبل

in future fil most'abal

فى المستقبل

G

gallon gālōn

جالون

game (cards etc) kotshayna

كوتشينة

(match) 'match'

ماتش

(meat) Sayd

صيد

garage (for fuel) maHaTTit banzeen

محطة بنزين

(for repairs) warshit Aarabayyāt

ورشة عربيّات

(for parking) mow'af Aarabayyāt

موقف عربيّات

garden gonayna

جنينة

garlic tōm

توم

gas gāz

جاز

(US) banzeen

بنزين

gas can SafeeHet banzeen

صفيحة بنزين

gas cylinder amboobit

botagāz

أنبوبة بوتاجاز

gas station maHaTTit banzeen

محطة بنزين

gate bawwāba

بوّابة

gearbox el fetees

الفتيس

gear lever Aamood el fetees

عمود

gears troos

تروس

general (adj) Aām

عام

gents (toilet) tawalet rigālee,

Hammām er-rigāl

تواليت رجالي، حمّام الرجال

genuine (antique etc) Ha'ee'ee

حقيقي

German almānee

ألماني

Germany almānya

ألمانيّة

get (fetch) gāb

جاب

could you get me another one,
please? (to man) momkin
tegeeb le waHda tania, low
samaHt?

ممكن تجيب لي
واحدة تانية، لوسمحت؟

(to woman) momkin tegeebee
le waHda tania, low
samaHtee?

ممكن تجيبي لي
واحدة تانية، لوسمحتى؟

how do I get to ...? izzay
arooH le ...?

إزاي أروح ل....؟

do you know where I can get
them? teAraf minayn a'dar
ageebhom?

تعرف منين أقدر اجيبهم

•••••• DIALOGUE ••••••

can I get you a drink? (to man/
woman) teshrab/teshrabee ay?

no, I'll get this one la', ana el-lee
HaTlob el marrādee

what would you like? (to man/
woman) teHeb/teHebbee teshrab/
teshrabee ay?

a glass of red wine kās nebeet aHmar

get back (return) ragaA

رجع

get in (arrive) waSal

وصل

get off nazal

نزل

where do I get off? anzil fayn?

أنزل فين؟

get on (to train etc) rakab

ركب

get out (of car etc) nazal

نزل

get up (in the morning) SaHā

صحى

gift hedaya

هديّة

gift shop maHal hadāya

محل هدايا

gin Jin

جن

a gin and tonic, please (to man/woman) Jin we tonik, low samaHt/samaHtee

جن وتونيك، لو سمحت/ سمحتى

girl bint

بنت

girlfriend SaHba

صاحبة

give ed-da

إدّى

can you give me some change? momkin teddeenee shwīyet fakka?

ممكن تدّينى شويّة فكة؟

I gave it to him ana eddithaloo

إدّيتها له

will you give this to ...? momkin teddee da le ...?

ممكن تدّى دا ل ...؟

•••••• DIALOGUE ••••••

how much do you want for this? (to man) Aayiz tebeeA el waHda bekām?

(to woman) Aīza tebeAee el waHda bekām?

I'll give it to you for five pounds (to man/woman) Haddeelak/ Haddeelik elwaHda bekhamsa geneeh

give back ragaA

رجع

glass (material) ezāz

قزاز

(tumbler) kobbāya

كوبّايا

(wine glass) **kās**

كاس

a glass of water **kās mīya**

كاس مية

glasses **naDDāra**

نضارة

go **raH**

راح

we'd like to go to the Opera
House **Aīzeen nerooH le dār
elobra**

عايزين نروح لدار الأوبرا

where are you going? (to man)
inta rīeH fayn?

إنت رايح فين؟

(to woman) **inti rīHa fayn?**

إنتى رايحة فين؟

where does this bus go? **fayn
rīeH el otobees da?**

فين رايح الأوتوبيس دا؟

let's go! **yalla
nimshee!**

يللا نمشى!

she's gone (left) **hayya
meshet**

هيّ مشت

where has he gone? **fayn raH
howa?**

فين راح هوّ؟

I went there last week
ana roHt hināk el esbōA el-

lee fāt

أنا رحت هناك
الأسبوع اللى فات

go away **emshee min hena**

إمشى من هنا

go away! **emshee!**

إمشى!

go back (return) **ragaA**

رجع

go down (the stairs etc) **nazal**

نزل

go in **dakhal**

دخل

go out: do you want to go out
tonight? (to man) **Aayiz
tokhrog e-laylade?**

عايز تخرج الليلة دى؟

(to woman) **Aīza tokhrogee
e-laylade?**

عايزة تخرجى الليلة دى؟

go through **mar**

مر

go up (the stairs etc) **TalaA**

طلع

goat **meAza**

معزة

god **rab**

رب

God **allāh**

الله

God willing **inshā'llāh**

إن شاء الله

goddess ilāha

إلاهة

goggles naDDara Tibbaya

نضّارة طبّية

gold dahab

ذهب

good kwayis

كويس

good! kwayis!

كويس!

it's no good mish kwayis

مش كويس

goodbye maAssalāma

مع السلامة

good evening masā' el khayr

مساء الخير

Good Friday el gomAa el Hazeena

الجمعة الحزينة

good morning SabāH el khayr

صباح الخير

good night masā' el khayr

مساء الخير

got: we've got to leave iHna lāzim nemshee

إحنا لازم نمشى

have you got any ...? (to man/woman) Aandak/Aandik aī ...?

عندَك/ عندِك أى ...؟

government Hokooma

حكومة

gradually shwīya shwīya

شويّة شويّة

gram(me) grām

جرام

granddaughter Hafeeda

حفيدة

grandfather gid

جد

grandmother gidda

جدة

grandson Hafeed

حفيد

grapefruit graybfroot

جريب فروت

grapefruit juice AaSeer graybfroot

عصير جريب فروت

grapes Aenab

عنب

(small, seedless) Aenab banātee

عنب بناتى

(large) Aenab fayyoomee

عنب فيّومى

grass Hasheesh

حشيش

grateful motshakkir

متشكر

gravy Tāgin

طاجن

great (excellent) AaZeem

عظيم

that's great! da AaZeem!

دا عظيم!

a great success nagāH kebeer

نجاح كبير

Great Britain beriTanya el AoZma

بريطانيا العظمى

Greece el yonān

اليونان

greedy TamaA

طمع

Greek yonānee

يونانى

green akhDar

أخضر

green card (car insurance) 'green card'

جرين كارد

greengrocer's (vegetable shop) khoDaree

خضرى

(fruit shop) fakahānee

فكهانى

grey romādee

رمادى

grilled mashwee

مشوى

grocer's ba'āl

بقال

ground arD (f)

أرض

on the ground Aalal arD

على الأرض

ground floor ed-dōr el arDee

الدور الأرضى

group magmooAa

مجموعة

guest (man/woman) Dayf/Dayfa

ضيف / ضيفة

When invited into someone's home, it's the custom to take your shoes off before entering the reception rooms. It's also customary to take a gift: sweet pastries (or tea and sugar in rural areas) are always acceptable. At a communal meal, it is important to use the right hand and not the left – Muslims use that hand for washing after going to the toilet.

guesthouse bansayōn

بنسيون

see hotel

guide (man/woman) morshid/ morshida

مرشد / مرشدة

Official guides can be engaged through branches of Misr Travel, American Express and Thomas Cook, local tourist offices and large hotels. You can also hire them on the spot at the Antiquities Museum in Cairo and the Pyramids of Giza. They normally charge a fixed hourly rate, which can be shared among a group of people, though obviously a group would be expected to make some sort of additional tip. Such professional guides can be useful at major sites, like the Valley of the Kings, where they will be able to ease your way through queues at the tombs.

Far more common are local, self-appointed guides, who fall into two main categories. At ancient sites there are often plenty of loungers-around, who will offer to show you 'secret tombs' or 'special reliefs', or just present themselves in tombs or temples, with palms outstretched. They don't have a lot to offer and you can usually get rid of them by reading aloud from a guide book.

The other kind – most often encountered in a small town or village – are people who genuinely want to help out foreigners, and maybe practise their English at the same time. They are often teenagers. Services offered could be escorting you from one taxi depot to another, or showing you the route to the market or a local site. The majority of people you meet in this way don't expect money and you could risk offence by offering. If people want money from you for such activities, they won't be shy about asking.

An official version of this kind of guiding is offered by members of the Tourist Friends Association, who often approach lost-looking foreigners at bus and train stations, and will swiftly produce their identity cards. They are generally students, very friendly and helpful, and not on the make. Be courteous, even if you don't want their help.

guidebook daleel sayāHee
دليل سياحى
guided tour gowla
mowwagaha
جولة موجّهة

→

guitar gitār

جيتار

Gulf: the Gulf States diwal el khaleeg el Aarabee

دول الخليج العربي

gum (in mouth) lessa

لسّة

gun (rifle) bondo'aya

بندقيّة

(pistol) mosaddas

مسدس

H

hair shaAr

شعر

hairbrush forshit shaAr

فرشة شعر

haircut Hilā'a

حلاقة

hairdresser's (men's) Hallā'

حلاق

(women's) kowafayr

كوافير

hairdryer seshwār

سشوار

hair spray mossabbit shaAr

مثبت شعر

half nos

نص

half an hour nos sāAa

نص ساعة

half a litre nos litr

نص لتر

about half that Hawālee nos da

حوالى نص دا

half board nos eQāma

نص إقامة

half-bottle nos ezāza

نص قزازة

half fare nos tazkara

نص تذكرة

half-price nos et-taman

نص التمن

ham werk khanzeer

ورك خنزير

hamburger 'hamburger'

هامبورجر

hand eed

إيد

handbag shanTit eed

شنطة إيد

handbrake farāmil yad

فرامل يد

handkerchief mandeel

منديل

handle (on door) okra

أُكرة

(on suitcase etc) eed

إيد

hand luggage shanTa

شنطة

hangover āsār esh-shorb

اثار الشرب

I've got a hangover (said by man/woman) ana mosāb/ mosāba biāsār esh-shorb

أنا مصاب/مصابة باثار الشرب

happen Hasal

حصل

what's happening? ayh el-lee momkin yeHsal?

إيه اللى ممكن يحصل؟

what has happened? ayh el-lee Hasal?

إيه اللى حصل؟

happy mabsooT

مبسوط

I'm not happy about this (said by man/woman) ana mish mabsooT/mabsooTA beda

أنا مش مبسوط/مبسوطة

harbour meena

ميناء

hard gāmid

جامد

(difficult) SaAb

صعب

hard-boiled egg bayDa masloo'a awee

بيضة مسلوقة قوى

hard lenses Aadasa lāSQa

عدسة لاصقة

hardly: hardly ever nādir

نادر

hardware shop maHal adawāt manzilaya

محل أدوات منزلية

hat Ta'aya

طاقية

hate (verb) karah

كره

have* akhad

أخذ

can I have a ...? momkin ākhod ...?

ممكن آخذ ...؟

do you have ...? fee Aandak/ Aandik ...?

فى عندك/عندك ...؟

what'll you have? (to man/ woman) Hateshrab/ Hateshrabee ay?

حتشرب/حتشربى إيه؟

I have to leave now ana lāzim amshee delwa'tee

أنا لازم أمشى دلوقتى

do I have to ...? lāzim ana ...?

لازم أنا ...؟

can we have some ...? momkin nākhod shwīyet ...?

ممكن ناخد شويّة ...؟

hayfever Homma el-'ash

حُمّى القش

he* howa

هوا

head rās (f)

راس

headache sodāA

صداع

headlights en-noor el oddamānee

النور القدّمانى

healthy seHHee

صحّى

health
Despite the potential health hazards of travel in Egypt, the majority of visitors experience nothing worse than a bout of diarrhoea. If symptoms persist more than a few days, seek medical help.
The main things to guard against are heatstroke and food poisoning, with rare meat and raw shellfish topping the danger list. Just use common sense, and accustom your stomach gradually to Egyptian cooking. Asking for dishes very hot ('sokhna awee') will reduce the risk of catching anything. Take prompt care of cuts and →

skin irritations, since flies can quickly spread infection. Many visitors experience problems with Egypt's intense heat; you can easily become dehydrated without realising it. Dehydration is exacerbated by alcohol, coffee and tea. Drink plenty of other fluids (at least three litres per day; twice as much if you're exerting yourself) and take a bit of extra salt with your food. Wear a hat and loose-fitting clothes (not synthetic fabrics), and a high factor sunscreen to protect yourself from sunburn. Try to avoid going out in the middle of the day and wear a T-shirt when snorkelling, as the sun burns you even quicker in the water.

hear simeA

سمع

•••••• DIALOGUE ••••••

can you hear me? (to man)
te'dar tismaAnee?
(to woman) te'daree tismaAeenee?
I can't hear you, could you repeat that? (to man/woman) ana mish samAak/samAik, momkin teAeed/teAeedee tānee?

heart alb

قلب

heart attack zabHa Sadrayya

ذبحة صدريّة

heat Harāra

حرارة

heatstroke Darbit shams

ضربة شمس

heavy ti'eel

تقيل

heel (of foot, of shoe) kaAb

كعب

could you heel these?
momkin terakkib lee kaAb fee dōl?

ممكن تركب لى كعب فى دول؟

heelbar tasleeH gezam

تصليح جزم

height (of person) Tool

طول

(mountain) Aolow

علو

helicopter 'helicopter'

هليكوبتر

hello ahlan

أهلاً

(answer on phone) aloo

ألو

helmet (for motorcycle) khōza

خوذة

help (noun) mosaAda

مساعدة

(verb) sāAid

ساعد

help! el Ha'oonay!

إلحقونى!

can you help me? momkin tesaAednee?

ممكن تساعدنى؟

thank you very much for your help (to man/woman) shokran giddan Aala mosaAdetak/ mosaAdetik laya

شكراً جداً على مساعدتك/مساعدتك لَيّا

helpful khadoom

خدوم

hepatitis eltihāb fil kibd

إلتهاب فى الكبد

her*: I haven't seen her mashoftahāsh

ماشوفتهاش

to her leha

ليها

with her maAāha

معاها

for her Aalashanha

علشانها

that's her da btaAha

دا بتاعها

that's her towel dee fooTit-ha

دى فوطتها

herbal tea shī Aashāb

شاى أعشاب

herbs aAshāb

أعشاب

here hena

هنا

here is/are ... hena el ...

هنا ال ...

here you are (to man/woman)

etfaDDal/etfaDDalee

إتفضّل / إتفضّلى

hers* btaAha

بتاعها

that's hers da btaAha

دا بتاعها

hey! (to man/woman) inta!/inti!

إنت! / إنتى!

hi! (hello) ahlan!

أهلا!

hide (verb) istakhabba

إستخبّى

hieroglyphics hayroghleefee

هيروغليفى

high Aālee

عالى

highchair korsee Aālee

كرسى عالى

highway eT-Taree' es-sareeA

الطريق السريع

hill maTlaA

مطلع

him*: I haven't seen him

mashofthoosh

ماشوفتهوش

to him leh

له

with him maAāh

معاه

for him Aalashānoo

علشانه

that's him howa da

هوّ دا

hip hansh

هنش

hire aggar

أجّر

for hire lil egār

للإيجار

where can I hire a car? fayn

a'dar a'aggar Aarabaya?

فين أقدر أأجر عربيّة؟

see rent

his*: it's his car Aarabeeto

عربيته

that's his da btāAo

بتاعه

hit (verb) Darab

ضرب

hitch-hike oto-stob

أوتوستوب

In the countryside and desert, where buses may be sporadic or non-existent, it is standard practice for lorries (Aarabayyāt na'l) and pick-up trucks (beejō) to carry and charge passengers. You may be asked to pay a little more than the locals, or have to bargain over a price, but it's straightforward enough. Getting rides in tractors is another possibility in rural areas.

hobby hewāya

هواية

hold (verb) masak

مسك

hole khorm

خرم

holiday agāza

أجازة

on holiday fi agāza

فى أجازة

Holland holanda

هولندا

home bayt

بيت

at home (in my house etc)

fil bayt

فى البيت

(in my country) baladee

بلدى

we go home tomorrow HanrowwaH bokra le baladna

حنروّح بكرة لبلدنا

honest ameen

أمين

honey Aasal naHl

عسل نحل

honeymoon shahr el Aasal

شهر العسل

hood (US: of car) kabboot

كبّوت

hope itmanna

إتمنّى

I hope so atmanna kida

أتمنّى كده

I hope not matmannāsh

ماتمنّاش

hopefully inshā'allāh

إن شاء الله

horn (of car) kalaks

كلاكس

horrible morAeb

مرعب

horse HoSān

حصان

horse-drawn buggy HanToor

حنطور

horse riding rikoob el khayl

ركوب الخيل

hospital mostashfa

مستشفى

hospitality karam

كرم

thank you for your hospitality

shokran Aala alkaram

شكراً على الكرم

hot (water etc) sokhn

سخن

(spicy) Hāmee

حامي

I'm hot (said by man/woman)

ana Harrān/Harrāna

أنا حرّان / حرّانة

it's hot eg-gow Harr

الجوّ حر

hotel fondo'

فندق

Egyptian hotels are loosely categorized by star ratings, ranging from five-star deluxe class down to one-star. Below this range there are also unclassified hotels and guesthouses, some of them tailored to foreign backpackers, others mostly used by Egyptians. The categoriza-→

tions tend to have more meaning in the higher bands; once you're down to one or two stars the differences are often hard to detect.

Deluxe hotels are almost exclusively modern and chain-owned with swimming pools, bars, restaurants, air-conditioning and all the usual international facilities. Four-star hotels can be more characterful, including some famous (and reconditioned) names from the old tradition of Egyptian tourism. There is the odd gem amongst three-star hotels, though most of them are 1970s towers, often becoming a little shabby. Facilities like air-conditioning and plumbing can be unreliable. At two- and one-star level, you rarely get air-conditioning, though better places will supply fans, and old-style buildings with balconies, high ceilings and louvred windows are well designed to cope with the heat. However, they can be distinctly chilly in winter, as they rarely have any form of heating.

Some of the cheaper hotels are classified as guesthouses (bansyōn) which makes little →

difference in terms of the facilities, but tends to signify family ownership and a friendlier ambience.

At the cheap end of the scale, in the most popular tourist towns, like Luxor and Hurghada, you also get 'student hostels', specifically aimed at backpackers. They are often quite well run and equipped, if a bit cramped.

Bookings for the four- and five- star hotels are best made through the central reservation office of the chain owning the hotel. At mid-range hotels, it is worth trying to book ahead if you want to stay in a particular place in Cairo, Alex, Aswan or Luxor. Elsewhere, – and at all the cheaper hotels – most people just turn up.

Most hotels levy a service charge (12 per cent) plus local taxes (2-15 per cent) on top of their quoted rates. Breakfast is generally provided and may or may not be included in the room rate. Extra charges most commonly turn up at mid-range hotels, which may add on a few pounds for a fan or air-conditioning, or a TV.

hotel room Hogrit fondo'

حجرة فندق

hour sāAa

ساعة

house bayt

بيت

how izzay

إزّاى

how many? ad ay?

قد إيه؟

how do you do? (to man/woman) Aāmil/Aāmla ay?

عامل/عاملة إيه؟

•••••• DIALOGUES ••••••

how are you? (to man/woman) izzayak/izzayik?

fine, thanks, and you? (to man/woman) bekhayr, shokran, winta/winti?

how much are they? bekām?

five pounds each elwaHda be khamsa geneeh

I'll take it iddeenee waHda

humid roTooba

رطوبة

hungry gooA

جوع

are you hungry? (to man) inta gaAān?

إنت جعان؟

(to woman) inti gaAāna?

إنتى جعانة؟

hurry (verb) istaAgil

إستعجل

I'm in a hurry (said by man/
woman) ana mistaAgil/
mistaAgila

أنا مستعجل/مستعجلة

there's no hurry Aala mehlak

على مهلك

hurry up! yalla besorAa!

يللا بسرعة!

hurt (verb) wagaA

وجع

it really hurts Ha'ee'ee
bitowgaA

حقيقى بتوجع

husband gōz

جوز

hydrofoil 'launch' maTTāT

مطاط

I

I ana

أنا

ice talg

ثلج

with ice bee talg

بالثلج

no ice, thanks min ghayr

talg, shokran

من غير ثلج، شكرا

ice cream Jelātee

جيلاتى

ice-cream cone Jelātee bee
baskōt

جيلاتى بيسكوت

iced coffee ahwa metalliga

قهوة متلّجة

ice lolly loleeta

لوليتا

idea fikra

فكرة

idiot ghabee

غبى

if low

لو

ignition tadweer

تدوير

ill Aīyān

عيّان

I feel ill (said by man/woman)
ana Aīyān/Aīyāna

أنا عيّان/عيّانة

illness maraD

مرض

imitation (leather etc) ta'leed

تقليد

immediately Hālan

حالاً

important mohim

مهم

it's very important da mohim awee

دا مهم قوى

it's not important da mish mohim

دا مش مهم

impossible mostaHeel

مستحيل

impressive mo'assir

مؤثّر

improve taHseen

تحسين

I want to improve my Arabic (said by man/woman) ana Aayiz/Aiza aHassin el Aarabee betāAee

أنا عايز/عايزة أحسّن العربى بتاعى

in: it's in the centre fee el wesT

فى الوسط

in my car fee Aarabeetee

فى عربيتى

in Cairo fil Qāhira

فى القاهرة

in two days from now khilāl yomayn

خلال يومين

in five minutes khilāl

khamas da'āye'

خلال خمس دقايق

in May fee mayoo

فى مايو

in English bil ingleezee

بالإنجليزى

in Arabic bil Aarabee

بالعربى

is he in? howa mowgood?

هوّ موجود؟

inch boosa

بوصة

include yeshmal

يشمل

does that include meals? da shāmel el wagabāt?

دا شامل الوجبات؟

is that included? da maHsoob fes seAr?

دا محسوب فى السعر؟

inconvenient mish molā'im

مش ملائم

incredible mod-hish

مدهش

Indian hindee

هندى

indicator eshārit noor

إشارة نور

indigestion soo' haDm

سوء هضم

indoor pool Hammām sibāHa

dākhelee

حمّام سباحة داخلى

indoors dākhelee

داخلى

inexpensive rekhees

رخيص

infection Aadwa

عدوى

infectious moAdee

معدى

inflammation eltihāb

إلتهاب

informal mish rasmee

مش رسمى

information maAlomāt

معلومات

do you have any information
about ...? (to man/woman)

Aandak/Aandik maAlomāt
Aan ...?

عندَك/عندِك معلومات
عن ...؟

information desk esteAlamāt

إستعلامات

injection Ho'na

حقنة

injured etgaraH

إتجرح

she's been injured hayya
etgaraHet

هىّ إتجرحت

innocent baree'a

بريئة

insect Hashara

حشرةّ

insect bite arSit Hashara

قرصة

do you have anything for
insect bites? (to man/woman)

Aandak/Aandik aī Hāga Did
ars el Hasharāt?

عندَك/عندِك أى حاجة
ضد قرص الحشرات

insecticide spray mobeed
Hasharee SiH-Hee

مبيد حشرى صحى

insect repellent Tārid lil
Hasharāt

طارد للحشرات

inside gowa

جوّه

inside the hotel gowa el
fondo'

جوّه الفندق

let's sit inside yalla no'Aod
gowa

يلا نقعد جوّه

insist: I insist ana moSir

أنا مصر

instant coffee naskafee

نسكافيه

instead badal

بدل

give me that one instead
eddeenee wāHid tānee
badal da
إدّيني واحد تاني بدل دا

instead of ... badal min ...
بدل من

insulin ansooleen
أنسولين

insurance ta'meen
تأمين

intelligent zakee
ذكى

interested: I'm interested in ...
ana mohtam be ...
أنا مهتم ب...

interesting momteA
ممتع

that's very interesting da
momteA awee
دا ممتع قوى

international Aālamee
عالمى

interpreter (man) motargim
fowree
مترجم فورى

(woman) motargima fowraya
مترجمة فورية

intersection taqāTOA Toro'
تقاطع طرق

interval (at theatre) estirāHa
إستراحة

into le
ل

I'm not into that ana
mabaHebbish da
أنا ماباحبّش دا

introduce Aarraf
عرّف

may I introduce ...? momkin
aAarrafak bee ...?
ممكن أعرّفك ب...؟

invitation (general) daAwa
دعوة

(for meal) Aezooma
عزومة

invite daAa
دعى

Iran irān
إيران

Iraq el Arā'
العراق

Ireland īrlanda
ايرلندا

Irish īrlandee
أيرلندى

I'm Irish (said by man/woman)
ana īrlandee/īrlandaya
أنا أيرلندى/أيرلندية

iron (for ironing) makwa
مكوى

can you iron these for me?
momkin tekwee dool

Aalashanee?

ممكن تكوى دول علشانى؟

is*

island gezeera

جزيرة

Israel isra'eel

إسرائيل

Israeli isra'eelee

إسرائيلى

it* howa/hayya (m/f)

هوَ/هى

it is ... da/dee ... (m/f)

دا/دى

is it ...? ... da/dee?

دا/دى؟

where is it? fayn da/dee?

فين دا/دى

it's him howa da

هوَ دا

it's her hayya dee

هىَ دى

it was ... kan/kānit ... (m/f)

كان/كانت

I like it baHebbo/
baHebbaha (m/f)

بحبه/بحبها

Italian eTālee

إيطالى

Italy eTālya

إيطاليا

itch: it itches bitakolnee

بتاكلنى

J

jacket Jākit

جاكت

jam mirabba

مربّى

jammed: it's jammed
maHshoor

محشور

January yanāyer

يناير

jar (noun) barTamān

برطمان

jaw fakk

فك

jazz moseeQa el Jāz

موسيقى الجاز

jealous ghīrān

غيران

jeans Jeenz

جينز

jeep jeb

جيب

jellyfish andeel baHr

قنديل بحر

Jerusalem el Qods

القدس

jetty raSeef

رصيف

jeweller's **megow**har**ā**tee

مجوهراتى

(also repairs) s**ā**yegh

صايغ

jewellery megowhar**ā**t

مجوهرات

Jewish yah**oo**dee

يهودى

job shoghl

شغل

joke nokta

نكتة

Jordan el ordon

الأردن

journey re**H**la

رحلة

have a good journey! re**H**la
sa**A**eeda!

رحلة سعيدة!

jug ebree'

إبريق

a jug of water shafsha' m**ī**ya

شفشق مية

July yolyo

يوليو

jump (verb) no**T**

نط

junction ta**Q**ā**T**o**A** **T**oro'

تقاطع طرق

June y**o**nyo

يونيو

just (only) bas

بس

just two itneen bas

إتنين بس

just for me laya ana bas

لّى أنا بس

just here bas hena

بس هنا

not just now mish delwa'tee

مش دلوقتى

we've just arrived e**H**na lessa
w**ā**sleen delwa'tee

إحنا لسّة واصلين دلوقتى

K

keep: keep the change kh**a**llee
el b**ā**'ee

خلّى الباقى

can I keep it? momkin
akhd**Q**?

ممكن أخذه؟

please keep it momkin
tekh**a**lleeh ma**A**āk

ممكن تخليه معاك؟

ketchup 'ketchup'

كيتش اب

kettle barr**ā**d

برّاد

key moft**ā****H**

مفتاح

the key for room 201, please

(to man/woman) **momkin**
**moftāH ōDa maytayn we
wāHid, low samaHt/
samaHtee**

ممكن مفتاح أوضة ٢٠١،
لو سمحت/سمحتي؟

keyring **Hala'it mafateeH**

حلقة مفاتيح

kidneys (in body) **kelā**

كلى

(food) **kalāwee**

كلاوى

kill **atal**

قتل

kilo **keelo**

كيلو

kilometre **kelomitr**

كيلومتر

how many kilometres is it
to ...? **kam kelomitr takhod
liHad ...?**

كم كيلومتر تاخذ لحد...؟

kind (generous) **kareem**

كريم

that's very kind **da zoo'
minnak**

دا ذوق منّك

•••••• D I A L O G U E ••••••

which kind do you want? (to man/
woman) **Aayiz/Aīza aī nōA?**
I want this kind (said by man/

woman) **ana Aayiz/Aīza
en-nōA da**

king **malik**

ملك

kiosk **koshk**

كشك

kiss (noun) **bōsa**

بوسة

(verb) **bās**

بس

---

kissing
Kissing and/or embracing in
public should be avoided in
Egypt; it is considered as a
criminal offence and could lead
to a civil court case.

---

kitchen **maTbakh**

مطبخ

Kleenex® **kleniks**

كلينكس

knee **rokba**

ركبة

knickers **libās Hareemee**

لباس حريمّي

knife **sikkeena**

سكّينة

knock (verb) **da'**

دق

knock over (object) **wa'aA**

وقع

(pedestrian) **khabaT**

خبط

he's been knocked over **howa etkhabaT**

هوّ إتخبط

know **Aaraf**

عرف

I don't know **maAarafsh**

ماعرفش

I didn't know that **ana maAaraftish da**

أنا ماعرفتش دا

do you know where I can find ...? **te'dar te'ollee fayn alā'ee ...?**

تقدر تقول لى فين الأقى ؟....

Koran **Qor'ān**

قران

Kuwait **al kowayt**

الكويت

L

label **tekit**

تيكت

ladies' room, ladies' (toilets) **tawalet Hareemee**

تواليت حريمى

ladies' wear **malābis**

Hareemee

ملابس حريمى

lady **madām**

مدام

lager **stella®**

ستيللا

see beer

lake **birka**

بركة

Lake Nasser **boHayrit nāSSer**

بحيرة ناصر

lamb (meat) **Dānee**

ضانى

lamp **lambba**

لمبة

lane (small road) **Hāra**

حارة

language **logha**

لغة

language course **kors logha**

كورس لغة

large **kebeer**

كبير

last **akheer**

أخير

last week **el isbooA el-lee fāt**

الإسبوع اللى فات

last Friday **el gomAa el-lee fāttit**

الجمعة اللى فاتت

last night **laylit imbbāreH**

ليلة إمبارح

what time is the last train to Alexandria? **imta āakhir aTr liskinderaya?**

إمتى آخر قطر لسكندريّة؟

late **mit'kh-khar**

متأخّر

sorry I'm late (said by man/ woman) **āsif/asfa Aala et-ta'kheer**

آسف/أسفة على التأخير

the train was late **el-'aTr kan mit'akh-khar**

القطر كان متأخّر

we must go – we'll be late **eHna lāzim nemshee – Hanit'akh-khar**

إحنا لازم نمشي، حنتأخّر

it's getting late **el wa't etakh-khar**

الوقت إتأخّر

later **baAdayn**

بعدين

I'll come back later **ana HargaA tanee**

أنا حارجع تاني

see you later **ashoofak**

بعدين أشوفك

later on **baAdayn**

بعدين

latest **akheer**

آخر

by Wednesday at the latest **Aala ela'all yōm elarbaA**

على الأقل يوم الأربع

laugh (verb) **DaHak**

ضحك

launderette, laundromat **maghsala afrangee**

مغسلة أفرنجي

laundry (clothes) **ghaseel**

غسيل

(place) **maghsala**

مغسلة

In Egypt no one goes to the laundry: if they don't do their own, they send it out to a **makwagee** (a person who washes clothes and irons them). Wherever you are staying, there will either be an in-house **makwagee**, or one close by to call on. Some low-budget hotels in Luxor, Aswan and Hurghada allow guests to use their washing machine for free or for a small charge. You can

→

buy washing powder at most pharmacies. Dry cleaners are confined to Cairo, Aswan and Hurghada.

lavatory tawalet

تواليت

law Qānoon

قانون

lawyer (man/woman) moHāmee/ mohamaya

محامي / محامية

laxative molayin

مليّن

lazy kaslān

كسلان

lead (electrical) silk kahraba

سلك كهربا

(verb) Qād

قاد

where does this lead to? da yewaddee Aala fayn?

دا يودّى على فين؟

leaf wara'it shagar

ورقة شجر

leaflet manshoor

منشور

leak (noun) rashH

رشح

(verb) rashaH

رشح

the roof leaks essa'af bayershaH

السقف بيرشح

learn daras

درس

least: not in the least eTlāQan

إطلاقا

at least 50 khamseen Aalal a'all

٥٠ على الأقل

leather gild

جلد

leave (verb) mashā

مشى

I am leaving tomorrow ana māshee bokra

أنا ماشى بكرة

he left yesterday howa mesha embbāriH

هوّ مشى إمبارح

may I leave this here? momkin aseeb da hena?

ممكن أسيب دا هنا؟

I left my jacket in the bar nasayt eJākit btāAee fil bār

نسيت الجاكت بتاعى فى البار

when does the bus for the airport leave? el otobees el-lee bayrooH elmaTār

bayTlaA imta?

الأوتوبيس اللى بيروح
المطار بيطلع إمتى؟

Lebanon **libnān**

لبنان

left **shimāl**

شمال

on the left **Aala esh-shimāl**

على الشمال

to the left **lesh-shimāl**

للشمال

turn left **Howid shimāl**

حود شمال

there's none left **mafDelshee
Haga**

مافضّلش حاجة

left-handed **ashwal**

أشول

left luggage (office) **maktab
amanāt**

مكتب أمانات

leg **rigl** (f)

رجل

lemon **lamoon**

لمون

lemonade **espatis®**

إسباتس

lemon juice **lamonāta**

لموناتة

lemon tea **shī be lamoon**

شاى باللمون

---

lend **sallif**

سلّف

will you lend me your ...? (to man/
woman) **momkin tesallifnee/
tesallifnee ... betāAak/betāAik?**

ممكن تسلفنى/تسلفينى
... بتاعك/بتاعك؟

lens (of camera) **Aadasa**

عدسة

less **a'all**

أقل

less than **a'all min**

أقل من

less expensive **arkhas**

أرخص

lesson **dars**

درس

let (allow) **yesmaH**

يسمح

will you let me know?
momkin teAarrafnee?

ممكن تعرفنى؟

I'll let you know **Hab'a
a'ool-lak**

حبقى أقول لك

let's go for something to eat
yalla nerooH nākol Haga

يلا نروح ناكل حاجة

let off **nazzil**

نزّل

will you let me off at ...?

momkin te**nazzil**nee **A**and ...?

ممكن تنزّلني عند ....؟

letter **gowāb**

جواب

do you have any letters for
me? fee a**ī gowab**āt **l**a**ya**?

فى أى جوابات لىّ؟

letterbox **sandoo' el bosTa**

صندوق البوسطة

see post office

lettuce **khas**

خس

lever (noun) **A**atala

عتلة

library **maktaba**

مكتبة

Libya **libya**

ليبيا

licence **rokhsa**

رخصة

lid **ghaTa**

غطا

lie (verb: tell untruth) **kazab**

كذب

lie down **yessaTTaH**

يسطّح

life **A**omr

عمر

lifebelt **Too' nagāh**

طوق نجاه

lifeguard **Hāris esh-shaT**

حارس الشط

life jacket **sotrit inqāz**

سترة إنقاذ

lift (in building) **asansayr**

أسانسير

could you give me a lift?

momkin te**wassal**nee
be**lA**ara**bayya**?

ممكن توصّلني بالعربيّة؟

would you like a lift? (to man)

Aayiznee a**wassal**ak?

عايزني أوصّلك؟

(to woman) **A**īzanee
a**wassal**ik?

عايزاني أوصّلك؟

light (noun) **noor**

نور

(not heavy) **khafeef**

خفيف

do you have a light? (for
cigarette) ma**A**ak **kabreet**?

معاك كبريت؟

light green **a**kh**Dar fāteH**

أخضر فاتح

light bulb **lamba**

لمبة

I need a new light bulb (said by man/woman) ana Aayiz/Aīza lamba gedeeda

أنا عايز/عايزة لمبة جديدة

lighter (cigarette) wallāAa

ولاعة

lightning bar'

برق

like (verb) Hab

حب

I like it baHebbo/baHebbaha (m/f)

بحبّه/بجبّها

I like going for walks baHeb atmashā

بحب أتمشّى

I like you (to man/woman) ana baHebbak/baHebbik

أنا بحبّك/بجبّك

I don't like it mabaHebboosh

مابجبّوش

do you like ...? (to man) inta betHeb ...?

إنت بتحب ...؟

(to woman) inti betHebbee ...?

إنتى بتحبّى ...؟

I'd like a beer (said by man/woman) ana Aayiz/Aīza beera

أنا عايز/عايزة بيرة

I'd like to go swimming (said by man/woman) ana Aayiz/Aīza aAoom

أنا عايز/عايزة أعوم

would you like a drink? (to man) inta Aayiz teshrab Haga?

إنت عايز تشرب حاجة؟

(to woman) inti Aīza teshrabee Haga?

إنتى عايزة تشربى حاجة؟

would you like to go for a walk? (to man) teHeb tetmasha?

تحب تتمشّى؟

(to woman) teHebbee tetmashee?

تحبّى تتمشّى؟

what's it like? hayya zay ay?

هيّا زى إيه؟

I want one like this (said by man/woman) ana Aayiz/Aīza waHda zay dee

أناعايز/عايزة واحدة زى دى

lime lamoon

لمون

line (on paper) SaTr

سطر

(phone) khaT

خط

could you give me an outside line? (to man/woman) momkin teftaHlee/teftaHelee khaT kharegee?

ممكن تفتح/تفتحى لى خط خارجى؟

lips shafayef

شفايف

lip salve zebdit kakow

زبدة كاكاو

lipstick alam rōj

قلم روج

liqueur sharāb mo'aTTar

شراب مقطر

listen ismaA

إسمع

litre litr

لتر

little soghīar

صغيّر

just a little, thanks shwīya soghīareen, shokran

شوية صغيّرين، شكراً

a little milk shwīyet laban

شوية لبن

a little bit more shwīya kamān

شوية كمان

live (verb) sakan

سكن

we live together eHna

sakneen maAa baAD

إحنا ساكنين مع بعض

•••••• DIALOGUE ••••••

where do you live? (to man) inta sākin fayn?

(to woman) inti sakna fayn?

I live in London (said by man/ woman) ana sākin/sakna fee 'London'

lively nasheeT

نشيط

liver (in body) kibd

كبد

(food) kibda

كبدة

loaf Aaysh

عيش

lobby (in hotel) madkhal

مدخل

lobster gambaree kebeer

جمبرى كبير

local maHallee

محلى

can you recommend a local restaurant? (to man/woman) momkin te'ollee/te'olelee fayn aHsan maTAam maHallee?

ممكن تقوللى/تقوليلى فين أحسن مطعم محلى؟

lock (noun) efl

قُفل

(verb) afal

قفل

it's locked ma'fool

مقفول

lock in afal Aala

قفل على

lock out afal Aala

قفل على

I've locked myself out (of room)

el bab et'afāl Aalaya

الباب إتقفل عليّ

locker (for luggage etc) amanāt

أمانات

lollipop massāsa

مصّاصة

London 'London'

لندن

long Taweel

طويل

how long will it take to fix it?

betākhod ad ay wa't

Aalashan tesallaH dee?

بتاخذ قد إيه وقت
علشان تصلّح دى؟

how long does it take?

betākhod ad ay?

بتاخذ قد إيه؟

a long time wa't Taweel

وقت طويل

one day/two days longer

yōm/yōmayn aTwal

يوم / يومين أطول

long-distance call mokalma

khārigaya

مكالمة خارجيّة

look: I'm just looking, thanks

ana batfarag bas, shokran

أنا باتفرج بس، شكرا

you don't look well (to man)

inta shaklak taAbān

إنت شكلك تعبان

(to woman) inti shaklik

taAbāna

إنتى شكلك تعبانة

look out! Hāsib!

حاسب

can I have a look? momkin

abos?

ممكن أبص

look after khalla bāloh

خلّى باله

look at bos Aala

بص على

look for dowar Aala

دوّر على

I'm looking for ... ana

badowar Aala ...

أنا بدوّر على ...

look forward to anTazir

أنتظر

I'm looking forward to it ana monTazir ashofoh

أنا منتظر أشوفه

loose (handle etc) sāyib

سايب

lorry loree

لورى

lose khesir

خسر

I'm lost, I want to get to ...
(said by man/woman) ana toht,
ana Aayiz/Aīza arooH le ...

أنا تهت، أنا عايز/عايزة أروح ل...

I've lost my bag DaAet shanTetee

ضاعت شنطتى

lost property (office) maktab mafQodāt

مكتب مفقودات

lot: a lot, lots keteer

كتير

not a lot mish keteer

مش كتير

a lot of people nās keteer

ناس كتير

a lot bigger akbar bekteer

أكبر بكتير

I like it a lot baHebbo/
baHebbaha keteer (m/f)

باحبّه/باحبّها كتير

lotion marham

مرهم

loud Aālee

عالى

lounge sāla

صالة

love (noun) Hob

حب

(verb) Hab

حب

I love Egypt ana baHeb maSr

أنا باحبّ مصر

lovely gameel

جميل

low (prices) rekheeS

رخيص

(bridge) wāTee

واطى

luck HaZ

حظ

good luck! HaZ saAeed!

حظ سعيد!

luggage shonaT

شنط

luggage trolley Aarabayyit shonaT

عربية شنط

lunch ghadā

غذاء

lungs ri'atayn

رئتين

Luxor lo'sor

الأقصر

luxurious fakhm

فخم

luxury fakhāma

فخمه

M

machine makana

مكنه

magazine magalla

مجله

maid (in hotel) khaddāmit el ghoraf

خدامة الغرف

mail (noun) bosTa

بوسطه

(verb) baAat

بعث

is there any mail for me? fee aī bosTa laya?

في اي بوسطه ليه؟

mailbox sandoo'el bosTa

صندوق البوسطه

see post office

main ra'eesee

رئيسي

main course elwagba elra'eesaya

الوجبه الرئيسيه

main post office maktab

elbareed elra'eesee

مكتب البوسطه الرئيسي

main road eT-Taree' er-ra'eesee

الطريق الرئيسي

make (brand name) marka

ماركه

(verb) Aemil

إعمل

what is it made of? maAmoola min ay?

معموله من إيه؟

make-up mikyāJ

مكياج

malaria malarīa

ملاريا

man rāgil

راجل

manager (man/woman) modeer/ modeera

مدير/مديره

can I see the manager? momkin ashoof el modeer?

ممكن اشوف المدير؟

mango manga

منجه

many keteer

كثير

not many mish keteer

مش كثير

map khareeTa

خريطه

General maps of Egypt are on sale in Cairo, Luxor and Aswan. City plans of Cairo are also available. Elsewhere, however, aside from fairly crude maps of Alexandria, Luxor, Aswan and Port Said, and photocopied handouts in Mersa Matrouh and Siwa Oasis, there are no town plans to be found.

March **māris**

مارس

margarine **zibda SinaAaya**

زبده صناعيه

market **soo'**

سوق

marmalade **nareng**

نارنج

married: I'm married (said by man/woman) **ana mitgowiz/mitgowiza**

أنا متزوج/متزوجه

are you married? (to man) **inta mitgowiz?**

إنت متزوج؟

(to woman) **inti mitgowiza?**

إنتي متزوجه؟

match (football etc) **'match'**

ماتش

matches **kabreet**

كبريت

material (fabric) **omāsh**

قماش

matter: it doesn't matter **maAlaysh**

معلش

what's the matter? **fee ay?**

فى إيه؟

mattress **martaba**

مرتبه

May **māyo**

مايو

may: may I have another one? **momkin ākhud wāHid tanee/waHda tania?** (m/f)

ممكن اخد واحد تانى/واحده تانيه؟

may I come in? **momkin adkhol?**

ممكن ادخل؟

may I see it? **momkin ashoofo/ashoofha?** (m/f)

ممكن اشوفه/اشوفها؟

may I sit here? **momkin aAod hena?**

ممكن اقعد هنا؟

maybe **yimkin**

يمكن

mayonnaise **mayonayz**

مايونيز

me* **ana**

أنا

that's for me **da/dee**

Aalashānee (m/f)

دا /دى علشانى

send it to me ibAathālee

إبعتها لى

me too wana kamān

وانا كمان

meal wagba

وجبه

•••••• DIALOGUE ••••••

did you enjoy your meal? (to man/
woman) Aagabak/Aagabik el akl?

it was excellent, thank you kan
momtāz, shokran

mean (verb) aSad

قصد

what do you mean? (to man/
woman) aSdak/aSdik ay?

قصدك /قصدِك إيه؟

•••••• DIALOGUE ••••••

what does this word mean?
ek-kelma dee maAnāha ay?

it means ... in English maAnāha ...
bil ingleezee

meat laHma

لحمه

Mecca makka

مكه

mechanic makaneekee

ميكانيكى

medicine dowa (m)

دواء

Mediterranean el baHr el
metowassiT

البحر المتوسط

medium (adj: size) metowassiT

متوسط

medium-dry noS gaffa

نصف جافة

medium-rare noS sewa

نصف سوا

medium-sized metowassiT

متوسط

meet ābil

قابل

nice to meet you forSa
saAeeda

فرصه سعيده

where shall I meet you? (to
man/woman) fayn momkin
a'ablak/a'ablik?

فين ممكن أقابلك/أقابلِك؟

meeting egtimāA

إجتماع

meeting place makān egtimāA

مكان إجتماع

melon shemmām

شمام

men reggāla

رجاله

mend sallaH

صلح

could you mend this for me?

(to man/woman) momkin
tesallaH / tesallaHee dee
laya?

ممكن تصلح/تصلحي
دى لى؟

men's room tawalet rigālee,
Hammām er-rigāl

حمام الرجال

menswear malābis regālee

ملابس رجالى

mention: don't mention it el
Aafw

العفو

menu elmenew

المنيو

may I see the menu, please?

(to man/woman) momkin
ashoof elmenew, low
samaHt/samaHtee

ممكن أشوف المنيو لو
سمحت/سمحتى؟

see menu reader page 249

message resāla

رساله

are there any messages for
me? fee rasā'il Aalashānee?

فى رسائل علشانى؟

I want to leave a message
for ... (said by man/woman) ana

Aayiz/Aīza aseeb resāla le ...

أنا عايز/عايزه أسيب
رساله ل ...

metal (noun) maAdan

معدن

metre mitr

متر

midday eD-Dohr

الظهر

at midday eD-Dohr

الظهر

middle: in the middle fen-noS

فى النصف

in the middle of the night fee
noS ellayl

فى نصف الليل

the middle one elwasTānee

الوسطانى

Middle Egypt wesT maSr

وسط مصر

midnight noS ellayl

نصف الليل

at midnight fi noS ellayl

فى نصف الليل

might: I might ana momkin

أنا ممكن

I might not ana momkin ma

أنا ممكن ما

I might want to stay another
day ana momkin a'Aud yōm

zayāda

أنا ممكن اقعد يوم زياده

mild (taste) mosh Hāmee

مش حامي

(weather) gameel

جميل

mile meel

ميل

milk laban

لبن

millimetre millimetr

ميليمتر

minaret ma'zana

مأذنه

mind: never mind maAlaysh

معلش

I've changed my mind ana
ghīyart ra'yee

أنا غيرت رايى

•••••• DIALOGUE ••••••

do you mind if I open the window?
(to man/woman) Aandak/Aandik
māneA low fataHt eshebbāk?
no, I don't mind la', maAandeesh
māneA

mine*: it's mine da btāAee/dee
btaAtee (m/f)

دا بتاعى/دى بتاعتى

mineral water mīya maAdanaya

ماء معدنيه

Bottled mineral water is widely
available, particularly Baraka
('Blessing'); the Siwa brand is
less common. If tourists request
water, it is assumed they mean
mineral water unless they
specifically ask for tap water
(mīya min elHanafaya), which
is safe to drink in major towns
and cities, but too chlorinated
for the average visitor's palate.
When buying bottled water, it
is wise to check that the seal
is intact.
see water

minibus menibos

ميني باص

minute de'ee'a

دقيقه

in a minute kamān shwīya

كمان شويه

just a minute de'ee'a waHda

دقيقه واحده

mirror mrāya

مرايا

Miss ānisa

آنسه

miss: I missed the bus rāH
Aalaya el otobees

راح علىَّ الأوتوبيس

missing DĀyiA

ضائع

one of my ... is missing waHid
min ... betooAee DayiA

واحد من ... بتوعي
ضائع

there's a suitcase missing fee
shanTa DayiAa

فى شنطه ضائعه

mist shabboora

شبوره

mistake (noun) ghalTa

غلطه

I think there's a mistake aZon
en fee ghalTa hena

أظن إن فى غلطة هنا

sorry, I've made a mistake (said
by man/woman) āsif/āsfa, ana
gheleTt

آسف/آسفه، أنا غلطت

mobile phone 'mobile phone'

موبايل فون

modern modayrn

مودرن

moisturizer kraym

كريم

moment: I won't be a moment
mish Hat'akhar

مش حاتأخر

monastery dayr

دير

ENGLISH ◆ ARABIC | Mi

Monday yōm el itnayn

يوم الإثنين

money floos (f)

فلوس

Egypt's basic unit of currency is
the Egyptian pound (geneeh),
written as £E or LE. Notes are
colour-coded as follows: £E1
(brown), £E5 (blue), £E10
(red), £E20 (green), £E50 (red),
£E100 (green). The Egyptian
pound is divided into 100
piastres (irsh), abbreviated by
Westerners to pt. There are 25pt
and 50pt notes, and variously
sized coins to the value of 5pt,
10pt, 20pt, 25pt, and 50pt; some
25pt coins have a hole in the
middle. Formerly each piastre
was divided into ten miliemes,
making 1,000 miliemes to the
pound. Though no longer in
circulation, this denomination
is still often expressed in prices
(which follow the custom of
using a comma instead of a
decimal point: for example
£E1,30).

Aside from ordinary spending,
hard cash (usually US dollars)
may be required for visas, border taxes etc. Do not bring New
Zealand dollars, Irish punts,

Scottish or Northern Irish pounds as these are not accepted by banks.

money belt **shan**Tit wesT

شنطة وسط

month **shahr**

شهر

monument(s) **asār**

آثار

moon **amar**

قمر

more* **tanee**

تانى

can I have some more water, please? (to man/woman)

momkin **ā**khod shwīyit **m**īya kamān, low sama**H**t/ sama**H**tee?

ممكن آخذ شوية ميه كمان، لو سمحت/ سمحتى؟

more interesting **m**omti**A** aktar

متع أكثر

more expensive **a**ghla

أغلى

more than 50 **a**ktar min khamseen

أكثر من خمسين

more than that **a**ktar min

keda

أكثر من كده

a lot more **a**ktar **b**ekteer

أكثر بكثير

•••••• DIALOGUE ••••••

would you like some more? (to man) te**H**ebb **tā**khod **tā**nee?

(to woman) te**H**ebbee **t**akhdee **tā**nee?

no, no more for me, thanks **la, la'** da kif**ā**ya, shokran

how about you? (to man/woman) **w**inta/**w**inti?

I don't want any more, thanks (said by man/woman) **a**na mish **A**ayiz/ **A**īza **t**anee, shokran

morning **e**s-**S**ob**H**

الصبح

this morning **e**nnaharda **e**s-**S**ob**H**

النهارده الصبح

in the morning **e**s-**S**ob**H**

صبح

Morocco **e**l **m**aghrib

المغرب

mosque **gā**mi**A**

جامع

Most of the mosques and their attached Islamic colleges (m**a**drasas) that you'll want to visit are in Cairo, and are mostly classified as historic monuments. They are open routinely to non-Muslim visitors, although anyone not worshipping should avoid prayer times. Elsewhere in the country, mosques are not used to tourists and locals may object to your presence.

At all mosques, dress is important. Shorts (or short skirts) and exposed shoulders are out, and in some places women may be asked to cover their heads (a scarf might be provided). Above all, remember to remove your shoes upon entering the precinct. They will either be held by a shoe custodian (small b**a**'sheesh (tip) expected) or you can just leave them outside the door, or carry them in by hand (if you do this, place the soles together, as they are considered unclean).

see **tip**

mosquitoes and bugs

Currently resurgent throughout Africa, malaria could become a problem in Egypt in the future. Consult your doctor who may recommend a prophylactic course of Chloroquine, starting two weeks before you leave home.

Beside the risk of malaria, mosquitoes can make your life a misery. Horribly ubiquitous over the summer these blood-sucking pests are never entirely absent – even in Cairo. The only solution is total war, using fans, mosquito coils, rub-on repellent and a plug-in device, sold at pharmacies. The best guarantee of a bite-less night's sleep is to bring a mosquito net with long tapes, to pin above your bed. Mosquitoes favour shady, damp areas, and anywhere around dusk.

Equally loathsome – and widespread – are flies, which transmit various diseases. Only insecticide spray or air-conditioning offer any protection.

mosquito namoosa

ناموسه

mosquito net shabakit namosaya

شبكة ناموس

mosquito repellent kraym Did
en-nāmoos

كريم ضد الناموس

most: I like this one most of all

ana bafaDDal da Aala aī

shay' tanee

انا بافضل دا على
أى شئ تانى

most of the time mōAzam el
wa't

معظم الوقت

most tourists mōAzam
elsowwāH

معظم السواح

mostly mōAzam

معظم

mother omm

أم

mother-in-law Hamāt

حمات

motorbike motosikl

موتوسكل

motorboat 'launch'

لنش

motorway eT-Taree' es-sareeA

الطريق السريع

mountain gabal

جبل

in the mountains fil gebāl

فى الجبال

mouse far

فار

moustache shanab

شنب

mouth bo'

بق

move (verb) itHarrak

إتحرك

he's moved to another room

howa na'al leōDa tania

هو نقل لأوضه تانيه

could you move your car? (to
man) momkin tin'il
Aarabeetak?

ممكن تنقل عربيتَك؟

(to woman) momkin tin'ilee
Aarabeetik?

ممكن تنقلى عربيتِك؟

could you move up a little? (to
man/woman) momkin teTlaA/
teTlaAee oddām shwīya?

ممكن تطلع/تطلعى قدام
شويه؟

movie 'film'

فيلم

movie theater 'cinema'

سينما

Mr ostāz

أستاذ

Mrs madām

مدام

much **ket**eer

كثير

much worse **mo'rif akt**ar

مقرف أكثر

much better **aHs**an bekteer

أحسن بكثير

much hotter **askh**an bekteer

أسخن بكثير

not much **mish ket**eer

مش كثير

not very much **mish ket**eer

awee

مش كثير قوى

I don't want very much (said by

man/woman) **mish Aay**iz/**Aīz**a

keteer **aw**ee

مش عايز/عايزه كثير

قوى

mud **Teen**

طين

mug (for drinking) **kobbāy**a

كبايه

I've been mugged **an**a

etsar'**at**

أنا إتسرقت

mum **omm**

ام

mummy (in tomb) **mom**ya

مومياء

mural **war**a' **Ha'iT**

ورق حائط

museum **mat-Haf**

متحف

Museums are generally open
daily 9am–5pm, except Friday
when they close at 4pm.

mushrooms **Aesh elghorāb**

عش الغراب

music **moseeQ**a

موسيقى

Muslim (adj) **mos**lim

مسلم

mussels **om el kholool**

ام الخلول

must* : I must ... **an**a **lāz**im ...

أنا لازم

I mustn't drink alcohol **an**a

mamnooA **min shorb**

elkohol

أنا ممنوع من شرب

الكحول

mustard **maSTard**a

مسطرده

my* : my ... ... **btāAee/btaAtee**

(m/f)

بتاعى /بتاعتى

myself: I'll do it myself

HaAmiloo benafsee

هاعملو بنفسى

by myself **benafsee**

بنفسى

N

nail (finger) Dofar

ظفر

name esm

إسم

my name's John esmee 'John'

إسمى جون

what's your name? (to man/woman) esmak/esmik ay?

إسمك/إسمك إيه؟

what is the name of this street? ay esm esh-shāriA da?

إيه إسم الشارع هذ دا؟

Literally 'father of' and 'mother of', **aboo** and omm are used both as honorific titles and also figuratively as a nickname. For example, if speaking to the father of someone called Magdi, you would address them as 'aboo Magdi' and his mother would be 'omm Magdi'; you would not use the surname and there is no direct equivalent of 'Mr' or 'Mrs'.

Sometimes Egyptians prefer to be called by their nicknames. Some names have fixed nicknames: for example, the nick-→

name for Muhammad or Ahmed is Hamada, whereas for Mustafa, the nickname is Darsh. see you

napkin fooTa

فوطه

nappy kafoola

كافوله

narrow (street) dīya'

ضيق

nasty fazeeA

فظيع

national dowlee

دولى

nationality ginsaya

جنسيه

natural TabeeAee

طبيعى

navy (blue) azra'

أزرق

near gamb

جنب

is it near the city centre? howa orīyib min wesT elbalad?

هو قريب من وسط البلد؟

do you go near the beach? inta bitAadee Aalal blāj?

إنت بتعدى على البلاج؟

where is the nearest ...? fayn

a'rab ...?

فين أقرب...؟

nearby orīyib awee

قريب قوى

nearly ta'reeban

تقريبا

necessary Darooree

ضرورى

neck (of body) ra'aba

رقبه

necklace Ao'd

عقد

necktie garafatta

جرافته

need: I need ... ana meHtāg ...

أنا محتاج...

do I need to pay? howa ana
lāzim adfaA?

هو أنا لازم أدفع؟

needle ibra

إبره

neither: neither (one) of them
wala wāHid/waHda minhom

ولا واحد/واحده منهم

neither ... nor ... la ... wala ...

لا ...ولا

nephew (brother's son) ibn akh

إبن أخ

(sister's son) ibn okht

إبن أخت

Netherlands Holandda

هولندا

never abadan

أبدآ

•••••• DIALOGUE ••••••

have you ever been to Alexandria?
(to man/woman) maroHtish/
maroHteesh liskinderaya
abadan?
no, never, I've never been there
la', maroHtish henāk abadan

new gedeed

جديد

news (radio, TV etc) akhbār (f)

أخبار

newsagent's bayyāA garayid

بياع جرائد

newspaper gornāl

جرنال

newspaper kiosk koshk
garayid

كشك جرائد

New Year essana eggedeeda

السنه الجديده

Happy New Year! Aam
gedeed saAeed!

عام جديد سعيد!

Many Egyptians celebrate the New Year with a party, especially in hotels and clubs. It is not advisable to park your car in the street on New Year's Eve, as Egyptians have a custom of throwing all their unwanted glass and china into the street to mark the end of the year.

New Year's Eve laylit rās es-sana

ليلة رأس السنه

New Zealand nyoozeelanda

نيوزيلاندا

New Zealander: I'm a New Zealander (said by man/woman) ana nyoozeelanddee/ nyoozeelanddaya

أنا نيوزيلاندي/ نيوزيلانديه

next ellay baAd

اللى بعد

the next street on the left esh-shāriA eggāa Aala eshimāl

الشارع الجاى على الشمال

at the next stop el-maHaTTa eggāya

المحطه الجايه

next week el isbooA eggī

الإسبوع الجاى

next to gamb

جنب

nice (food) TeAem

طعم

(looks, person) kwayis

كويس

(view) gameel

جميل

niece (brother's daughter) bint akh

بنت أخ

(sister's daughter) bint okht

بنت أخت

night layl

ليل

at night bil layl

بالليل

good night tisbaH Aala khayr

تصبح على خير

•••••• DIALOGUE ••••••

do you have a single room for one night? (to man/woman) Aandak/ Aandik ōDa lemoddit layla waHda

yes, madam īwa, ya hānim

how much is it per night? bekām ellayla?

it's sixty pounds for one night

besetteen geneeh fellayla
thank you, I'll take it shokran,
Hakhodha

nightclub kabarayh

كباريه

nightdress amees nōm

قميص نوم

night porter ghafeer

غفير

Nile nahr en-neel

نهر النيل

Nile Valley wadee en-neel

وادى النيل

no la'

لا

I've no change maAandeesh
fakka

معنديش فكه

there's no ... left mafeesh ...
ba'ee

مفيش.... باقى

no way! abadan!

أبدا!

oh no! (upset) akh!

أخ!

nobody mafeesh Had

مفيش حد

there's nobody there mafeesh
Had henāk

مفيش حد هناك

noise dowsha

دوشه

noisy: it's too noisy da dowsha
awee

دا دوشه قوى

non-alcoholic min ghayr koHol

من غير كحول

none mafeesh

مفيش

nonsmoking compartment
mamnooA et-tadkheen

ممنوع التدخين

noon Dohr

ظهر

at noon feD-Dohr

فى الظهر

no-one mafeesh Had

مفيش حد

nor: nor do I walana

ولا انا

normal Aādee

عادى

north shamāl

شمال

in the north fesh-shamāl

فى الشمال

to the north lesh-shamāl

للشمال

north of Cairo shamāl
el-Qāhira

شمال القاهره

northeast shamāl shar'

شمال شرق

Northern Ireland īrlanda esh-shamalaya

أيرلنده الشماليه

northwest shamāl gharb

شمال غرب

Norway en-norwayg

النرويج

Norwegian norwaygee

نرويجى

nose manakheer

مناخير

not* mish

مش

no, I'm not hungry la', ana mish gaAān

لا ، أنا مش جعان

I don't want any, thank you la' mish Aayiz khālis, shokran

لا مش عايز خالص، شكرا

it's not necessary mish lāzim

مش لازم

I didn't know that makontish aAraf keda

ما كنتش أعرف كده

not that one – this one mish da – da

مش دا – دا

note (banknote) wara'

ورق

notebook (paper) noota

نوته

nothing mafeesh Hāga

مافيش حاجه

nothing for me, thanks mafeesh Hāga laya, shokran

مافيش حاجه لى، شكرا

nothing else mafeesh Haga tania

مافيش حاجه تانيه

November novamber

نوفمبر

now delwa'tee

دلوقتى

number raQam

رقم

(figure) nimra

نمره

I've got the wrong number maAaya raQam ghalaT

معايا رقم غلط

what is your phone number? (to man/woman) ay raQam telefōnak/telefōnik?

إيه رقم تليفونَك/ تليفونِك؟

number plate nimar elAarabaya

نمر العربيه

nurse (man/woman) momarreD/

momarreDa

ممرض / ممرضه

nuts gōz

جوز

O

oasis wāHa

واحه

occupied (toilet, telephone)
maJghool

مشغول

o'clock* es-sāAa

الساعه

October oktōbar

أكتوبر

odd (strange) ghareeb

غريب

of* min

من

off (lights) ma'fool

مقفول

it's just off Tal'at Harb Street
taHweeda waHda min shāriA
TalAat Harb

تحويده واحده من شارع
طلعت حرب

we're off tomorrow iHna
Aanddinā agāza bokra

إحنا عندنا أجازه بكره

office (place of work) maktab

مكتب

officer (said to policeman)
afanddim

أفندم

often dīman

دايما

not often aHyānan

أحيانا

how often are the buses? ay
maād magee' el otobeesāt?

أيه ميعاد مجيئ
الأوتوبيسات؟

oil (for car, for salad) zayt

زيت

ointment marham

مرهم

OK kwayis

كويس

are you OK? (to man) inta
kwayis?

إنت كويس؟

(to woman) inti kwayisa?

إنتي كويسه؟

is that OK with you? (to man/
woman) da kwayis maAāk/
maAākee?

دا كويس معاك / معاكى؟

is it OK to ...? momkin ...?

ممكن...؟

that's OK, thanks da tamām,

shokran

دا تمام، شكرا

I'm OK ana bekhayr

أنا بخير

I feel OK (said by man/woman)

ana kwayis/kwayisạ

أنا كويس/كويسه

is this train OK for ...? el aTr

da monāsib le ...?

القطر دا مناسب لـ...؟

old (person) Aagooz

عجوز

(thing) adeem

قديم

•••••• DIALOGUE ••••••

how old are you? (to man/woman)

Aandak/Aandik kam sana?

I'm 25 ana Aandee khamsa

weAeshreen sana

and you? (to man/woman) winta/

winti?

old-fashioned mōDa adeema

موضه قديمه

old town (old part of town)

elmadeena eladeema

المدينه القديمه

in the old town fil madeena

eladeema

فى المدينه القديمه

olive oil zayt zatoon

زيت زيتون

olives zatoon

زيتون

black/green olives zatoon

eswid/akhDar

زيتون إسود/أخضر

Oman Aomān

عمان

omelette omlit

اومليت

on* Aala

على

on the street Aala eT-Taree'

على الطريق

on the beach Aalal blāj

على البلاج

is it on this road? howa AaT-

Taree' da?

هو على الطريق دا؟

on the plane Aala eT-Tīara

على الطياره

on Saturday yōm es-sabt

يوم السبت

on television fee

et-telayfizyōn

فى التليفزيون

I haven't got it on me mish

maAāya

مش معايا

this one's on me (drink) el

mashroob da Aala Hesābee

المشروب دا على حسابي

the light wasn't on en-**noor**
kan ma**Tfee**

النور كان مطفى

what's on tonight? fee ay en-
naharda?

في إيه النهارده؟

once (one time) ma**rra waH**da

مره واحده

at once (immediately) AalaT**ool**
delwa'tee

على طول دلوقتى

one* wā**Hid** (m), waH**da** (f)

واحد/واحده

the white one el'**abyaD** (m),
elbay**Da** (f)

الأبيض/البيضاء

one-way ticket tazkara waHda

تذكره واحده

only bas

بس

only one wā**Hid** bas

واحد بس

it's only 6 o'clock es-s**āAa**
sitta bas

الساعه سته بس

I've only just got here **a**na
lessa wā**sil**

أنا لسه واصل

on/off switch kobs en-**noor**

كبس النور

open (adj) maf**tooH**

مفتوح

(verb) fataH

فتح

when do you open? (to man/
woman) betif**taH**/betif**taHee**
imta?

بتفتح/بتفتحى إمتى؟

I can't get it open mish **ā**dir
af**taH**-ha

مش قادر أفتحها

in the open air felkha**la**

فى الخلاء

opening times mawa**Aeed**
el**fatH**

مواعيد الفتح

open ticket tazkara maf**tooHa**

تذكره مفتوحه

opera **o**bra

أوبرا

operation (medical) Aama**la**ya

عمليّة

operator (telephone: man/woman)
Aamil telefo**nāt**/**Aam**lit
telefo**nāt**

عامل تليفونات/
عاملة تليفونات

The number for the inland
operator is 10; for the international operator it is 120.

opposite: the opposite direction
enaHya et-tania

الناحيه الثانيه

the bar opposite elbār ellay
fee enaHya et-tania

البار اللى فى الناحيه
الثانيه

opposite my hotel oddām
elfondo' betāAee

قدام الفندق بتاعى

or ow

أو

orange (fruit) borto'ān

برتقال

(colour) borto'ānee

برتقالى

fizzy orange AaSeer borto'ān
ghāzee

عصير برتقال غازى

orange juice AaSeer borto'an

عصير برتقال

order: can we order now? (in
restaurant) momkin noTlob
delwa'tee?

ممكن نطلب دلوقتى؟

I've already ordered, thanks
ana Talabt khalāS, shokran

انا طلبت خلاص، شكرا

I didn't order this ana
maTalabtish da

انا مطلبتش ده

out of order AaTlān

عطلان

ordinary Aādee

عادى

other tanee

ثانى

the other one et-tānee

الثانى

the other day el yōm
et-tanee

اليوم الثانى

I'm waiting for the others ana
mistannee elbā'yeen

أنا مستنى الباقيين

do you have any others? (to
man/woman) Aandak/Aandik
ghayrha tanee?

عندك/عندِك غيرها
ثانى؟

otherwise walla

وإلا

our* btaAna

بتاعنا

ours* btaAna

بتاعنا

out: he's out howa barra

هو بره

three kilometres out of town
talat kilomitrāt khārig
elbalad

ثلاث كيلومترات خارج
البلد

outside barra

بره

can we sit outside? momkin no'Aod barra?

ممكن نقعد بره؟

oven forn

فرن

over: over here hena

هنا

over there henak

هناك

over 500 aktar min khomsmaya

أكثر من خمسمائة

it's over intahit

إنتهت

overcharge: you've overcharged me (to man) inta daffaAtenee floos keteer

أنت دفعتني فلوس كتير

(to woman) inti daffaAteenee floos keteer

إنتى دفعتيني فلوس كتير

overnight (travel) Tool ellayl

طول الليل

owe: how much do I owe you? (to man/woman) ana Aalaya kam leek/leekee?

انا عليّ كام لك/لكى؟

own: my own ... ... btaAee/ btaAtee (m/f)

بتاعى/بتاعتى...

are you on your own? (to man) inta lewaHdak?

إنت لوحدك؟

(to woman) inti lewaHdik?

إنتى لوحدكِ؟

I'm on my own ana lewaHdee

أنا لوحدى

owner (man/woman) mālik/ malka

مالك/مالكه

oyster maHār

محار

P

pack (verb) Aabba

عبّأ

a pack of cigarettes Aelbit sagāyer

علبة سجاير

package (parcel) Tard

طرد

package holiday reHla shamla

رحله شامله

packed lunch ghada moAabba'

غذاء معبأ

packet bāko

باكو

page (of book) SafHa

صفحه

could you page Mr ...?

momkin tinādee elostāz ...?

ممكن تنادى الأستاذ....؟

pain wagaA

وجع

I have a pain here Aandee

wagaA hena

عندى وجع هنا

painful mo'lim

مؤلم

painkillers mosakkin

مُسكِّن

painting Soora

صوره

pair: a pair of ... gōz ...

جوز

Pakistani bākistānee

باكستانى

palace aSr

قصر

pale (face) miSfer

مصفر

(colour) fāteH

فاتح

pale blue azra' fāteH

ازرق فاتح

Palestine felesTeen

فلسطين

pan Halla

حَلّه

panties libās Hareemee

لِباس حريمى

pants (underwear: men's) libās

لِباس

(women's) libās Hareemee

لباس حريمى

(US: trousers) banTaloon

بنطلون

pantyhose sharāb Haraymee

Taweel

شراب حريمى طويل

paper wara'

ورق

(newspaper) gornāl

جرنال

a piece of paper Hettit

wara'a

حتة ورقه

paper handkerchiefs manadeel

wara'

مناديل ورق

papyrus wara' el bardee

ورق البردى

parcel Tard

طرد

pardon (me)? (didn't understand/

hear) afanddim?

أفندم؟

parents ahl

أهل

park (noun) mow'af

موقف

(verb) **rakan**

ركن

can I park here? **momkin
arkin hena?**

ممكن أركن هنا؟

parking lot **mow'af
Aarabayyāt**

موقف عربيات

part (noun) **goz'**

جزء

partner (boyfriend) **sāHib**

صاحب

(girlfriend) **saHbah**

صاحبة

party (group) **magmooAa**

مجموعة

(celebration) **Hafla**

حفلة

passenger (man/woman) **rākib/
rākba**

راكب/راكبة

passport **basbōr**

باسبور

All visitors to Egypt must hold
passports that are valid for
at least six months beyond
the proposed date of entry to
the country.

Most Arab countries except
Egypt and Jordan will deny
entry to anyone whose passport
→

shows evidence of a visit to
Israel, so if you are travelling
around the Middle East, be sure
to visit Israel after you have
been to Syria, Lebanon or
wherever.

Once in Egypt you should always
carry your passport with you:
you'll need it to register at
hotels, change money, collect
mail and possibly to show at
police checkpoints. It's a good
idea to photocopy the pages
recording your particulars, just
in case you lose your passport.

past* : in the past **min zamān**

من زمان

just past the information office
**yadōbak baAd maktab
elmaAloomāt**

يا دوبك بعد مكتب
المعلومات

path **mamar**

ممر

pattern **batrōn**

باترون

pavement **raseef**

رصيف

on the pavement **Aala
er-raseef**

على الرصيف

pay (verb) **dafaA**

دفع

can I pay, please? (to man/woman) **momkin adfaA, low samaHt/samaHtee?**

ممكن أدفع لو سمحت/ سمحتي؟

it's already paid for **el Hisāb khālis**

الحساب خالص

•••••• DIALOGUE ••••••

who's paying? **meen HayedfaA?**

I'll pay **ana HadfaA**

no, you paid last time, I'll pay (to man/woman) **la', inta/inti dafaAt/dafaAtee elmarra ellay fātit, ana HadfaA elmarra dee**

payphone **telefōn Aomoomee**

تليفون عمومى

peaceful **silmee**

سِلمى

peach **khōkh**

خوخ

peanuts **fool soodānee**

فول سودانى

pear **kommitra**

كمثرى

peculiar (strange) **ghareeb**

غريب

peg (for washing) **maJbak**

مشبك

(for tent) **watad**

وتد

pen **alam**

قلم

pencil **alam rosās**

قلم رصاص

penfriend (man/woman) **sādee' morasla/sādee'it morasla**

صديق مراسله/صديقة مراسله

penicillin **bensileen**

بنسلين

people **nās**

ناس

the other people in the hotel **en-nās et-tanyeen fil fondo'**

الناس الثانيين فى الفندق

too many people **nās keteer**

ناس كثير

pepper (spice) **felfil eswid**

فلفل إسود

per: per night **fil layla**

فى الليله

how much per day? **bekam fil layla?**

بكام فى الليله؟

per cent **nisba me'awaya**

نسبه مئويه

perfect tamām

تمام

perfume reeHa

ريحه

perhaps gāyez

جايز

perhaps not momkin la'

ممكن لا

period (of time) modda

مده

(menstruation) el Aāda
esh-shahraya

العاده الشهريه

permit (noun) taSreeH

تصريح

person shākhs

شخص

personal stereo kassit
soghīyar

كاسيت صغير

petrol banzeen

بنزين

petrol can SafeeHet banzeen

صفيحة بنزين

petrol station maHaTTit
banzeen

محطة بنزين

pharmacy agzakhana

أجزاخانه

For minor health complaints a
visit to a pharmacy is likely to
be sufficient. Pharmacies are
found in every town and Egyptian pharmacists are well
trained and dispense a wide
range of drugs, including many
available only on prescription
in Europe. They usually speak
English.

Pharaoh farAōn

فرعون

phone (noun) telefōn

تليفون

(verb) ettaSal

إتصل

All towns and cities have at
least one 24-hour telephone
and telegraph office (maktab
et-telfonāt/sentrāl) for calling
long distance and abroad.
Usually, you book the call
through the exchange, giving the
number to a clerk and paying in
advance, either for a set amount
of time or you make a deposit,
settling the bill afterwards.
Many telephone offices (and
some airports and stations) now
have orange direct-dial phones
that take phonecards (sold on
→

the premises), enabling you to avoid the system of booking long-distance and international calls through the exchange. Phonecard rates are slightly dearer than calls booked through the exchange, but you only pay for the time used; calls over six minutes during peak hours (8am–8pm local time) cost triple the normal rate.

You can also make calls through a hotel with a trunk or direct international line (most places with three or more stars have them); this costs between 15-100 per cent above the normal rate. Always check the rate first. Regular phone boxes really only serve for local calls which cost 25pt (though some kiosks only accept the old 5pt coins). You can also make local calls on semi-public phones owned by shopkeepers or hoteliers, who charge 50-100pt. Only in Cairo will you find payphones for dialling abroad.

phone book daleel telefōnāt

دليل تليفونات

phone box kabeenit telefōn

كابينة تليفون

phonecard kart telefōn

كارت تليفون

phone number raQam telefōn

رقم تليفون

photo soora

صوره

excuse me, could you take a photo of us? (to man/woman) baAd iznak/iznik, momkin tessowarna/tessowarina?

بعد إذنك/ إذنك، ممكن تصورنا/تصورينا؟

Before taking a photograph of someone, ask their permission first, especially in the more remote regions where you can cause genuine offence. Say: 'momkin akhod soora?' (can I take a photo?). You may also find that people stop you from taking photos that show Egypt in a 'poor' or 'backward' light. On a more positive front, taking a photograph of (and sending it to) someone you've struck up a friendship with, or exchanging photographs, is often greatly appreciated. Avoid photographing anything militarily sensitive (bridges, train stations, dams etc).

phrasebook daleel sayāHee

دليل سياحى

piano bayānoo

بيانو

piastre ersh

قرش

pickpocket (man/woman) nashāl/
nashāla

نشال/نشاله

pick up: will you be there to pick
me up? (to man) momkin
tekoon henak Aalashan
tewaSSalnee?

ممكن تكون هناك علشان
توصلنى؟

(to woman) momkin tekoonee
henak Aalashan
tewaSSalinee?

ممكن تكونى هناك
علشان توصلينى؟

picnic (noun) nozha

نزهه

picture Soora

صوره

piece Hetta

حته

a piece of ... Hettit ...

حتة...

pigeon Hamāma

حمامه

pillow makhadda

مخده

pillow case kees makhadda

كيس مخده

pin (noun) dabboos

دبوس

pineapple ananās

أناناس

pineapple juice AaSeer ananās

عصير أناناس

pink bambee

بمبى

pipe (for smoking) bebba

بيبه

(for water) masoora

ماسوره

pistachio fosto'

فستق

pity: it's a pity maAlesh

معلش

pizza beetza

بيتزا

place (noun) makān

مكان

at your place (to man/woman)

fee baytak/baytik

فى بيتك/بيتك

at his place fee bayto

فى بيته

plain (not patterned) sāda

ساده

plane Tīyāra

طياره

by plane beT-Tīyāra

بالطياره

plant nabāt

نبات

plasters blastar

بلاستر

plastic blastik

بلاستك

plastic bag shanTa blastik

شنطه بلاستك

plate Taba'

طبق

platform raSeef

رصيف

which platform is it for Tahrir station? raSeef nimra kam lemidān et-taHreer?

رصيف نمره كام لميدان التحرير؟

play (verb) laAab

لعب

(noun: in theatre) masraHaya

مسرحيه

pleasant mofriH

مفرح

please (to man/woman) low samaHt/samaHtee

لو سمحت/سمحتى

yes, please īwa, low samaHt/samaHtee

أيوه لو سمحت/سمحتى

could you please ...? momkin ... low samaHt/samaHtee?

ممكن...لو سمحت/سمحتى؟

please don't ma ... low samaHt/samaHtee

ما...لو سمحت/سمحتى

pleased: pleased to meet you Tesharrafna

تشرفنا

pleasure: my pleasure aī khidma

أى خدمه

plenty: plenty of ... keteer min ...

كثير من ...

there's plenty of time fee wa't keteer

فى وقت كثير

that's plenty, thanks da kifāya, shokran

دا كفايه ,شكرا

plug (electrical) feesha

فيشه

(in sink) saddādit HōD

سدادة الحوض

plumber sabbāk

سباك

pm*

poached egg bayD masloo'

بيض مسلوق

pocket gayb

جيب

point: there's no point mafeesh

fīda

مفيش فائده

poisonous mosammim

مسمم

police bolees

بوليس

call the police! etessil bil

bolees!

إتصل بالبوليس

Egypt has various police forces.
The Municipal Police have a
monopoly on law and order in
smaller towns. Their uniform
(khaki in winter, tan or white in
summer) resembles that of
the Traffic Police, who wear
striped cuffs. Both get involved
in accidents and can render
assistance in emergencies. However, relatively few officers
speak anything but Arabic.
If you've got a problem or need
to report a crime, always go to
the Tourist Police. The ordinary
ranks wear the regular khaki
uniform with a Tourist Police
armband; officers wear black →

uniforms in winter and white in
summer. Found at tourist sites,
museums, airports, stations and
ports, they often speak a foreign
language (usually English).
The fourth force is the Canal
Security police (dressed in black
and armed with Kalashnikovs)
who guard embassies, banks
and highways. To guard vital
utilities there are also Electricity, Airport and River Police
forces; the last is responsible
for overseeing felucca journeys
between Aswan and Luxor.
The emergency phone number
for the police is 122.

policeman rāgil bolees

رجل بوليس

police station esm esh-shorTa

قسم الشرطه

polite mo'addab

مؤدب

polluted millawis

ملوث

pomegranate rommān

رمان

pool (for swimming) Hammām

sibāHa

حمام سباحه

poor (not rich) fa'eer

فقير

(quality) mish **kway**is

مش كويس

pop music mo**see**Qa afran**gee**

موسيقى أفرنجى

(Western) mo**see**Qa ghar**bay**a

موسيقى غربيه

pop singer (man/woman)

mo**ghan**nee/mogha**na**ya

مغنى/مغنيه

popular ma**Hboob**

محبوب

pork khan**zeer**

خنزير

port (for boats) **mee**na

ميناء

porter (in hotel) shī**yāl**

شيال

Port Said bor sa**Aeed**

بور سعيد

posh (restaurant) **fā**khir gid**dan**

فاخر جدا

(people) foo' **awee**

فوق قوى

possible **mom**kin

ممكن

is it possible to ...?

momkin ...?

ممكن...؟

as ... as possible bee ... ma
yomkim

ب...ما يمكن

post (noun: mail) **bos**Ta

بوسطه

(verb) ba**Aat**

بعث

could you post this for me?

momkin **ter**mee lee
eg-ga**wāb** da fee el **bos**Ta?

ممكن ترمى لى الجواب دا
فى البوسطه؟

postcard kart

كارت

postcode ramz ba**ree**dee

رمز بريدى

poster **soo**ra

صوره

(advert) e**Alān**

إعلان

poste restante see post office

post office **bos**Ta

بوسطه

Post offices are generally open daily (except Fridays) 8am–2pm (Ramadan 9am–3pm), though central offices may stay open until 8pm.

When sending mail from Egypt, it speeds up the delivery if you get someone to write the name of the country in Arabic. As a rule, around 15 per cent of correspondence (in either direction) never arrives; letters

→

containing photos or other items are especially prone to go astray.

It's best to send letters from a major city or hotel; blue mailboxes are for overseas airmail, red ones for domestic post. Airmail (bareed gowee) stamps can be purchased at post offices, hotel shops and post-card stands, which may charge slightly above the normal rate. Registered mail can be sent from any post office. Selected post offices in the main cities also offer an Express Mail Service (36hr to Europe, 48hr to the US).

To send a parcel, take the goods unwrapped to a major post office for customs inspection, weighing and wrapping.

Receiving letters poste restante is a bit of a lottery, since post office workers don't always file letters under the surname. Ask for all your initials to be checked (including M for Mr, Ms, etc). To pick up mail you'll need your passport.

potato baTāTis (f)

بطاطس

pottery (objects) khazaf

خزف

pound (money: Egyptian) geneeh

جنيه

(British) estirleenee

إسترلينى

(weight) wazn

وزن

power cut el kaharaba ma'TŌAa

الكهرباء مقطوعه

power point bareeza

بريزه

practise: I want to practise my Arabic (said by man/woman) Aayiz/Aīza a'owwee elAarabee betāAee

عايز/عايزه أقوى العربى بتاعى

prawns gambaree

جمبرى

prefer: I prefer … ana afaDDal …

أنا أفضّل …

pregnant Hāmil

حامل

prescription (for medicine) roshetta

روشته

present (gift) hidaya

هديه

president (of country: man/woman)

ra'ees/ra'eesa

رئيس/رئيسه

pretty gameel

جميل

it's pretty expensive da

ghālee awee

دا غالى قوى

price taman

ثمن

prickly heat Hamw en-neel

حمو النيل

prime minister (man/woman)

ra'ees wozarā'/ra'eesit

wozarā'

رئيس وزراء/رئيسة وزراء

prince ameer

أمير

princess ameera

أميره

printed matter maTbooaāt

مطبوعات

private khās

خاص

private bathroom Hammām

khās

حمام خاص

probably gāyiz

جائز

problem moshkila

مشكله

no problem! mafeesh

moshkila!

مفيش مشكله!

program(me) barnāmig

برنامج

pronounce: how is this

pronounced? izzay tenTa'/

tenTa'ee dee?

إزاى تنطق/تنطقى دى؟

properly (repaired, locked etc)

kwayis

كويس

protection factor (of suntan lotion)

marham Hemāya

مرهم حمايه

Protestant brotistantee

بروتستانتى

public holiday agāza rasmaya

أجازه رسميه

Egypt abounds in holidays and festivals of all kinds, both Muslim and Christian, national and local. Ramadan, the month when all Muslims observe a total fast from dawn to sunset, can pose big problems for travellers because transport services may be limited. But the celebratory evenings are good times to hear music and to enjoy Egyptian hospitality.

If you are a non-Muslim you are not expected to observe
→

Ramadan, but it is good to be sensitive about not eating or drinking (and especially not smoking) in public.

All Islamic holidays and festivals follow the Islamic calendar. This is lunar based, so dates vary each year in relation to the Western calendar.

The Islamic festivals are:
Ramadan
Eid al-Fitr
Eid al-Adha
Islamic New Year
Birthday of Prophet Muhammad

Fixed public holidays are as follows:

1 January	New Year's Day
25 April	Liberation Day
1 May	Labour Day
23 July	Revolution Day
6 October	Armed Forces Day
23 October	Suez Day
23 December	Victory Day

pull shad

شد

pullover boloovar

بلوفر

puncture (noun) khorm

خرم

purple banafsigee

بنفسجى

purse (for money) bok

بوك

(US: handbag) shanTit eed

شنطة يد

push za'

زق

pushchair Aarabayit Tefl

عربية طفل

put HaT

حط

where can I put ...? aHoT ... fayn?

أحط....فين؟

could you put us up for the night? momkin nenām hena ellaylādee?

ممكن ننام هنا الليلة دى؟

pyjamas bJāma

بيجامه

pyramid haram

هرم

Q

Qatar Qatar

قطر

quality nōA

نوع

quarter robA

ربع

quayside: on the quayside Hafit
elmarsa

حافة المرسى

queen malika

ملكه

question so'āl

سؤال

queue (noun) Taboor

طابور

quick sareeA

سريع

that was quick da sareeA
awee

دا سريع قوى

which is the quickest way
there? aī Taree' elasraA?

إيه الطريق الأسرع؟

quickly bisorAa

بسرعه

quiet (place, hotel) hādee

هادى

quiet! hidoo'!

هدوء!

quite (fairly) ta'reeban

تقريبا

(very) giddan

جداً

that's quite right da ta'reeban
SaHeeH

دا تقريباً صحيح

quite a lot keteer awee

كتير قوى

R

rabies dā' elkalb

داء الكلب

Rabies is endemic in Egypt, so
avoid touching any strange
animal, wild or domestic. Treatment must be given between
exposure to the disease and the
onset of symptoms; once these
appear, rabies is invariably
fatal. To err on the side of
caution, consider having a
rabies jab before going to Egypt.
It will not avoid the need for
treatment altogether, should
you become infected, but fewer
injections will be required.

race (for runners, cars) sebā'

سباق

radiator radyatayr

راديتير

radio radyo

راديو

on the radio Aala er-radyo

على الراديو

rail: by rail bes-sikka el
Hadeed

بالسكه الحديد

railway es-sikka el Hadeed

السكه الحديد

rain (noun) naTara

مطره

in the rain fen-naTara

فى المطره

it's raining betnaTTar

بتمطر

raincoat balTo maTar

بالطو مطر

raisins zebeeb

زبيب

Ramadan RamaDān

رمضان

rape (noun) eghtesāb

إغتصاب

rare (uncommon) nādir

نادر

(steak) mish mistewee awee

مش مستوى قوى

rash (on skin) TafH

طفح

raspberry toot

توت

rat far

فار

rate (for changing money) seAr

سعر

rather: it's rather good shaklaha maa'ool

شكلها معقول

I'd rather ... ana afaDDal ...

أنا أفضل

razor makanit Hila'a

مكنة حلاقه

razor blades amwās Hila'a

أمواس حلاقه

read ara

قرا

ready gāhiz

جاهز

are you ready? (to man) inta mostaAid?

إنتَ مستعد؟

(to woman) inti mostaAidda?

إنتى مستعده؟

I'm not ready yet (said by man/woman) ana lessa mish mostaAid/mostaAidda

أنا لسه مش مستعد / مستعده

•••••• DIALOGUE ••••••

when will it be ready? Hatkoon gahza imta?

it should be ready in a couple of days Hatkoon gahza khilāl yōmayn

real Ha'ee-ee

حقيقى

really awee

قوى

I'm really sorry (said by man/
woman) ana āsif/āsfa begad

أنا آسف/آسفه بجد

that's really great da SaHeeH
shay' AaZeem

دا صحيح شئ عظيم

really? (doubt) SaHeeH?

صحيح؟

(polite interest) maA'ool?

معقول؟

rear lights el loomaD el
warrānaya

اللمض الورانيه

rearview mirror mrāya warrānaya

مرايه ورانيه

reasonable (prices etc) maA'ool

معقول

receipt wasl

وصل

recently min orīyib

من قريب

reception (in hotel) este'bāl

إستقبال

at reception Aand eleste'bāl

عند الإستقبال

reception desk maktab
elesti'bāl

مكتب الإستقبال

receptionist (man/woman)
mowaZZaf/mowaZZafit
este'bāl

موظف/موظفة إستقبال

recognize etAarraf Aala

إتعرف على

recommend: could you
recommend ...? (to man/woman)
momkin te'ollee/
te'olelee ...?

ممكن تقول لى/
تقولى لى ....؟

record (music) isTwāna

إسطوانه

red aHmar

أحمر

Red Sea el baHr elaHmar

البحر الأحمر

red wine nebeet aHmar

نبيذ أحمر

refund (noun) targeeA

ترجيع

can I have a refund? momkin
akhod feloosee tanee?

ممكن أخد فلوسى تانى؟

region manTe'a

منطقه

registered: by registered mail
bareed mosaggal

بريد مسجل

registration number nimrit
elAarabayya

نمرة العربيه

religion deen

دين

remains (of city etc) kharabāt

خرابات

remember: I don't remember

mish fākir

مش فاكر

I remember ana fākir

أنا فاكر

do you remember? (to man)

inta fākir?

إنت فاكر؟

(to woman) inti fakra?

إنتى فاكره؟

rent (noun: for apartment etc)

eegār

إيجار

(verb: car etc) aggar

أجّر

to rent lil egār

للإيجار

• • • • • • DIALOGUE • • • • • •

I'd like to rent a car (said by man/woman) ana Aayiz/Aīza a'aggar Aarabayya

for how long? lemoddit ad ay?

two days yomayn

this is our range dee mooAaddalatna

I'll take the … Hākhod el…

is that with unlimited mileage? dee ellay maAalhāsh Hodood lessafar?

it is īwa

can I see your licence, please? (to man) momkin ashoof rokhsitak, low samaHt?

(to woman) momkin ashoof rokhsitik, low samaHtee?

and your passport (to man/woman) we basborak/basborik?

is insurance included? shāmil et-ta'meen?

yes, but you pay the first fifty pounds (to man) īwa, bas inta lāzim tedfaA khamseen geneeh fee el-'owil

(to woman) īwa, bas inti lāzim tedfaAee khamseen geneeh fee el-'owil

can you leave a deposit of thirty pounds? (to man/woman) momkin teseeb/teseebee talateen geneeh Aarboon?

rented car Aarabayya mit'aggara

عربيه متأجره

repair (verb) SallaH

صلح

can you repair it? momkin tisallaH da?

ممكن تصلح دا؟

repeat Aād

عاد

could you repeat that? momkin teAeed tanee?

ممكن تعيد تانى؟

reservation Haġz

حجز

I'd like to make a reservation
(said by man/woman) Aayiz/Aīza
aHgiz

عايز / عايزه أحجز

• • • • • **DIALOGUE** • • • • •

I have a reservation ana Hagazt
hena
yes sir, what name please? HaDir
yafanddem, taHt esm meen?

reserve (verb) Hagaz

حجز

• • • • • **DIALOGUE** • • • • •

can I reserve a table for tonight?
momkin aHgiz Tarabayza
lel-layla dee?
yes madam, for how many people?
HaDir ya madām, lekam waHid?
for two letnayn
and for what time? wessāAa kām?
for eight o'clock essāAa tamaniya
**and could I have your name
please?** momkin ākhod ismik,
low samaHtee?

rest: **I need a rest** (said by man/
woman) ana meHtāg/
meHtāga istirāHa

أنا محتاج / محتاجة إستراحه

the rest of the group bā'ee el

magmooAa

باقى المجموعه

restaurant maTAam

مطعم

Eating out falls into two camps.
At a local level there are cafés
and diners, and loads of street
stalls, which sell one or two
simple dishes. More formally
and expensively, restaurants
cater to middle-class Egyptians
and tourists. The latter have
menus (most cafés don't) offering a broader range of dishes,
and sometimes specialising in
foreign cuisine. They will also
invariably add a service charge
and taxes to your bill, which
can increase the total by 10-12
per cent. You are also expected
to tip.

The classic Egyptian restaurant
or café meal is either a lamb
kabab or kofta (spiced mince
patties), accompanied or pre-
ceded by a couple of dips.
The dips are usually houmous
(made from chickpeas),
TeHeena (tahini, paste made
from sesame seeds) and baba
ghan-noog (tahini with auber-
gine).

In a basic place, salad, fool

→

medammis (brown beans) and bread could also be on offer and chicken (frākh) is a standard, both in cafés and as a takeaway food from spit-roast stands. Pigeon (Hamām) is common too, most often served with spicy wheat (freek) stuffing. In slightly fancier places you may also encounter pigeon in a Tāgin, stewed with onions, tomatoes and rice in an earthenware pot.

More expensive restaurants feature these same dishes, plus a few that are more elaborate. Some may precede main courses with a larger selection of dips, plus olives, stuffed vine leaves and so on. Soups too, are occasionaly featured, most famously molokhayya, which is made from stewing Jew's mallow in chicken stock. Two common main dishes are maHshee, comprising stuffed vegetables (tomatoes, aubergines etc), and Torlee, a mixed vegetable casserole with chunks of lamb, or occasionally beef. Fish (samak) is featured on restaurant menus in Alexandria, Aswan, the Red Sea coast and Sinai. You may also find →

squid (sob-bayT), shrimps (gambaree) and octopus (ekhTaboot).

One confusion you'll often run up against is that pasta, rice, chips (French fries) and even crisps (potato chips) are interchangeable. Order rice and you'll get chips, and your querying of the matter will be regarded as inexplicable.

restaurant car Aarabayyit el akl
عربية الأكل

resthouse istirāHa
إستراحه

Chiefly found in the Western Desert oases, government resthouses offer basic triple-bed rooms and cold showers at very reasonable prices. Guests may have to share with strangers unless they're willing to pay for beds to be kept unoccupied. Apart from tourists, resthouses are mostly used by truckers.

rest room tawalet
تواليت

retired: I'm retired ana Aalal maAāsh
أنا على المعاش

return: a return to Aswan
tazkarit Aowda le Aswān

تذكرة عوده لأسوان

return ticket tazkarit Aowda

تذكرة عوده

see ticket

reverse gear marshidayr

مارشدير

revolting mo'rif

مقرف

rice roz

رز

rich (person) ghanee

غني

(food) dasim

دسم

ridiculous mish maA'ool

مش معقول

right (correct) SaH

صح

(not left) yemeen

يمين

you were right (to man) inta
kont Aala Ha'

إنت كنت على حق

(to woman) inti kontee Aala
Ha'

إنتى كنتى على حق

that's right da SaH

دا صح

this can't be right da mish

momkin yekoon SaH

دا مش ممكن يكون صح

right! SaH!

صح!

is this the right road for ...? da
eT-Taree' eS-SaHeeH le ...?

دا الطريق الصحيح
لـ ...؟

on the right Aalal yemeen

على اليمين

to the right lelyemeen

لليمين

turn right Howid yemeen

حود يمين

right-hand drive dereksayoon
Aalal yemeen

دريكسيون على اليمين

ring (on finger) khātim

خاتم

I'll ring you (to man/woman)
HātesSil beek/beekee

حاتصل بيك/بيكى

ring back ettaSal baAdayn

إتّصل بعدين

ripe (fruit) mistaywee

مستوى

risky khaTar

خطر

river nahr

نهر

road Taree'

طريق

is this the road for ...? da
Taree' le ...?

دا طريق ل ...؟

down the road fee ākhir esh-
shāreA

فى آخر الشارع

road map KhareeTit Toro'

خريطة طرق

rob: I've been robbed ana
etsara't

أنا إتسرقت

rock Hagar

حجر

(music) moseeQa rok

موسيقى روك

on the rocks (with ice) bee talg

بالتلج

roll (bread) Aaysh fayno
medowwar

عيش فينو مدوّر

Roman romānee

رومانى

roof (of house) SaT-H

سطح

(of car) sa'f

سقف

room ōDa

أوضة

in my room fee oDtee

فى أوضتى

•••••• DIALOGUE ••••••

do you have any rooms? (to man/
woman) Aandak/Aandik aī ewaD
faDya

for how many people? lekām
wāHid

for one/for two lewāHid/letnayn

yes, we have rooms free īwa,
Aandina ewaD faDya

for how many nights will it be?
lekām layla?

just for one night layla waHda

how much is it? bekām?

... with bathroom and ... without
bathroom ... beHammām we ...
min ghayr Hammām

can I see a room with bathroom?
momkin ashoof ōDa
beHammām?

OK, I'll take it okay, Hākhod dee

room service khedma lil ewaD

خدمة للاوض

rope Habl

حبل

rosé (wine) wardee

وردى

roughly (approximately)
ta'reeban

تقريبا

round: it's my round da dōree

دا دورى

round-trip ticket tazkarit Aowda

تذكرة عودة

route Taree'

طريق

what's the best route? ay aHsan Taree'?

إيه أحسن طريق؟

rubbish (waste) zebāla

زبالة

(poor quality goods) nōA mish kwayis

نوع مش كويّس

rubbish! (nonsense) da kalām fāDee!

دا كلام فاضى!

rucksack shanTit Dahr

شنطة ضهر

rude mish mo'addab

مش مؤدّب

ruins kharabāt

خرابات

rum ram

رم

rum and Coke® ram we kakoola

رم وكاكولا

run (verb: person) geree

جرى

sad Hazeen

حزين

saddle (for bike) korsee

كرسى

(for horse) sirg

سرج

safe (not in danger) ameen

أمين

(not dangerous) amān

أمان

Sahara SaHara

صحرا

sail (noun) shirāA

شراع

sailboarding 'sailboarding'

سيلبوردنج

salad salāTa

سلاطة

salad dressing Salsa les-salāTa

صلصة للسلاطة

sale: for sale lil bayA

للبيع

salt malH

ملح

same: the same zī

زى

the same as this zī da

زى دا

the same again, please (said by

man/woman) wāHid tānee, low
samaHt/samaHtee

واحد تانى، لو سمحت/
سمحتى

it's all the same to me koloo
zī baADoo ben nesbālee

كلّه زى بعضه بالنسبة لى

sand ramla

رملة

sandals Sandal

صندل

sandstorm Aāsifa ramlaya

عاصفة رملية

sandwich sandawitsh

ساندوتش

sanitary napkins/towels fewoT
SeHHaya

فوط صحيّة

Saturday yōm es-sabt

يوم السبت

Saudi Arabia es-soAodaya

السعوديّة

sauce Tagin

طاجن

saucepan Halla

حلّة

saucer Taba' fongān

طبق فنجان

sausage sodo'

سجق

say āl

قال

how do you say ... in Arabic?
izzay ti'ool ... bil Aarabee?

إزّاى تقول ... بالعربى؟

what did he say? howa āl ay?

هوّ قال إيه؟

she said ... hayya ālit ...

هيّ قالت ...

could you say that again? (to
man/woman) momkin teAeed/
teAeedee ellay oltu/oltee
tanee?

ممكن تعيد/تعيدى
اللى قلته/قلتيه تانى؟

scarf (for neck) talfeeAa

تلفيعة

(for head) asharb

أشارب

scenery manZar

منظر

schedule (US: timetable) gadwal
el mowāAeed

جدول المواعيد

scheduled flight reHla yōmaya

رحلة يوميّة

school madrasa

مدرسة

scissors ma'as

مقص

scorpion Aa'rab

عقرب

scorpions and snakes

The danger from scorpions and snakes is minimal as most species are nocturnal and generally avoid people, However, you shouldn't go barefoot, turn over any rocks or stick your hands into dark crevices anywhere off the beaten track. If stung, cold-pack the area and get to a doctor.

All snake bites should be washed immediately. Stay calm, as panicking sends the venom through your bloodstream more quickly, and get immediate help.

scotch weskee

ويسكى

Scotch tape® solotabe

سولوتيب

Scotland eskotlanda

إسكتلندا

Scottish eskotlandee

إسكتلندى

I'm Scottish (said by man/woman)

ana eskotlandee/
eskotlandaya

أنا إسكتلندى/
إسكتلندية

scrambled eggs bayD ma'lee

بيض مقلى

scuba-diving 'scuba diving'

سكوبا دايفينج

sea baHr

بحر

by the sea gamb el baHr

جنب البحر

seafood wagabāt baHaraya

وجبات بحريّة

seafront wag-hit el baHr

واجهة البحر

on the seafront Aala wag-hit
el baHr

على واجهة البحر

seasick: I feel seasick (said by
man/woman) Hāsis/Hassa
bidowarān

حاسس/حاسّة بدوران

I get seasick baygeelee
dowarān

بيجيلى دوران

seaside: by the seaside gamb
el blāʒ

جنب البلاج

seat korsee

كرسى

is this seat taken? Had aAid
hena?

حد قاعد هنا؟

second (adj) et-tānee

التانى

(in time) sanya

ثانية

just a second! **sanya waHda**

ثانية واحدة

second-class (travel etc) **daraga tania**

درجة تانية

second-hand mostaAmal

مستعمل

see shāf

شاف

can I see? **momkin ashoof?**

ممكن أشوف

have you seen ...? (to man/woman) **shoft/shoftee ...?**

شفت/شفتى ؟...

I saw him this morning **ana shoftoo eS-SobHaya**

أنا شفته الصبحيّة

see you! **netlā'a baAdayn!**

نتلاقى بعدين!

I see (I understand) **īwa**

أيوه

self-service khedma zātaya

خدمة ذاتيّة

sell bāA

باع

do you sell ...? (to man/woman) **betbeeA/betbeeAee ...?**

بتبيع بتبيعى ؟...

send baAat

بعت

I want to send this to England

(said by man/woman) **ana Aayiz/Aīza abAat da lingilterra**

أنا عايز/عايزة أبعت دا لإنجلترا

separate monfasil

منفصل

separately (pay, travel) **lewaHdee**

لوحدى

September sebtamber

سبتمبر

serious (problem, illness) **khaTeer**

خطير

service charge (in restaurant) **rasm el khedma**

رسم الخدمة

service station maHaTTit banzeen

محطّة بنزين

set menu Qīmit TaaĀm moHadadda

قائمة طعام محدّدة

several keteer

كتير

sew khīyaT

خيّاط

could you sew this back on? (to man/woman) **momkin tekhīyaT/tekhīyaTee da?**

ممكن تخيّط/تخيّطى دا؟

sex gins

جنس

sexy moghray

مغرى

shade: in the shade feD-Dil

فى الضل

shallow (water) mish ghoweeT

مش غويط

shame: what a shame! Haga
teksif!

حاجة تكسف!

shampoo (noun) shamboo

شامبو

share (verb: room, table etc) assim

قسِم

sharp (knife) Hāmee

حامى

shaver makanit Hilā'a

مكنة حلاقة

shaving foam kraym Hilā'a

كريم حلاقة

shaving point bareeza li
makanit el Hilā'a

بريزة لمكينة الحلاقة

she* hayya

هيّ

is she here? hayya hena?

هيّ هنا؟

sheep kharoof

خروف

sheet (for bed) mlāya

ملايا

shelf raff

رف

shell Sadafa

صدفة

shellfish Sadafa

صدفة

ship (big) safeena

سفينة

(small) markib

مركب

by ship bes-safeena

بالسفينة

shirt amees

قميص

shit! ellaAna!

اللعنة!

shock (noun) Sadma

صدمة

I got an electric shock from
the ... ana etkahrabt min ...

أنا إتكهربت من ...

shocking fazeeA

فظيعة

shoe fardit gazma

فردة جزمة

a pair of shoes gazma

جزمة

shoelaces robaT gazma

رباط جزمة

shoe polish warneesh

ورنيش

shoe repairer gazmagee

جزمجى

shop maHal

محل

(small, local) dokkān (f)

دكان

> Shops generally open at 9.30 or 10am. Most shops close at 10pm, though some may be open until midnight or even 24 hours a day. Many shops close in the afternoon between 1.30–4 pm.

shopping: I'm going shopping
ana rīeH ashteree Hagāt

أنا رايح أشترى حاجات

shop window vatreenit el maHal

فاترينة المحل

shore shaT

شط

short osīyar

قصير

shorts short

شورت

should: what should I do?
aAmil ay?

أعمل إيه؟

you should ... mafrooD innak ...

مفروض إنّك ...

you shouldn't ... mish

mafrooD innak ...

مش مفروض إنّك ...

he should be back soon
howa mafrooD yekoon hena baAd shwīya

مفروض يكون هنا بعد شوية

shoulder kitf

كتف

shout (verb) zaA-Aa'

زعّق

show (in theatre) AarD masraHee

عرض مسرحى

could you show me? momkin tewarreenee?

ممكن تورّينى؟

shower (in bathroom) dosh

دش

(of rain) shita

شتا

with shower beddosh

بالدش

shrine DareeH

ضريح

shut (verb) afal

قفل

when do you shut? (to man/ woman) biti'fil/biti'filee imta?

بتقفل/بتقفلى إمتى؟

when does it shut? baye'fil
imta?

بيقفل إمتى؟

they're shut a'fleen

قافلين

I've shut myself out el bab
et'efil wana barra

الباب إتقفل وانا بره

shut up! ekhras!

إخرس!

shutter (in camera) monaZZim
fatHet el Aadasa

منظّم فتحة العدسة

(on window) sheesh

شيش

sick (ill) Aīyān

عيّان

I'm going to be sick (vomit)
ana HaraggaA

انا حارجّع

side gamb

جنب

the other side of the street el
gamb el tanee meshāriA

الجنب التانى من الشارع

side street shāriA gānaybee

شارع جانبى

sidewalk raSeef

رصيف

on the sidewalk Aala
er-raSeef

على الرصيف

sight: the sights of ... manāZer
el ...

مناظر ال. . .

sightseeing: we're going
sightseeing rīHeen fee
gowla sayāHaya

رايحين فى جولة سياحيّة

sightseeing tour gowla
sayāHaya

جولة سياحيّة

sign (roadsign etc) ishāra

إشارة

silk Hareer

حرير

silly ahbal/habla (m/f)

أهبل/هبلة

silver (noun) faDDa

فضّة

similar zī

زى

simple (easy) sahl

سهل

since: since last week min el
esbooA ellay fāt

من الأسبوع اللى فات

since I got here min sāAit ma
waSalt hena

من ساعة ما وصلت هنا

sing ghanna

غنّى

singer (man/woman)
moghannee/

moghanaya

مغنّي/مغنّية

single: a single to ... tazkara
le ...

تذكرة لـ...

I'm single (said by man/woman)
ana Aāzib/Aazba

أنا عازب/عازية

single bed sireer faraDānee

سرير فرضاني

single room ōDa le wāHid

أوضة لواحد

single ticket tazkara waHda

تذكرة واحدة

sink (in kitchen) HōD

حوض

sister okht

أخت

sister-in-law neseeba

نسيبة

sit: can I sit here? momkin
aAod hena?

ممكن أقعد هنا؟

is anyone sitting here? fee
Had āAed hena?

فى حد قاعد هنا؟

sit down aAad

قعد

sit down! o'Aod!

قُعد !

size Hagm

حجم

(clothing) ma'āss

مقاس

skin gild

جلد

skin-diving ghōs

غوص

skinny rofīyaA awee

رُفيّع قوى

skirt gonilla

جونلة

sky sama

سما

skyscraper naT-Het seHāb

ناطحة سحاب

sleep (verb) nām

نام

did you sleep well? (to man/
woman) nimt/nimtee kwayis?

نمت/نمتى كويّس؟

sleeper (whole train) atr en-nōm

قطر النوم

sleeping bag 'sleeping bag'

سليبنباج

sleeping car Aarabayyit nōm

عربية نوم

sleeve komm

كم

slide (photographic) 'slide'

سلايد

slow baTee'

بطئ

  slow down! (driving) haddee
es-soraa!

هدّى السرعة!

slowly berrāHa

بالراحة

  very slowly baTee' awee

بطئ قوى

small soghīyar

صغيّر

smell: it smells (smells bad)
reHetha weHsha

ريحتها وحشة

smile (verb) ebtasam

إبتسم

smoke (noun) dokhān

دخّان

  do you mind if I smoke?
momkin adakhan?

ممكن أدّخن؟

  I don't smoke
mabadakhansh

مابدّخنش

  do you smoke? (to man/woman)
betdakhan/betdakhanee?

بتدّخن/بتدخنى؟

snack akla khafeefa

أكلة خفيفة

snake teabān

تعبان

sneeze (noun) yeatas

يعطس

snorkel 'snorkel'

سنوركل

snorkelling ghōs

غوص

so: it's so good momtāz
giddan

ممتاز جدا

  it's so expensive da ghālee
awee

دا غالى قوى

  not so much mish awee

مش قوى

  not so bad mish weHesh
awee

مش وحش قوى

  so am I, so do I ana kaman

أنا كمان

  so-so yaanee

يعنى

soaking solution (for contact
lenses) maHlool let-tanDeef

محلول للتنضيف

soap saboon

صابون

soap powder mashoo'
ghaseel

مسحوق غسيل

sock fardit sharāb

فردة شراب

socket (electrical) **bareeza**

بريزة

soda (water) 'soda'

صودا

sofa **kanaba**

كنبة

soft (material etc) **nāAim**

ناعم

soft-boiled egg **bayD breshtoh**

بيض بريشته

soft drink **mashroob ghayr koHollee**

غير كوحولى

---

soft drinks

Every main street has a couple of stand-up juice bars, recognisable by their displays of fruit. Normally you order and pay at the cash desk before exchanging a token for your drink at the counter; it's usual to leave a tip. Street vendors also sell iced, strong, sweet lemonade (**AaSeer lamoon**), bitter-sweet liquorice water and deliciously refreshing tamarind (**tamr hind-dee**). Western-style soft drinks, including Coca Cola and 7-Up (called Seven) are available everywhere. You have to pay a deposit on the bottle to take one away.

---

soft lenses **Aadasāt lasQa**

عدسات لاصقة

sole (of shoe) **naAl**

نعل

(of foot) **baTn er-rigl**

بطن الرجل

could you put new soles on these? **momkin terakkib naAl gedeed le dool?**

ممكن تركّب نعل جديد لدول؟

some: can I have some? **momkin ākhod shwīya?**

ممكن آخذ شويّة؟

can I have some water? **momkin shwīyit mīya?**

ممكن شويّة ميّة؟

somebody, someone **Had**

حد

something **Haga**

حاجة

something to eat **Haga tettākil**

حاجة تتاكل

sometimes **aHyānan**

أحيانا

somewhere **fee Hitta moAayana**

فى حتّة معيّنة

son ibn

إبن

song oghnaya

أغنية

son-in-law neseeb

نسيب

soon Hālan

حالا

I'll be back soon HargaA
besoraA

حارجع بسرعة

as soon as possible be'asraA
ma yomkin

بأسرع ما يمكن

sore: it's sore betewgaA

بتوجع

sore throat wagaA fee ez-zōr

وجع فى الزور

sorry: I'm sorry (said by man/
woman) ana āsif/āsfa

أنا آسف/أسفة

sorry? (didn't understand/hear)
afanddim?

أفنّدم؟

sort: what sort of ...? aī nōA
min ...?

أى نوع من....؟

soup shorba

شوربة

sour (taste) Hāmid

حامض

south ganoob

جنوب

in the south fil ganoob

فى الجنوب

South Africa ganoob afreQya

جنوب أفريقيا

South African: I'm South African
(said by man/woman) ana
ganoob afreeQee/afreQaya

أنا جنوب أفريقى/أفريقيّة

southeast el ganoob
es-shar'ee

الجنوب الشرقى

southwest el ganoob el
gharbee

الجنوب الغربى

souvenir tizkār

تذكار

Spain asbania

أسبانيا

Spanish asbānee

أسبانى

spare tyre Aagala estebn

عجلة إستبن

speak: do you speak English? (to
man/woman) betikkallim/
betikkallimee ingleezee?

بتتكلّم/بتتكلمى
إنجليزى؟

I don't speak ... ana
mabakkallimsh ...

أنا مابتكلّمش...

can I speak to ...? momkin
akkallim ...?

ممكن أتكلّم...؟

•••••• DIALOGUE ••••••

can I speak to Magdi? momkin
akallim magdi?
who's calling? meen maɅaya?
it's Patricia 'Patricia'
I'm sorry, he's not in, can I take a
message? (said by man/woman)
ana āsif/āsfa, howa mish
mowgood, teHebbee teseebee
resāla?
no thanks, I'll call back later la'
shokran, ana Hattesil baɅdayn
please tell him I called momkin
te'ollo ennay ittasalt

spectacles naDDāra

نضّارة

spend Saraf

صرف

sphinx abol hōl

أبو الهول

spider Ankaboot

عنكبوت

spirits

For serious drinking, Egyptians
get stuck into spirits. The
favoured tipple is brandy, known
by the slang name of jaz (literally bottle), which comes under
three labels: aHmar (the cheapest), maɅatta' (the best) and
vin (the most common). zebeeb
is similar to Greek ouzo, but
drunk neat. Avoid Egyptian-
made gin and whisky, whose
labels are designed to resemble
famous Western brands. Imported spirits are sold at
duty-free shops in the main
resorts for modest sums.

spoon maɅla'a

معلقة

sport rayāDa

رياضة

sprain: I've sprained my ... ana
lawayt ...

أنا لويت...

spring (season) er-rabeeA

الربيع

in the spring fer-rabeeA

فى الربيع

square (in town) medān

ميدان

squid sobbayT

سبيط

stairs salālim (f)

سلالم

stale mish Tāza

مش طازة

stamp (noun) TābeA

طابع

•••••• DIALOGUE ••••••

a stamp for England, please (to
man/woman) TābeA lingiltera,
low samaHt/samaHtee
what are you sending? (to man)
Aayiz tebAat ay?
(to woman) Aīza tebAatee ay?
this postcard el kart da
see post office

standby Qīmit el entizār

قائمة الإنتظار

star nigma

نجم

start (noun) el bedāya

البداية

(verb) bada'

بدأ

when does it start? bayebda'
imta?

ببدأ إمتى؟

the car won't start el
Aarabayya mabiddorsh

العربيّة مابتدورش

starter (food) fateH lil shahaya

فاتح للشهيّة

station (train) maHaTTit es-
sekka el Hadeed

محطّة السكة الحديد

(bus) mow'af otobees

موقف أوتوبيس

statue temsāl

تمثال

stay: where are you staying? (to
man) inta nazil fayn?

إنت نازل فين؟

(to woman) inti nazla fayn?

إنتى نازلة فاين؟

I'm staying at ... (said by man/
woman) ana nazil/nazla fee ...

أنا نازل/نازلة فى ...

I'd like to stay another two
nights (said by man/woman)
Aayiz/Aīza aAod layltayn
tanyeen

عايز/عايزة أقعد
ليلتين تانيين

steak felay

فيليه

steal sara'

سرق

my bag has been stolen
shanTitee etsara'it

شنطتى إتسرقت

steep (hill) metdaHdar

متدحدر

step: on the steps Aala
essalālim

على السلالم

sterling estirlaynee

إسترليني

steward (on plane) moDeef

مضيف

stewardess moDeefa

مضيفة

still: I'm still here ana lessa
hena

أنا لسّة هنا

is he still there? howa lessa
henāk?

هوّ لسّة هناك؟

keep still! esbat maHallak!

إثبت محلك!

sting: I've been stung ana
et'arasT

أنا إتسرقت

stockings sharāb Haraymee
Taweel

شراب حريمي طويل

stomach meAda

معدة

stomachache maghaS

مغص

stone (rock) Hagar

حجر

stop (verb) wa'af

وقف

please, stop here (to taxi driver
etc) o'af hena, low samaHt

أقف هنا، لو سمحت

do you stop near ...? bito'af
orīyib min ...?

بتوقف قريّب من ....؟

stop it! baTTal da!

بطّل دا!

stopover 'transit'

ترانزيت

storm Aāsifa

عاصفة

straight (whisky etc) 'straight'

ستريت

it's straight ahead AalaTool

على طول

straightaway Towālee

طوّالى

strange (odd) ghareeb

غريب

stranger (man/woman) ghareeb/
ghareeba

غريب/غريبة

strap (on watch) ostayk

أستيك

(on dress, suitcase) Hezām

حزام

strawberry farowla

فراولة

stream magra

مجرى

street shāriA

شارع

on the street feshāriA

فى الشارع

streetmap khareeTit Toro'

خريطة طرق

string khayT

خيط

strong shedeed

شديد

(taste) Hāmee

حامى

(drink) morakkaz

مركز

stuck maznoo'

مزنوق

it's stuck etzana'it

إتزنقت

student (male/female) Tālib/
Tāliba

طالب/طالبة

stupid ghabee

غبى

suburb DaHya

ضاحية

Sudan essodān

السودان

suddenly fag'a

فجأة

suede shamwā

شموا

Suez es-sways

السويس

Suez Canal Qanāt es-sways

قنال السويس

sugar sokkar

سكر

suit (noun) badla

بدلة

it doesn't suit me (jacket etc)

ma bitnasibneesh

ماتناسبنيش

it suits you (to man/woman)

Helwa Aalayk/Aalaykee

حلوة عليك/عليكى

suitcase shanTit safar

شنطة سفر

summer Sayf

صيف

in the summer feS-Sayf

فى الصيف

sun shams (f)

شمس

in the sun fesh-shams

فى الشمس

out of the sun feDDil

فى الضل

sunbathe Hammām shams

حمّام شمس

sunblock (cream) kraym DeD
esh-shams

كريم ضد الشمس

sunburn lafHet shams
لفحة شمس

sunburnt maHroo' min esh-
shams
محروق من الشمس

Sunday yōm el Had
يوم الحد

sunglasses naDDāra shamsaya
نضارة شمسية

sun lounger korsay lil blāJ
كرسي للبلاج

sunny: it's sunny moshmisa
مشمسة

sunset ghroob esh-shams
غروب الشمس

sunshade tanda
تندة

sunshine shoAāA esh-shams
شعاع الشمس

sunstroke Darbit shams
ضربة شمس

suntan samār min esh-shams
سمار من الشمس

suntan lotion marham
lesh-shams
مرهم للشمس

suntanned ismar min
esh-shams
إسمر من الشمس

suntan oil zayt lesh-shams
زيت للشمس

super lazeez
لذيذ

supermarket 'supermarket'
سوبرماركت

supper Aashā
عشا

supplement (extra charge) rasm
iDāfee
رسم إضافى

sure: are you sure? (to man) inta
mota'akid?
إنت متأكّد؟

(to woman) inti mota'akida?
إنتى متأكّدة؟

sure! okay!
أوكى!

surname esm el Aayla
إسم العيلة

swearword sheteema
شتيمة

sweater swaytar
سويتر

sweatshirt fanilla
فانلة

Sweden es-swayd
السويد

Swedish swaydee
سويدى

sweet Helw
حلو

sweets Halawayāt

حلويّات

swim (verb) Aām

عام

I'm going for a swim (said by man/woman) ana rīH/rīHa aAoom

أنا رايح/رايحة أعوم

let's go for a swim yalla nerooH neAoom

يللا نروح نعوم

swimming costume mayoo Haraymee

مايوه حريمي

swimming pool Hammām sibāHa

حمّام سباحة

swimming trunks mayoo rigālee

مايوه رجالي

switch (noun) kobs

كوبس

switch off Taf-fa

طفّى

switch on wallaA

ولّع

swollen werim

ورم

Syria sorya

سوريا

T

table tarabayza

ترابيزة

a table for two tarabayza litneen

ترابيزة لتنين

tablecloth mafrash tarabayza

مفرش ترابيزة

table tennis bing bong

بنج بونج

tailor tarzee

ترزي

take akhad

أخذ

can you take me to the ...? (to man/woman) momkin takhodnee/takhdenee lil ...?

ممكن تاخذني /تاخذيني لل ....؟

do you take credit cards? (to man/woman) betākhod/ betakhdee 'credit card'?

بتاخذ/بتاخذي كريدت كارد؟

fine, I'll take it Tayib, Hakhdoo

طيّب حاخذه

can I take this? (leaflet etc) momkin ākhod da?

ممكن آخذ دا؟

how long does it take?
betākhod ad ay wa't?

بتاخذ قد إيه وقت؟

it takes three hours betākhod
talat saAāt

بتاخذ تلات ساعات

is this seat taken? fee Had
āAid hena?

فى حدّ قاعد هنا؟

talcum powder bodrit talk

بودرة تلك

talk (verb) etkallim

إتكلم

tall (person) Taweel

طويل

(building) Aālee

عالى

tampons 'Tampax'®

تامباكس

tan (noun) samār min
esh-shams

سمار من الشمس

to get a tan esmar

إسمر

tap Hanafaya

حنفيّة

taste (noun) TaAm

طعم

can I taste it? momkin
adoo'oo?

ممكن ادوقه؟

taxi taksee

تاكسى

service taxi taksee khidma

تاكسى خدمة

will you get me a taxi? (to man/
woman) momkin tegiblee/
tegibelee taksee?

ممكن تجيبلى/تجيبيلى
تاكسى؟

where can I find a taxi? fayn
momkin alā'ee taksee?

فين ممكن ألاقى تاكسى؟

•••••• DIALOGUE ••••••

to the airport/to the ... Hotel, please
lil maTār/lefondo' el ..., low
samaHt

how much will it be? Haykoon
bekām?

fifteen pounds bekhamastashar
geneeh

that's fine right here, thanks hena
kwayis, shokran

Collective service taxis are one
of the best features of Egyptian
transport. They operate on a
wide variety of routes, are
generally quicker than buses
and trains, and fares are very
reasonable.
The taxis are usually big
Peugeot saloons carrying seven
→

passengers or minibuses seating a dozen people. Most business is along specific routes, with more or less non-stop departures throughout the day on the main ones, while cross-desert traffic is restricted to early morning and late afternoon. As soon as the right number of people are assembled, the taxi sets off. On established routes service taxis keep to fixed fares for each passenger. Alternatively, you can charter a whole taxi for yourself or a group – useful for day excursions, or on odd routes. You will have to bargain hard to get a fair price.

Equally ubiquitous are four-seater taxis (black and white in Cairo, black and yellow in Alexandria) which often pick up extra passengers heading in the same direction. As meters are rarely used (or work), the trick is to know the fare and to pay on arrival, rather than ask or haggle at the beginning. Above all, don't confuse these cabs with larger special taxis (usually Peugeot 504s or Mercedes) which cost three times more and prey on tourists.

→

You will also come across carettas – horse-drawn buggies, also known as HanToor. These are primarily tourist transport, and you'll be accosted by drivers in Alexandria, a few parts of Cairo and most of all in Luxor and Aswan. Fares are high by local taxi standards and, despite supposed tariffs set by the local councils, are in practice entirely negotiable. In a few small towns, mostly in Middle Egypt, carettas remain part of the local city transport. Ask locals the price of fares before climbing on board.

---

taxi-driver sowā' taksee
سوّاق تاكسى
taxi rank mow'af taksayāt
موقف تاكسيّات
tea (drink) **shī**
شاى
tea for one/two, please (to man/woman) **wāHid/itnayn shī, low samaHt/samaHtee**
واحد / إتنين شاى،
لو سمحت/سمحتى

Tea is Egypt's national beverage and it is generally made by boiling the leaves, and served

→

black and sugared to taste –
though posher cafés use teabags
and may supply milk (ask for shī
bel-laban if you want milk). A
glass of mint tea (shī ben
neAnāA) is refreshing when the
weather is hot. You may also
enjoy herbal teas like fenugreek
(Helba), aniseed (yansoon) or
cinnamon (erfa).
A drink characteristic of Egypt
is karkaday, a deep red infusion
of hibiscus flowers. Most popular in Luxor and Aswan, it is
equally refreshing drunk hot or
cold. Elsewhere they tend to
use dehydrated extract instead
of real hibiscus, so it doesn't
taste as good.

teabags kayās shī

كياس شاي

teach: could you teach me? (to
man/woman) momkin
teAallimnee/teAallimenee?

ممكن تعلّمني/تعلّميني؟

teacher (man/woman) modariss/
modarissa

مدرّس/مدرّسة

team faree'

فريق

tearoom Hogrit shī

حجرة شاي

teaspoon maAla'it shī

معلقة شاى

tea towel fooTit shī

فوطة شاى

teenager (male/female) morāhiQ/
morahQa

مراهق/مراهقة

telephone telefoon

تليفون

see phone

television teleefizyōn

تليفزيون

tell: could you tell him ...? (to
man/woman) momkin to'ol
loo/laha ...?

ممكن تقول له/لها ...؟

temperature (weather) dargit el
Harāra

درجة الحرارة

(fever) Homma

حُمّى

temple (religious) maAbad

معبد

tent khayma

خيمة

term (at university, school) faSl

فصل

terminal mow'af

موقف

terminus (rail) mow'af

موقف

terrible faZeeA

فظيع

terrific momtāz

ممتاز

than* min

من

smaller than asghar min

أصغر من

thank: thanks, thank you shokran

شكرا

thank you very much shokran giddan

شكراً جدّا

thanks for the lift shokran Aala eltowSeela

شكراًعلى التوصيلة

no thanks la' motshakkir

لأ متشكّر

•••••• DIALOGUE ••••••

thanks shokran

that's OK, don't mention it Aafwan, mafeesh mashākil

that: that boy el walad da

الولد دا

that girl el bint dee

البنت دى

that one da/dee (m/f)

دا/دى

I hope that ... atmanna keda ...

أتمنّى كده

that's nice da gameel

دا جميل

is that ...? da/dee ...?

دا/دى ...؟

that's it (that's right) SaH

صح

the* el

ال

theatre masraH

مسرح

their* btaAhom

بتاعهم

theirs* btaAhom

بتاعهم

them* homma

همّا

for them leehom

ليهم

with them maAāhom

معاهم

to them leehom

ليهم

who? - them? meen? - homma

مين؟ - همّا

then (at that time) baAdayn

بعدين

(after that) we baAdayn

وبعدين

there henāk

هناك

over there henāk

هناك

up there foo' henāk

فوق هناك

is/are there ...? fee ...?

فى ....؟

there is/are ... fee ...

فى ...

there you are (giving something) itfaDal

إتفضّل

Thermos® flask tormos

ترمس

these* dōl

دول

they* homma

همّا

thick Tekheen

تخين

(stupid) ghabee

غبى

thief (man/woman) Harāmee/ Haramaya

حرامى/حراميّة

thigh fakhd

فخد

thin rofīyaA

رفيّع

thing Hāga

حاجة

my things Hagātee

حاجاتى

think fakkar

فكّر

I think so Aala mazon

على ما ظن

I don't think so maAtaQedsh

ماعتقدش

I'll think about it Hafakkar fee elmowDOOA

حافكّر فى الموضوع

third-class daraga talta

درجة تالتة

thirsty: I'm thirsty ana AaTshān

أنا عطشان

this: this boy el walad da

الولد دا

this girl el bint dee

البنت دى

this one da/dee (m/f)

دا/دى

this is my wife dee mrātee

دى مراتى

is this ...? da/dee ...?

دا/دى...؟

those* dōl

دول

thread (noun) khayT

خيط

throat zōr

زور

throat pastilles bastilya

خلال

through khilāl

باستيليا

does it go through ...? (train,
bus) bayAaddee Aala ...?

بيعدّى على ....؟

throw (verb) rama

رمى

throw away (verb) ramā

رمى

thumb es-sobaA el kebeer

الصبع الكبير

thunderstorm Aāsifa raAadaya

عاصفة رعديّة

Thursday yōm el khamees

يوم الخميس

ticket tazkara

تذكرة

•••••• DIALOGUE ••••••

a return to Aswan tazkarit
Aowdah le aswān

coming back when? weHatergaA
imta?

today/next Tuesday ennaharda/
yōm el talāt el gī

that will be two hundred pounds
da Haykōn bemaytayn geneeh

ticket office (bus, rail) maktab

tazākir

مكتب تذاكر

tie (necktie) garafatta

جرافتّة

tight (clothes etc) dīya'

ضيّق

it's too tight da dīya' awee

دا ضيق قوى

tights sharāb Haraymee
Taweel

شراب حريمى طويل

time* wa't

وقت

what's the time? es-sāAa
kām?

الساعة كم؟

this time el marrādee

المرّة دى

last time el marra el-lee fātit

المرّة اللى فاتت

next time el marra eg-gīya

الجايّة

three times talāt marāt

تلات مرّات

Time is a more elastic concept
than Westerners are used to. In
practice, 'five minutes' often
means an hour or more, 'later'
(baAdayn), the next day; and
'tomorrow' (bokra) an indefinite wait for something that
→

may never happen. Remember that Western abruptness strikes Egyptians as rude; never begrudge the time it takes to say 'peace be upon you' (essalāmo Alaykom) or to return a greeting.

timetable gadwal el
mowāAeed
جدول المواعيد
tin (can) Aelba
علبة
tinfoil wara' solofān
ورق سولوفان
tin-opener fattāHit Aelab
فتّاحة علب
tiny Soghīyar awee
صغيّر قوى
tip (to waiter etc) ba'sheesh
بقشيش

As a presumed-rich foreigner (khawāga), you will be expected to be liberal with ba'sheesh. The most common form this takes is tipping: a small reward for a small service, which can encompass anyone from a waiter or lift operator to someone who unlocks a tomb or museum room. A small sum is expected – between £E2 and £E5. In →

restaurants, you tip 10–12 per cent in expensive places, giving a higher percentage where the sums involved are trifling. In juice bars and diners, customers simply put 50-100pt on a plate by the exit.

A second type of ba'sheesh is more expensive: rewarding the bending of rules. Examples might include letting you into an archeological site after hours, finding you a sleeper on a train when the carriages are 'full', and so on. This should not be confused with bribery, which is a more serious business with its own etiquette and risks best not entered into.

The last kind of ba'sheesh is alms giving. The disabled are traditional recipients of such gifts; children, however, are a different case, pressing their demands only on tourists.

tire (US) kowetsh
كاوتش
tired taAbān
تعبان
I'm tired (said by man/woman)
ana taAbān/taAbāna
أنا تعبان/تعبانة

tissues kleniks

كلينكس

to: to Cairo/London lil Qāhira/
'London'

للقاهرة/لندن

to Egypt/England le masr/
ingiltera

لمصر/ إنجلترا

to the post office le maktab
elbosTa

لمكتب البوسطة

toast (bread) 'toast'

توست

today en-naharda

النهارده

toe SobaA rigl

صبع رجل

together maAa baAD

مع بعض

we're together (in shop etc)
eHna maAa baAD

إحنا مع بعض

toilet tawalet

تواليت

where is the toilet? fayn
et-tawalet?

فين التواليت؟

I have to go to the toilet ana
lāzim arooH let-tawalet

أنا لازم أروح للتواليت

toilet paper wara' tawalet

ورق تواليت

tomato TamāTem

طماطم

(in Cairo) ooTa

قوطة

tomato juice Aaseer TamaTem

عصير طماطم

tomb ma'bara

مقبرة

tomorrow bokra

بكرة

tomorrow morning bokra es-
sobH

بكرة الصبح

the day after tomorrow baAd
bokra

بعد بكرة

tongue lisān

لسان

tonic (water) mīya maAdanaya

ميّة معدنيّة

tonight ellaylādee

الليلة دى

too (excessively) awee

قوى

(also) kamān

كمان

too hot Har awee

حر قوى

too much keteer awee

كتير قوى

me too wana kamān

وانا كمان

tooth sinna

سنّة

toothache wagaA senān

وجع سنان

toothbrush forshit senān

فرشة سنان

toothpaste maAgoon senān

معجون سنان

top: on top of ... foo' el ...

فوق ال ...

at the top of the ... Aalal ...

على ال ...

top floor ed-dōr el fo'ānee

الدور الفوقانى

torch baTTaraya

بطّاريّة

total (noun) magmooA

مجموع

tour (noun) gowla

جولة

is there a tour of ...? fee gowla le ...?

فى جولة ل ...؟

tour guide (man) morshid sayāHee

مرشد سياحى

(woman) morshida sayāHaya

مرشدة سياحيّة

tourist (man/woman) sayeH/ sayHa

سايح/سايحة

tourist information office maktab es-sayāHa

مكتب السياحة

In Egypt, you'll get a variable service from local tourist offices. The most knowledgable and helpful ones are in Cairo, Aswan, Luxor, Alexandria, and the oases of Siwa and Dakhla. Elsewhere, most provincial offices are good for a dated brochure, if nothing else.

In towns and cities, travel agencies can advise on (and book) transport, accommodation and excursions.

Receptionists at hotels can also be a source of information, and maybe practical assistance. In Luxor, Hurghada and some of the Western Desert oases, most guesthouses double as information exchanges and all-round 'fixers', as do campsites and backpackers' hotels in Sinai.

tour operator maktab sayāHa

مكتب سياحة

towards tegāh

تجاه

towel fooTa

فوطة

town madeena

مدينة

in town fee wesT el balad

فى وسط البلد

just out of town fee DawaHee
el madeena

فى ضواحى المدينة

town centre wesT elbalad

وسط البلد

toy leAba

لعبة

track (US) raseef

رصيف

traditional aslee

أصلى

traffic moroor (f)

مرور

traffic jam zaHmit moroor

زحمة مرور

traffic lights isharat el moroor

إشارات المرور

train aTr

قطر

by train bil aTr

بالقطر

Covering a limited network of
routes, trains are best used for
long hauls between the major
cities, when air-conditioned
services offer a more comfortable alternative to buses and
→

taxis. For shorter journeys
however, trains are slower and
less reliable.

Air-conditioned trains nearly
always have two classes of
carriage. The most comfortable
option is first class (daraga
oola) which has waiter service,
reclining armchairs and no
standing in the aisles. Unfortu-
nately for those trying to sleep,
they also screen videos until
midnight. Air-conditioned second class superior (daraga
tania momtaza) is less plush
and more crowded, but at two
thirds of the price of first class
it's a real bargain.

Seats are reservable up to seven
days in advance. There is occasional double booking but a little ba'sheesh to the conductor
usually sorts out any problem.
One common difficulty is that
return-trip bookings can't be arranged at the point of origin, so
if you're travelling back to Cairo
or Aswan/Luxor (or vice versa),
it's best to book your return seat
the day you arrive. Most travel
agencies sell first-class tickets
for a small commission, which
saves you having to queue.

•••••• DIALOGUE ••••••

is this the train for Luxor? howa da
aTr lo'sor?

سّ أحنا بنتجوّل

sure akeed

no, you want that platform there
(to man) la', Aayiz er-raSeef
ellay henāk

(to woman) la', inti Aīza er-raSeef
ellay henāk

trainers (shoes) gazma kowetsh
جزمة كاوتش

train station maHaTTit aTr
محطة قطر

tram tormī
ترماى

translate targim
ترجم

could you translate that? (to
man/woman) momkin
tetargim/tetargimee
da?
ممكن تترجم/تترجمى دا؟

translator (man/woman)
motargim/motargima
مترجم/مترجمة

trash zebāla
زبالة

travel safar
سفر

we're travelling around eHna

benetgowil
إحنا بنتجوّل

travel agent's wikālit safar
وكالة سفر

traveller's cheque sheek
sayāHee
شيك سياحى

Carry the bulk of your money in
a well-known brand of traveller's
cheque, with credit cards and/
or Eurocheques for backup.
American Express, Barclays,
Citibank and Bank of America
traveller's cheques are accepted
by most banks and exchange
offices. Any other brand will
prove more trouble than it's
worth. Eurocheques backed by
a Eurocard can be cashed at
most branches of the Banque
Misr.

tray Sanaya
صينيّة

tree shagara
شجرة

trim: just a trim, please (to man/
woman) taHdeed bass, low
samaHt/samaHtee
تحديد بس لو
سمحت/سمحتى

trip (excursion) reHla

رحلة

I'd like to go on a trip to ...

(said by man/woman) ana Aayiz/
Aīza aTlaA reHla lee ...

أنا عايز/عايزة أطلع
رحلة ل ...

trolley 'trolley'

ترولى

trouble (noun) mashākil

مشاكل

I'm having trouble with ... ana
Aandee mashākil maAa ...

أنا عندى مشاكل مع ...

trousers banTaloon

بنطلون

true Ha'ee'ee

حقيقى

that's not true da mish SaH

دا مش صح

trunk (US: of car) shanTa

شنطة

try (verb) Hāwil

حاول

can I try it? (food) momkin
adoo'oo?

ممكن أدوقه؟

try on garrab Aala

جرّب على

can I try it on? momkin

agarrabo Aalaya?

ممكن أجرّبه علىّ؟

T-shirt fanilla nos kom

فانلة نص كم

Tuesday yōm et-talāt

يوم التلات

Tunisia toonis

تونس

tunnel nafa'

نفق

Turkey torkaya

تركيا

Turkish torkee

تركى

Turkish coffee ahwa torkee

قهوة تركى

Turkish delight malban

ملبن

turn: turn right Howid yemeen

حوّد يمين

turn left Howid shimāl

حوّد شمال

turn off (TV etc) afal

قفل

where do I turn off? fayn
a'fil el ...?

فين أقفل ال ....؟

turn on (TV etc) wallaA

ولّع

turning (in road) taHweed

التحويده

twice marritayn

مرّتين

twice as much eD-DeAf

الضعف

twin beds sireerayn

سريرين

twin room ōDa litnayn

أوضة لتنين

twist: I've twisted my ankle ana
lowayt kaAbee

أنا لويت كعبى

type (noun) nōA

نوع

another type of ... nōA tanee
min ...

نوع تانى من ...

typhoid tīfood

تيفود

typical aSlee

أصلى

tyre kowetsh

كاوتش

U

ugly weHesh awee

وحش قوى

UK elmamlaka elmottaHida

المملكة المتّحدة

umbrella shamsaya

شمسيّة

uncle (father's brother) Aamm

عم

(mother's brother) khāl

خال

under (in position) taHt

تحت

(less than) a'all min

أقل من

underdone (meat) nīya

نيّة

underground (railway) nafa'

نفق

underpants libās

لباس

understand: I understand ana
fāhim

أنا فاهم

I don't understand mish
fāhim

مش فاهم

do you understand? (to man)
inta fāhim?

إنت فاهم؟

(to woman) inti fahma?

إنتى فاهمة؟

unemployed AāTil

عاطل

United States amreeka

أمريكا

university gamAa

جامعة

unleaded petrol banzeen ghayr

monaQQa

بنزين غير منقّى

unlimited mileage masāfa
ghayr maHdooda

مسافة غير محدودة

unlock fataH

فتح

unpack faDDa

فضّى

until leHad

لحد

unusual shāz

شاذ

up foo'

فوق

up there foo'

فوق

he's not up yet (not out of bed)
howa lessa maS-Heesh

هوّ لسّة ماصحيش

what's up? (what's wrong?) fee
ay?

فى إيه؟

Upper Egypt wagh eblee

وجه قبلى

(colloquial) eS-SeAeed

الصعيد

upset stomach wagaA baTn

وجع بطن

upside down ma'loob

مقلوب

upstairs foo'

فوق

urgent mistaAgil

مستعجل

us * lena

لينا

with us maAana

معانا

for us lena

لينا

USA elwelāyāt el mottaHada
el amreekaya

الولايات المتّحدة
الأمريكيّة

use (verb) estaAmil

إستعمل

may I use ...? momkin
astaAmil ...?

ممكن أستعمل ...؟

useful mofeed

مفيد

usual Aādee

عادى

V

vacancy: do you have any
vacancies? (hotel: to man/woman)
fee Aandak/Aandik aī ewaD
faDiya?

فى عندك/عندك أيّ
أوض فاضية؟

vacation (from university) agāza

أجازة

on vacation fee agāza

فى أجازة

vacuum cleaner moknesa bil kahraba

مكنسة بالكهرباء

valid (ticket etc) SalHa

صالحة

how long is it valid for? SalHa le'ad ay?

صالحة لقد إيه؟

valley wadee

وادى

Valley of the Kings wadee el mlook

وادى الملوك

valuable (adj) sameen

ثمين

can I leave my valuables here? momkin aseeb momtalakātee hena?

ممكن أسِيب ممتلكاتي هنا؟

value (noun) eema

قيمة

van Aarabayyit na'l

عربيّة نقل

vary: it varies betikhtelif

بتختلف

vase vāza

فازة

vegetables khoDār

خضر

vegetarian (noun: man/woman) nabātee/nabātaya

نباتى/نباتيّة

The concept of vegetarianism is totally incomprehensible to most Egyptians, and you'll be hard pushed to exclude meat from your diet. If you do get across that you 'don't eat meat', you're likely to be offered chicken or fish as a substitute.

very awee

قوى

very little for me Haga baSeeTa Aalashānee

حاجة بسيطة علشانى

I like it very much ana baHebbo/baHebbaha keteer awee (m/f)

أنا بحبّه/بحبّها كتير قوى

via Aan Taree'

طريق

video 'video'

فيديو

video recorder gihāz tasgeel

'video'
جهاز تسجيل فيديو

view manẓar
منظر

village Qarya
قرية

vinegar khal
خل

viper fībar
فيبر

visa veeza
فيزة

Almost all Europeans, North Americans and Australasians must obtain tourist visas for Egypt. Regular tourist visas are available from Egyptian consulates abroad, or on the spot at Cairo, Luxor and Hurghada airports. Though you might have to wait a bit, the process is generally painless and cheaper than getting a visa through a consulate. Both the single-visit and multiple-entry types of visa entitle you to stay in Egypt for one month, though the latter allows you to go in and out of the country three times within this period.

Tourists who overstay their (regular) visa are allowed a
→

fifteen day period of grace in which to renew it. After this they're fined unless they can present a letter of apology from their embassy (which may in itself cost something). Visitors anticipating an extended stay may apply for a tourist residence visa, valid for up to six months at a time.

visa extension tamdeed veeza
تمديد فيزا

visit (verb) zār
زار

I'd like to visit ... (said by man/woman) ana ʌayiz/ʌīza azoor ...
أنا عايز/عايزة أزور

vodka 'vodka'
فودكا

voice sōt
صوت

voltage volt
فولت

see electricity

vomit raggaʌ
رجّع

W

waist wesT

وسط

wait estanna

إستنّى

wait for me estannānee

إستنّانى

don't wait for me

matistananeesh

ماتستنانيش

can I wait until my wife gets
here? momkin astanna
leHad ma tegee mrātee?

ممكن أستنّى لحد ما
تيجى مراتى؟

can you do it while I wait? (to
man/woman) momkin
teAmiloo/teAmilha wana
hena?

ممكن تعمله/تعملها
وأنا هنا؟

could you wait here for me?
momkin testannānee hena?

ممكن تستنّانى هنا؟

waiter garsōn

جرسون

waiter! low samaHt!

لو سمحت!

waitress garsōna

جرسونة!

waitress! low samaHtee!

جرسونة! لو سمحتى!

wake: can you wake me up at
5.30? momkin tesaHHeenee
es-sāAa khamsa wenos?

ممكن تصحّينى الساعة
٥,٣٠؟

Wales 'Wales'

ويلز

walk: is it a long walk? hayya
masāfa Taweela?

هىّ مسافة طويلة

it's only a short walk da mish
beAeed

دا مش بعيد

I'll walk ana Hamshee

أنا حامشى

I'm going for a walk ana
khārig atmasha

أنا خارج أتمشّى

wall HayTa

حيطة

wallet maHfaZa

محفظة

want Aāz

عاز

I want a ... (said by man/woman)
ana Aayiz/Aīza ...

أنا عايز/عايزة ...

I don't want any ... ana mish

Aayiz/Aīza aī ...

أنا مش عايز عايز
/عايزة أي ...

I want to go home ana Aayiz/
Aīza arowaH

أنا عايز/عايزة أروّح

I don't want to ana mish
Aayiz/Aīza

أنا مش عايز/عايزة

he wants to ... howa Aayiz ...

هو عايز ...

what do you want? (to man/
woman) Aayiz/Aīza ay?

عايز/عايزة إيه؟

war Harb

حرب

ward (in hospital) Aambbar

عنبر

warm dāfee

دافي

was* : he was howa kān

هوّ كان

she was hayya kānit

هيّ كانت

it was kān/kānit ... (m/f)

كان/كانت

wash (verb) ghasal

غسل

can you wash these? (to man/
woman) momkin teghsil/

teghsillee dōl?

ممكن تغسل/تغسلى دول

washhand basin HŌD

حوض

washing (clothes) ghaseel

غسيل

washing machine ghassāla

غسّالة

washing powder mas-Hoo'
ghaseel

مسحوق غسيل

washing-up: do the washing-up
yeghsil elmowaAeen

يغسل

washing-up liquid sā'il leghasl
elmowaAeen

سائل لغسل المواعين

wasp dabboor

دبّور

watch (wristwatch) sāAa

ساعة

will you watch my things for
me? (to man) momkin tākhod
bālak min Hagātee?

ممكن تخذ بالك من
حاجاتى؟

(to woman) momkin takhdee
bālik min Hagātee?

ممكن تاخذى بالك من
حاجاتى؟

water mīya

ميّة

may I have some water?
momkin shwīyit mīya?

ممكن شويّة ميّة؟

The tap water in Egyptian towns and cities is mostly safe to drink, but heavily chlorinated. In rural areas, Sinai campsites and desert resthouses there's a fair risk of contaminated water. Consequently most tourists stick to bottled mineral water, which is widely available. However, excessive fear of tap water is unjustified. Once you have adjusted, it's usually OK to drink it without further purification. What you should avoid is any contact with stagnant water that might harbour bilharzia. Irrigation canals and the slower stretches of the River Nile are notoriously infested with these minute worms. Don't drink or swim there, walk barefoot in the mud or even on grass that's wet with Nile water. But it's OK to bathe in the saline pools of the desert oases.

see mineral water

watermelon baTTeekh

بطيخ

waterproof (adj) Did el mīya

ضد الميّة

waterskiing 'waterskiing'

ووتر سكيينج

wave (in sea) mōga

موجة

way: it's this way fil ettegāh da

فى الإتّجاه دا

it's that way fil ettegāh da

فى الإتّجاه دا

is it a long way to ...? howa eTTaree' beAeed le ...?

هوّ الطريق بعيد ل ...؟

no way! abadan!

أبداً!

•••••• DIALOGUE ••••••

could you tell me the way to ...? (to man/woman) momkin te'ollee/ te'olelee eTTaree' le ...?
go straight on until you reach the traffic lights imshee Aala Tool leHad matlā'ee esharāt elmroor
turn left Howid/Howidee shmāl
take the first on the right owil Taree' Aala eedak/eedik el yemeen

we° eHna

إحنا

weak (person) DaAeef

ضعيف

(drink) khafeef

خفيف

weather gow

جو

wedding Haflit gowāz

حفلة جواز

wedding ring khātim eg-gowāz

خاتم الجواز

Wednesday yōm el arbaA

يوم الأربع

week esbooA

إسبوع

a week (from) today baAd esbooA min ennaharda

بعد أسبوع من النهارده

a week (from) tomorrow baAd esbooA min bokra

بعد أسبوع من بكرة

weekend ākhir elesbooA

آخر الأسبوع

at the weekend yōm eg-gomAa

يوم الجمعة

weight wazn

وزن

weird ghareeb

غريب

welcome: you're welcome (don't mention it) Aafwan

عفوا

well: I don't feel well (said by man/

woman) ana taAbān/taAbana shwīya

أنا تعبان/تعبانة شويّة

she's not well hayya taAbana shwīya

هي تعبانة شويّة

you speak English very well (to man) inta bititkallim/ ingleezee kwayis awee

إنت بتتكلم إنجليزى كويس قوى

(to woman) inti bititkallimee ingleezee kwayis awee

إنتى بتتكلمى إنجليزى كويس قوى

well done! Aafārim Aalayk!

عفارم عليك

this one as well wedee kamān

ودى كمان

well well! (surprise) mish maA'ool!

مش معقول!

•••••• DIALOGUE ••••••

how are you? (to man/woman) izzayak/izzayik?

very well, thanks (said by man/ woman) kwayis/kwayisa, shokran

and you? (to man/woman) winta/ winti?

well-done (meat) maTbookha kwayis

مطبوخة كويس

Welsh welzee

ويلزى

I'm Welsh (said by man/woman)

ana welzee/welzaya

أنا ويلزى/ويلزيّة

were*: we were konna

كنّا

you were kont

كنت

they were kāno

كانوا

west gharb

غرب

in the west fil gharb

فى الغرب

Western (from Europe, US) afrangee

أفرنجى

wet mablool

مبلول

what? ay?

إيه؟

what's that? ay da?

إيه دا؟

what should I do? a'Amil ay?

أعمل إيه؟

what a view! manZar

gameel!

منظر جميل!

what bus do I take? ākhod aī otobees?

آخذ الأوتوبيس؟

wheel Aagala

عجلة

wheelchair korsee lil Aagaza

كرسى للعجزة

when? imta?

إمتى؟

when we get back lamma nergaA

لمّا نرجع

when's the train/the ferry? imta el aTr/el 'launch'?

إمتى بيجى القطر/اللنش؟

where? fayn?

فين؟

I don't know where it is mish Aārif hiya fayn

مش عارف هىّ فين

•••••• DIALOGUE ••••••

where is the Greek Museum? fayn elmat-Haf elyonānee?

it's over there howa henak

could you show me where it is on the map? momkin tewarrehoolee Aala el khareeTa?

it's just here howa hena bez-ZabT

which: which bus? aī otobees?

أىّ أوتوبيس؟

•••••• DIALOGUE ••••••

which one? aī wāHid?
that one da
this one? dowwa?
no, that one la', da

while: while I'm here wana
hena

ونا هنا

whisky weskee

ويسكى

white abyaD

أبيض

white wine nebeet abyaD

نبيت أبيض

who? meen?

مين؟

who is it? meen?

مين؟

the man who ... er-rāgil el-
lee ...

... الراجل اللى

whole: the whole week el
isbooA kolloo

الأسبوع كله

the whole lot kollohom

كلّهم

whose: whose is this? da bitaA

meen?

دا بتاع مين؟

why? lay?

ليه؟

why not? la' lay?

لأ ليه؟

wide AareeD

عريض

wife: my wife mrātee

مراتى

will*: will you do it for me? (to
man/woman) momkin
teAmelhoolee/
teAmelihoolee?

ممكن تعملهولي/
تعمليهولى؟

wind (noun) reeH (f)

ريح

window shebbāk

شبّاك

near the window gamb esh-
shebāk

جنب الشبّاك

in the window (of shop) fil
vatreena

فى الفاترينة

window seat korsee gamb
esh-shebbāk

كرسى جنب الشبّاك

windsurfing 'windsurfing'

وندسرفنج

wine nebeet

نبيت

can we have some more wine?

momkin nebeet tanee?

ممكن نبيت تانى؟

> A half-dozen or so Egyptian
> wines are produced at Giancolis,
> near Alexandria. The most com-
> monly found are Omar Khayyam
> (a dry red), Cru des Ptolémées
> (a dry white) and Rubis d'Egypt
> (a rosé).

wine list Qīmit en-nebeet

قايمة نبيت

winter sheta

شتا

in the winter fesh-sheta

فى الشتا

with maAa

مع

I'm staying with ... ana a-īd
maAa ...

أنا قاعد مع

without min ghayr

من غير

witness (man/woman) shāhid/
shahda

شاهد / شاهدة

will you be a witness for me?
(to man/woman) momkin tesh-
hadlee/tesh-hadi lee?

ممكن تشهد / تشهدى لى؟

woman sit

ست

women

Many women visitors do a range
of things that no respectable
Egyptian woman would con-
sider: dressing 'immodestly',
showing shoulders and cleavage,
sharing rooms with men to
whom they are not married,
drinking alcohol in bars or restaurants, smoking, even travelling alone on public transport,
without a relative as an escort.
Though some Egyptians know
enough about Western ways to
realize that this does not signify
a prostitute (as it would for an
Egyptian woman), most are
ready to think the worst. There
are a few steps you can take to
improve your image (see dress
page 74).
On public transport, try to sit
with other women – who may
often invite you to do so. On the
Cairo Metro and trams in Alexandria there are carriages
reserved for women. If you're
travelling with a man, wearing
a wedding ring confers respect-
→

ability, and asserting that you're married is better than admitting to be 'just friends'. As anywhere, looking confident and knowing where you're going is a major help in avoiding hassle. Problems – most commonly hissing or groping – tend to come in downtown Cairo and in the public beach resorts (except Sinai's Aqaba coast or Red Sea holiday villages which are more or less the only places where you'll feel happy about sunbathing).

Some women find that verbal hassle is best ignored, while others may prefer to use an Egyptian brush-off like 'khalās!' (that's it!). If you get groped the best response is to yell 'sebnee le waHdee!' (leave me alone!) which will shame any assailant in public, and may attract help.

---

wonderful rā'eA

رائع

won't* : it won't start mabaydorsh

مابيدورش

wood (material) khashab

خشب

wool Soof

صوف

word kelma

كلمة

---

work (noun) shoghl

شغل

(verb) shagh-ghal

شغّال

it's not working mish shaghghāl

مش شغّال

worry: I'm worried ana al'ān

أنا قلقان

worse: it's worse da aswa'

دا أسوأ

worst el aswa'

الأسوأ

would: would you give this to ...? momkin teddee da lee ...?

ممكن تدّى دا ل ....؟

wrap: could you wrap it up? (to man/woman) momkin teleffoo/teleffeeh?

ممكن تلفه/تلفيه؟

wrapping paper wara' lil laf

ورق للفّ

wrist resgh

رسغ

write katab

كتب

could you write it down? (to man/woman) momkin tektiboo/tektibeeh?

ممكن تكتبه/تكتبيه؟

writing paper wara' lil ketāba

ورق للكتابة

wrong: it's the wrong key da
mish elmoftāH eSaHeeH

دا مش المفتاح الصحيح

this is the wrong train da
mish el aTr eSaHeeH

دا مش القطر الصحيح

the bill's wrong el fatoora
ghalaT

الفاتورة غلط

sorry, wrong number (said by
man/woman) āsif/āsfa, el
nimra ghalaT

آسف/أسفة، النمرة غلط

sorry, wrong room āsif/āsfa,
el ōDa ghalaT

آسف/أسفة، الأوضة غلط

there's something wrong
with ... fee Aayb fee ...

في عيب في...

what's wrong? fee Haga ghalaT?

في حاجة غلط؟

Y

yacht yakht

يخت

yard (measurement) yarda

ياردة

year sana

سنة

yellow aSfar

أصفر

Yemen el yaman

اليمن

yes īwa

أيوه

yesterday embāreH

إمبّارح

yesterday morning embāreH
es-SobH

إمبّارح الصبح

the day before yesterday

owel embāreH

أوّل إمبّارح

yet leHad delwa'tee

لحد دلوقتى

•••••• DIALOGUE ••••••

is it here yet? hayya mowgooda
delwa'tee?

no, not yet la', lessa

you'll have to wait a little longer yet
lāzim testanna shwīya tanyeen

yoghurt zabādee

زبادى

you* (to man/woman) inta/inti

إنت/إنتى

(to more than one person) intoo

إنتو

this is for you (to man/woman)

da Aalashanak/Aalashanik

دا علشانُك/علشانِك

with you (to man/woman)
maAak/maAakee

معاك/معاكى

If you are addressing a woman or an elderly man, avoid 'inta' or 'inti' (you), as it may be considered disrespectful. If you are speaking either to an older person, someone of the opposite sex, or to a person for the first time, use words such as 'afanddim' (sir/madam), 'Hadretak' (you: formal said to a man) and 'Hadretek' (you: formal, said to a woman).

---

young shāb

شاب

your* (m/f object, male owner)
btāAak/btaAtak

بتاعك/بتاعتك

(m/f object, female owner) btāAik/
btaAtik

بتاعك/بتاعتك

your camera (to man/woman)
kamiretak/kamiretik

كاميرتك/كاميرتك

yours* (m/f object, male owner) da
btāAak/dee btaAtak

دا بتاعك/دى بتاعتك

(m/f object, female owner) da
btāAik/dee btaAtik

دا بتاعك/دى بتاعتك

youth hostel bayt shabāb

بيت شباب

Egypt's youth hostels are cheap but their drawbacks are considerable. A day-time lock-out and night-time curfew are universal practice; so too is segregating the sexes and (usually) foreigners and Egyptians. The better hostels are in Cairo, Sharm el-Sheikh and Ismailiya.
see **hotel** and **resthouse**

Z

zero sifr

صفر

zip sosta

سوستة

could you put a new zip on?
(to man/woman) momkin
terakkib/terakkibee sosta
gedeeda?

ممكن تركّب/تركّبى
سوستة جديدة؟

zip code ramz bareedee

رمز بريدى

zoo gonaynit el Hīyowanāt

جنينة الحيوانات

Arabic-English

COLLOQUIALISMS

The following are words you might well hear. You shouldn't be tempted to use any of the stronger ones unless you are sure of your audience.

abadan! no way!
āllah wa akbar! God almighty!
āllah yenowar! well done!
ekhras! shut up!
ekhs Alayk! shame on you!
ellaAna! damn!
fa'r! shit!
ghebee! fool!, idiot!
hala hala! well, well!, well I never
Hasib! look out!
intaAama? are you blind?
khallee balak take care
mish teHasib? can't you watch what you're doing?
momtāz excellent
ra'iA great
salām? is that right?
Toz? so what?
ya salām! my goodness! (lit: oh peace!)

The alphabetical order in this section is:

a, ā, A, b, d, D, e, f, g, h, H, i, ī, j, l, k, l, m, n, o, ō, Q, r, s, S, t, T, w, y, z, Z

a

a'all less
a'all min under, less than
aAad sit down
aAma blind
ab father
abadan never; ever
abAad further
abl before
abol hōl sphinx
aboo father of
abyaD white
ad ay? how many?
adeem old; ancient
afal close; shut; lock; turn off
afanddim sir; madam
  afanddim? pardon (me)?, sorry?
afaS basket
a'fleen they're shut
afrangee Western (from Europe, US)
agāza holiday, vacation
agāza rasmaya public holiday
aggar rent, hire
aghla more expensive
aghosTos August
agnabaya (f) foreigner
agnabee (m) foreign; foreigner
agzakhana chemist's, pharmacy

ahbal silly
ahl parents
ahlan hello; welcome
ahlan bik/biki hello; welcome (to man/woman)
ahlan bikom hello; welcome (to more than one person)
ahlan wa sahlan welcome
ahwa coffee; café, coffee house
aHmar red
aHsan better; best
aHyānan sometimes, not often
aī what; which
aī Had anybody
aī Hāga anything
  aī Hāga tania? anything else?
aī khidma my pleasure
akh brother
akhad take, accept; collect; have
akhbār (f) news
akhd el HaQā'ib baggage claim
akhDar green
akheer last
akheeran eventually
akkid confirm
akl food
aktar more
  aktar bekteer a lot more
  aktar min more than, over
alam pen
alam gāf ballpoint pen
alam rosāS pencil
alAa fortress, citadel; castle
alb heart
alf thousand
alfayn two thousand

almānee German
aloo hello
amar moon
amān safe (not dangerous)
ameen safe (not in danger);
  honest
ameeS shirt
amreeka United States,
  America
amrekānee American
ana I; me
ara read
arbaAa four
arbaAtāshar fourteen
arbiAeen forty
arD (f) floor; ground
arkhaS less expensive
arSa bite
arSit Hashara insect bite
asansayr lift, elevator
asār archeology; monument
asāsee essential
asbānee Spanish
ash'ar blond
asharb scarf (for head)
ashoof? can I see?
asmar dark (hair)
assim share
aswa' worse
  el aswa' worst
aSfar yellow
aSlee traditional; typical
aSr palace
atal kill
atmanna keda I hope so; I
  hope that
aTaA cut (verb)
aTfāl children
aTr train

aTr en-nōm sleeper
aTrash deaf
awee too; really, very
ay? what?
ay ... ow ... either ... or ...
azra' blue

ā

ābil meet
āfil closed
ākheer latest
ākhir bottom
ākhir elesbooA weekend
āl say
āllah Allah, God
ānisa Miss
āsif/āsfa sorry; excuse me
  (said by man/woman)

A

Aabr across
Aadee ordinary
Aadwa infection
AaDDa bite (by animal)
AaDm bone
Aafsh zāyid excess baggage
Aafwan you're welcome,
  don't mention it
Aagala bicycle; wheel
Aagooz/Aagooza old (person);
  senior citizen (man/woman)
Aala on
Aalal on; at the top
Aalashanha for her
Aalashanna for us
Aalashān because
Aalashānoo for him

AalaTool frequent; straight ahead

AalaTool delwa'tee at once, immediately

Aamal do

Aam gedeed saAeed! Happy New Year!

Aamm uncle (father's brother)

Aamma aunt (father's sister)

Aan about

Aand at

Aandak/Aandik ...? have you got any ...? (to man/woman)

Aan Taree' via

Aa'rab scorpion

Aarabayya car

Aarabayya beHsān horse-drawn buggy

Aarabayya HanToor horse-drawn buggy

Aarabayya mit'aggara rented car

Aarabayyit aTr carriage

Aarabayyit bidoon tadkheen nonsmoking compartment

Aarabayyit el akl buffet car

Aarabayyit na'l van

Aarabayyit nōm sleeping car

Aarabayyit shonaT luggage trolley

Aarabee Arab

Aarboon deposit

AarD fair (adj)

AarD masraHee show (in theatre)

AareeD wide

Aarraf introduce

Aasha dinner, evening meal; supper

Aashara ten

Aashar talāf ten thousand

Aash-shaT ashore

Aaskar camp

Aasree modern

AaTal break down

AaTlān out of order

AaTshān thirsty

Aayāda clinic

Aayiz: ana Aayiz I want (said by man)

Aayiz ay? what do you want? (to man)

Aayla family

Aayn (f) eye

Aaysh bread

Aazba single (woman)

AaZeem great, excellent

Aād repeat

Aādee normal, usual, ordinary

Aālam world

Aālamee international

Aālee high; loud; tall

Aām general (adj); swim

Aāmil/Aāmla ay? how do you do? (to man/woman)

Aāraf know

Aāsifa storm

Aāsifa raAdaya thunderstorm

Aāsifa ramlaya sandstorm

Aātil unemployed

Aāzib single (man)

Aeed milād birthday

Aeed milād el meseeH Christmas

Aeed milād saAeed! merry Christmas!; happy birthday!

Aeed sham el neseem Easter

Aelba can; small tin; pack
Aelbit sagāyer a pack of
  cigarettes
Aemil make
Aezooma invitation (for meal)
Ainwān address
Aishreen twenty
Aīyān ill, sick
Aīza: ana Aīza I want (said by
  woman)
  Aīza ay? what do you want?
  (to woman)
Aoboor cruise; crossing (by
  sea)
Ao'd necklace
Aolow height (mountain)
Aomla coin
Aomr life; age

b

ba'āl delicatessen; grocer's
baAat send; post, mail
baAd after
baAdak/baAdik after you (to
  man/woman)
baAdayn afterwards, later
  (on); then
baAd bokra the day after
  tomorrow
baAd eD-Dohr afternoon
bab door
baba dad
bada' start, begin
badal instead
badawee Bedouin
badree early
baHebbo/baHebbaha I like it
  (m/f object)

baHr sea
  el baHr elaHmar Red Sea
  el baHr el metowassiT
  Mediterranean
balad country, nation
baladee national
bambee pink
banafsigee purple
bango marijuana
banseeyōn boarding house,
  guesthouse
banTaloon trousers, pants
banyo bath
banzeen petrol
bar' lightning
baraka blessing
bard cold (noun)
bardān cold (adj)
bareed mail
bareed gowee airmail
bareed mosaggal by
  registered mail
barra outdoors; outside
barTamān jar
bas just, only
ba'sheesh tip, gratuity; bribe;
  alms
bas hena just here
bas keda nothing else
batrōn pattern
baTee' slow
baTn er-rigl sole (of foot)
baTTal da! stop it!
baTTanaya blanket
baTTaraya battery; torch,
  flashlight
bawwāba gate
bayDa egg
bayn among; between

bayt house; home

bayt shabāb youth hostel

bayyāA garayid newsagent's

bāA sell

bāko packet

bāligh/balgha adult (man/ woman)

be'asraA ma yomkin as soon as possible

beAeed far; in the distance

bebalāsh free (no charge)

bebba pipe (for smoking)

beddosh with shower

bedāAa Horra duty-free (goods)

bekam? how much is it?

bekhayr OK, fine

bekteer a lot

belHa' fairly

benafsee by myself

berrāHa slowly

bes-safeena by ship

bes-sikka el Hadeed by rail

betelloo beef; veal

betHeb: inta betHeb ...? do you like ...? (to man)

betHebee: inti betHebbee ...? do you like ...? (to woman)

betnaTTar it's raining

beT-Tīyāra by plane

beZZabT! exactly!

bil: bil Aarabayya by car
bil Aarabee in Arabic
bil ingleezee in English

bil bareed eg-gowee by airmail

bil layl in the evening; at night

bint girl; daughter

bint akh niece (brother's daughter)

bint Aamm cousin (on father's side: uncle's daughter)

bint Aamma cousin (on father's side: aunt's daughter)

bint khala cousin (on mother's side: aunt's daughter)

bint khāl cousin (on mother's side: uncle's daughter)

bint okht niece (sister's daughter)

birka lake

bisabab e-... because of ...

bisorAa quickly

biTa'it SoAood boarding pass

blāj beach

blooza blouse

bo' mouth

boHayrit nāSSer Lake Nasser

bok purse (for money)

bokra tomorrow

bokra eS-SobH tomorrow morning

bonnay brown

bosTa post office; post, mail

boS Aala look at

bowwāb doorman

btaA: da btaA meen? whose is this?

btaAha her; hers

btaAhom theirs; their

btaAitkoo your; yours (m object, to more than one person)

btaAna ours; our

btaAtee my; mine (f object)

btaAtkoo your; yours (f object, to more than one person)

btāAee my; mine (m object)

btāAak/btaAtak your; yours (m/ f object, male owner)

btāAik/btaAtik your; yours (m/f object, female owner)

btāAo his (m/f object)

d

da this; that; this one; that one; it is; this/that is (m object)
  da ...? is this/that ...?; is it ...?

daAa invite

da Aalashanak/Aalashanik this is for you (to man/woman)

daAwa invitation

dada baby-sitter, child-minder

dafaA pay

dahab gold

dakhal go in

daleel telefōnāt phone book; directory enquiries

dameem ugly

damm blood

da'n (f) chin; beard

daraga oolā first-class

daraga talta third-class

daraga tania economy class, second-class

daraga tania momtāza second-class superior

daras learn

dars lesson

dayr monastery

dayr 'ebTee Coptic monastery

dā' elkalb rabies

dāfee warm

dākhelee indoors

dee (f) this; that; this one;

that one; this/that is; it is
  dee ...? is this/is that ...?; is it ...?

de'ee'a minute
  de'ee'a waHda just a minute

deen religion

delwa'tee now

dibbāna fly

dīman often; always

dokhān smoke

dokkān (f) shop (small, local)

dolāb cupboard

dort el mīya toilet, rest room

dosh shower (in bathroom)

dowa (m) medicine; drug

dowlee national

dowrit el mīya toilet, rest room

dowsha noise

dōl those/these

dōr floor, storey

drāA arm

D

Dahr back (of body)

Dahr el markib deck

DaHya suburb

Dakhm enormous

Darbit shams sunstroke, heatstroke

DareeH shrine

Darooree necessary

Dayf/Dayfa guest (man/woman)

DāyiA missing

Dānee lamb (meat)

Did against

Dohr noon

e

ebree' jug
ebTee Coptic
ed-da give
ed-dōr el arDee ground floor, (US) first floor
ed-dōr el awwal first floor, (US) second floor
ed-dōr el fo'ānee top floor
ed-dōr et-taHtānee downstairs
eD-DeAf twice as much
eD-Dohr midday; at midday
eD-Dohraya this afternoon
eed hand; handle
eegār rent
eema value
efl lock
eggazā'ir Algeria
eHna we
eHwid shimāl turn left
ekhtafa disappear
ekhtelāf difference
el the
el Aafw don't mention it
el Hamdoo lillāh I'm fine (lit: praise be to Allah)
ellay baAd next
ellaylādee tonight; this evening
elmadeena eladeema old town
elmamlaka elmottaHida UK
elmenew menu
elwagba elra'eesaya main course
embāreH yesterday
embāreH eS-SobH yesterday morning

emshee warāya follow me
en-naharda today
  en-naharda eS-SobH this morning
ensāb injured
er-rabAa (f) fourth
er-rabeeA spring
er-rābiA (m) fourth
esbooA week
  el esbooA eggī next week
esm name; first name
esmak/esmik ay? what's your name? (to man/woman)
  esmee ... my name is ...
esm el Aayla surname
esm esh-shorTa police station
essalāmo Alaykom hello (lit: peace be upon you)
essana eggedeeda New Year
es-sāAa o'clock
  es-sāAa kām? what's the time?
es-sikka el Hadeed railway
estaAmil use
estanna wait
este'bāl reception
estirleenee pound (British)
eswid black
eS-SaHara' esh-shar'aya Eastern Desert
eS-SeAeed Upper Egypt
eS-SobH in the morning
  eS-SobH badree early in the morning
etAarraf Aala recognize
etfaDDal/etfaDDalee here you are (to man/woman)
etgaraH injured
etkallim talk

ettafa'na it's a deal
et-talta (f) third
et-tania (f) second
et-tālit (m) third
et-tānee second (adj); the
 other one
ettaSal phone, call
ettaSal baAdayn ring back
ettigāh direction
eTlāQan not in the least
eT-Taree' er-ra'eesee main
 road
eT-Taree' es-sareeA motorway,
 freeway, highway
ezāz glass (material)
ezāza bottle

f

faDDa silver
fa'eer poor (not rich)
fag'a suddenly
fagr dawn
fahim: ana fahim I understand
fakahānee greengrocer's (fruit
 shop)
fakhm luxurious
fakkar think
fallāheen: el fallāheen country,
 countryside
falooka Egyptian sailboat
fanilla noS kom T-shirt
fann art
far rat; mouse
faransa France
faransāwee French
farAōn Pharaoh
fardit gazma shoe
fardit sharāb sock

faree' team
faSl term (at university, school)
fataH unlock; open
fateH lil shahaya starter,
 appetizer
fatoora bill
faTāTree pastry shop
fawākih fruit
fayn? where?
 fayn da/dee? where is it?
faZeeA terrible, awful
fāDee empty
feD-Dil in the shade
feD-Dohr at noon
feD-Dohraya in the afternoon
fee in; at; on
 fee ... there is/are ...
 fee el wesT in the centre
fee ay? what's up?, what's the
 matter?
fee Aandak/Aandik ...? do you
 have ...?
fee Aayb faulty
fee SeHHetak! cheers!
felesTeen Palestine
fen-noS in the middle
feTār breakfast
fibrīer February
fil in; at; on
 fil 'ākher at the back
 fil mo'addima at the front
fil khareg abroad
fil layla per night
fiaDān flood
fībar viper
floos (f) money
fondo' hotel
foo' up; up there; upstairs;
 above

foo' el ... on top of ...

foo' henāk up there

fooTa towel; serviette, napkin

fooTit Hammām bath towel

forn oven; bakery

forsha brush

forSa saAeeda nice to meet you

fostān dress

frākh chicken

g

ga come in

gabal mountain

gadwal el mowāAeed timetable, schedule

gamal camel

gamārek Customs

gamAa university

gamb side; next to; near

gamb el baHr by the sea

gameel pretty, lovely, beautiful; exciting; nice; mild

ganāza funeral

ganoob south

fil ganoob in the south

el ganoob el gharbee southwest

el ganoob es-shar'ee southeast

garafatta tie, necktie

garrab Aala try on

garrāH asnān dentist

garsōn waiter

garsōna waitress

gayb pocket

gazma shoes

gazmagee shoe repairer

gazzār butcher's

gāb get, fetch; bring

gāhiz ready

gāmiA mosque

gāmid hard

gāyiz perhaps; probably

gedeed new

geneeh Egyptian pound

geree run

gezeera island

ghabee thick, stupid; idiot

ghadā lunch

ghalaT confusion, mix-up; wrong, incorrect

el nimra ghalaT wrong number

ghalTa mistake

ghanee rich (person)

ghanna sing

gharāma fine (punishment)

gharb west

fil gharb in the west

ghareeb/ghareeba strange, weird, peculiar; stranger (man/woman)

ghasal wash

ghaseel washing, laundry

ghassāla washing machine

ghaTa lid; cap

ghayr Aādee extraordinary

ghāba forest

ghālee expensive

ghoraf rooms

ghorfa room

ghoweeT deep

ghōs snorkelling; skin-diving

ghroob esh-shams sunset

gid grandfather

gidda grandmother
giddan very, extremely
gild skin; leather
gins sex
ginsaya nationality
gism body
gomAa: el gomAa Friday
gomrok custom
gonayna garden
gonaynit el Hīowanāt zoo
gonilla skirt
gooA hungry
gornāl newspaper
gornālgee newsagent's
gow dull (weather)
gowa inside
gowabāt letters
gowāb letter
gowla tour
gowla mowwagaha guided
tour
gowla sayāHaya sightseeing
tour
goz' part
gōz husband; double; a pair
of; a couple of

h

habla (f) silly
hansh hip
haram pyramid
hayya she; her; it
hādee quiet
hedaya gift
hedoom clothes
hena here; over here
    hena ... here is/are ...
    hena taHt down here

henāk there; over there
hidaya present, gift
hidoo'l quiet!
homma they; them
howa he; him; it; air

H

Hab like; love
Habba Habba gradually
Habl ghaseel clothes line
Had somebody, someone
Hadsa accident
HaDretak/HaDretik you (formal: to
man/woman)
Ha'ee'ee real; true; genuine
Hafeed grandson
Hafeeda granddaughter
Hafit elmarsa on the quayside
Hafla party (celebration)
Haflit gowāz wedding
Haga something
Hagar stone, rock
Hagaz reserve, book
Hagm size
Hagz reservation
Hala'a circle
Halawanee cake shop,
patisserie
Hama father-in-law
Hamāt mother-in-law
HammaD develop
Ham-mām bathroom
Ham-māmāt toilets, rest room
Ham-mām dākhil el ghorfa en-
suite bathroom
Ham-mām er-rigāl men's
room, gents (toilet)
Ham-mām khās private

bathroom
Ham-mām shams sunbathe
Ham-mām sibāHa (swimming)
  pool
Ham-mām sibāHa lel aTfāl
  children's pool
Hanafaya tap; fountain (for
  drinking)
HanToor horse-drawn buggy;
  donkey-drawn cart
Hara' burn
Harāmee/Haramaya thief (man/
  woman)
Harāra heat
Harb war
Haree'a fire
Hareer silk
HareeS careful
Harrān hot
Haseerit blāj beach mat
Hashara insect
Hasheesh grass
HaSal happen
HatDallim it's getting dark
Hateshrab/Hateshrabee ay?
  what'll you have? (to man/
  woman)
HaT put
HayTa wall
Hazeen sad
Haz luck
  Haz saAeed! good luck!
Hādis sir'a burglary
Hādsa crash
Hāga thing
Hāga tania something else
Hālan soon; immediately
Hāmee strong (taste); hot,
  spicy; sharp (knife)

HāmiD sour
Hāmil pregnant
Hāra lane
Hāsib charge
Hāsib! look out!
Hātee kebab house
Hāwil try
Hebbee friendly
Hedood border
Hel'ān earrings
Helm dream
Helw sweet, dessert; nice
Hetta bit, piece
Hetta tania somewhere else
Hettit ... a bit/piece of ...
Hidāshar eleven
Hizām belt; strap
Hīawān animal
Hob love
HOD bathtub; washhand basin;
  sink
Hogrit fondo' hotel room
Hogrit nōm bedroom
Hogrit shī tearoom
Homār donkey
HoSān horse
Howālee about, approximately
Howid turn

i

ibn son
ibn akh nephew (brother's son)
ibn Aamm cousin (on father's
  side, uncle's son)
ibn Aamma cousin (on father's
  side, aunt's son)
ibn khāla cousin (on mother's
  side, aunt's son)

ibn khāl cousin (on mother's side, uncle's son)

ibn okht nephew (sister's son)

ibreel April

ikhtār choose

iktashaf find out

ilāha goddess

imta? when?

ingiltera Britain; England

ingleezee British; English

inshā'allāh hopefully; God willing

inta/inti you (to man/woman)

intal/inti! hey!

intoo you (to more than one person)

iQāma kamla full board

irsh piastre

isAāf ambulance

isAāf awwalee first aid

isboAayn fortnight

ishtara buy

iskinderaya Alexandria

ismaA listen

istaAgil hurry

istirāHa resthouse

iswera bracelet

itfaDal/itfaDalee come in; help yourself; here you are (to man/woman)

itHarrak move

itmanna hope

itnayn both; couple (two people)

itnāshar twelve

'ītaA cut (noun)

izzay how

izzayak/izzayik? how are you?; how do you do? (to man/woman)

ī

īwa yes

j

jeb jeep

J

jelātee ice cream

k

kaAb ankle; heel

kabeena cabin

kabeenit telefōn phone box

kabreet matches

kahraba electricity

kalb dog

kallif cost

kamān too, also

  kamān shwīya in a minute

kamirit tasgeel camcorder

kanaba sofa, couch

kareem kind, generous

karsa disaster

kart card; business card; postcard

kartōn carton

kart sheekāt cheque card

kart telefōn phonecard

kasar break

kashaf check

kaslān lazy

kassit Soghīyar personal
  stereo
katab write
kays cash desk
kān he was; it was
kānit she was; it was
kāno they were
kās glass
kāzeno bar and tea room,
  usually along the Nile
kebeer large, big
kees carrier bag
kees makhadda pillow case
kelma word
kelomitr kilometre
keteer a lot, lots; many;
  several; much
  keteer awee too much, too
  many; quite a lot
  keteer min ... lots/plenty of ...
khabeer experienced
khad cheek (on face); take,
  accept
khadoom helpful
khafeef light (not heavy); weak
khalaS finish
khalāS already
  khalāS Hashtreeha it's a deal
khaleeg bay
khallee bālak! be careful!
khamastāshar fifteen
khamsa five
  el khamsa (f) fifth
khamseen fifty
kharabāt ruins; remains
kharaz beads
khareef autumn, (US) fall
khareeTa map
kharoof sheep

kharrab damage
kharrabt damaged
khashab wood (material)
khaT line
khaTar dangerous
khaTeeb/khaTeeba fiancé/
  fiancée
khaTeer serious
khawāga foreigner
khayma tent
khayT string; thread
khazaf ceramics; pottery
khāl uncle (mother's brother)
khāla aunt (mother's sister)
khāmis: el khāmis (m) fifth
khās private
khātim ring
khāTeb engaged (to be married:
  man)
khedma lel ewaD room
  service
khedma zātaya self-service
khesir lose
khilāl through
khoDaree greengrocer's
  (vegetable shop)
khoDār vegetables
khomsomaya five hundred
khorm hole; puncture
khoroog exit
khoSooSan especially
kifāya enough
kitāb book
kobbāya glass; mug
kobree bridge
kobs switch
kol each, every; eat
kol Hāga everything
kol Hetta everywhere

kolohom the whole lot; all of them; altogether
koloo all of it
kol wāHid everyone
konna we were
kont you were
kornaysh corniche, coastal road
korsee chair; seat; saddle (for bike)
korsee blāj deckchair
kosharee snack bar selling **kosharee**, an Egyptian rice speciality
kotshayna game
kowetsh tyre, (US) tire
kōra ball
kōrit Qadam football
kwayis good; OK, all right; fine; nice; properly
inta kwayis? are you OK? (to man)
inti kwayisa? are you OK? (to woman)

l

la' no
la'! don't!
la' lay? why not?
la' motshakkir no thanks
la' shokran no thanks
la' TabAan certainly not; of course not
laAab play
laban milk
lafHet shams sunburn
lagha cancel
lahab fire (blaze)

laHma meat
lamba lamp; lightbulb
la ... wala ... neither ... nor ...
lay? why?
layl night
laylit imbbāreH last night
laylit rās es-sana New Year's Eve
lazeez delicious
lākin but
lāzim: ana lāzim ... I must ...
le to; into
leehom for them
leh to him
leha to her
lehom to them
leHad until
leHad delwa'tee yet
lena us; for us
lesh-shamāl to the north
lesh-shimāl to the left
lewaHdee separately
lil to the
lil bayA for sale
lil egār to rent; for hire
lil khareg abroad
lil yemeen to the right
lisān tongue
logha language
logha Aarabayya Arabic
lokanda small hotel
lo'sor Luxor
low if
low samaHt/samaHtee please; excuse me (to man/woman)
lōn colour

m

ma'āss size (clothing)
maʌa with
maʌa baʌD together
maʌada except
maʌak kabreet? do you have a light? (for cigarette)
ma ʌamaltish didn't
maʌana with us
maʌandeesh: maʌandeesh khālis I don't have any
maʌassalāma goodbye
maʌād appointment
maʌāh with him
maʌāha with her
maʌāhom with them
maʌāk/maʌākee with you (to man/woman)
maʌabad temple (religious)
maʌadan metal
maʌala'a spoon
maʌala'it shī teaspoon
maʌalaysh it doesn't matter; it's a pity
maʌalomāt information
maʌ'ool reasonable
maʌ'ool? really?
maʌaraD trade fair; exhibition
maʌarafsh I don't know
maʌataqedsh I don't think so
mabaHebboosh I don't like it
mabakkallimsh ... I don't speak ...
ma'bara tomb
mablool wet
mabna building
mabrook! congratulations!
mabsooT happy
ma'dartish ... I couldn't ...; I

can't ...
madām lady; Mrs
madeena town; city
madfan cemetery (historic, Islamic)
madkhal entrance; lobby
madrasa school
mafDelshee Haga there's none left
mafeesh none; there isn't any
mafeesh ... ba'ee there's no ... left
mafeesh Had no-one, nobody
mafeesh Hāga nothing
mafeesh Haga tania nothing else
mafeesh moshkila! no problem!
ma'fool off
mafrooD innak ... you should ...
maftooH open
magalla magazine
magaree express (train)
magāl field
maghāra cave
maghrib: el maghrib Morocco
maghsala laundry (place)
magmooʌ total
magmooʌa party, group
magnoon crazy
magra stream
mahfoof crazy
mahragān festival
maHal shop
maHal ʌaSeer juice bar
maHal be'āla food shop/store
maHal hadāya gift shop
maHallee local
maHal toHaf antique shop

maHaTTa destination
maHaTTit aTr train station
maHaTTit banzeen petrol station, gas station
maHaTTit es-sekka el Hadeed railway station
maHaTTit otobees bus station; bus stop
maHboob popular
maHfaza wallet
maHroo' min esh-shams sunburnt
malbak peg (for washing)
malghool busy; engaged, occupied
makana machine
makān place
makhadda pillow; cushion
makhbaz cake shop
makhTooba engaged (to be married: woman)
maksoor broken
maktab office
maktaba bookshop, bookstore; library
maktab amanāt left luggage (office)
maktab bareed post office
maktab elbareed (elra'eesee) main post office
maktab elesti'bāl reception desk
maktab es-sayāHa tourist information office
maktab et-telfonāt 24-hour telephone office
maktab sentrāl 24-hour telephone office
maktab Sarf bureau de change

maktab tazākir ticket office
makwa iron
makwagee person who takes in laundry
mala fill up; fill in
malAab playground
malH salt
malha laylee nightclub
malyān full
mamar path
manakheer nose
manshoor leaflet; brochure
manTe'a district, area, region
manZar view; scenery
mar go through
maraD illness; disease
marham lotion; ointment
marHaban lil ... welcome to ...
markib boat; ship
markib Sayd fishing boat
markib Soghīyar dinghy
marra once
  el marra eg-gīya next time
  el marra el-lee fātit last time
  marra tania again
  marra waHda once
marrādee: el marrādee this time
marritayn twice
marwaHa fan
masak hold; catch
masā' el khayr, masā' en-noor good evening; good night
masāfa distance
masākin eT-Talaba student hostel
mashā leave
mashākil trouble
mashbak ghaseel clothes peg

mash-hoor famous

mashroob non-alcoholic drink

mas-Hoo′ ghaseel washing powder, soap powder

masraH theatre

masraHaya play (in theatre)

maSr Egypt

maSree Egyptian

maSr el adeema Old Cairo

maSr el farAoonaya Ancient Egypt

mat-Haf museum

matmannāsh I hope not

maTār airport

maTAam restaurant

maTbakh kitchen

maTlaA hill

maya hundred

ma′zana minaret

maznoo′ stuck

mazraAa farm

mazzeeka music

mazbooT accurate

mālik/malka owner (man/woman)

māris March

mās diamond

māt die

māyo May

meAaddaya ferry

meAda stomach

meAza goat

medān square (in town)

meen? who?

meena harbour; port

mesa evening

meseeHee Christian

mestaAgil express (mail)

metarrab dusty

meTala′ divorced

millawis polluted

milowwin colour

min than; of; from

min isbooA a week ago

min abl already

minayn: inta/inti minayn? where are you from? (to man/woman)

min faDlak excuse me

min ghayr without

min ghayr koHol non-alcoholic

mish not

mish awee not so much

mish delwa′tee not just now

mish fāhim I don't understand

mish kwayis bad; poor; badly

mish lāzim it's not necessary

mish maA′ool ridiculous; surprising

mish mo′addab rude

mish modhish amazing, surprising

mistaAgil urgent

mitayn two hundred

mitgowiz married

mit′kh-khar late

mīya water

mīya maAdanaya mineral water

mīya min elHanafaya tap water

mīyit dead

mīyit shorb drinking water

mlāya sheet (for bed)

mo′addab polite

mo′addam in advance

mo′assir impressive

mobāshir direct

modariss/modarissa teacher (man/woman)

modda period (of time)

modeer/modeera manager (man/woman)

modhish fantastic, incredible

moDeef/moDeefa steward; stewardess

mofaDDal favourite

mofeed useful

mofriH pleasant

moftāH key

moghray sexy

mohim important

mokalma khārigaya long-distance call

mokhaddarāt drugs (narcotics)

mokhtalif different

molā'im convenient

mo'lim painful

momil boring

momkin possible

momkin ...? may I ...?; please could you ...?; is it OK to ...?

momkin inta/inti ...? can you ...? (to man/woman)

momtāz excellent

momteA enjoyable; interesting

momyā mummy (in tomb)

monfasil separate; apart from

moolid fair

morakkaz strong (drink)

moraeb horrible

moreeH comfortable

mo'rif dreadful, revolting, disgusting

mo'rif aktar much worse

morshid (sayāHee)/morshida

(sayāHayya) tour guide (man/woman)

mosaAda help

mosallee funny, amusing

mosammim poisonous

mosaTTaH flat (adj)

moseeQa music

moseeQa afrangee pop music (Western)

moseeQa gharbaya pop music (Egyptian)

moseeQa SeAeedee folk music (in Upper Egypt)

moseeQa shaAbaya folk music

moseer exciting

moshkila problem

mostaAid ready

mostaAmal second-hand

mosta'bal future

mostaHeel impossible

mostanad document

mostashfa hospital

moSir: ana moSir I insist

motowaSSiT medium, medium-sized

motshakkir: la' motshakkir no thanks

mow'af park; rail terminus

mow'af Aarabayyāt car park, parking lot

mow'af otobees bus station

mow'af taksayāt taxi rank

mowāfi' accept; agree

mowQiA elmoAaskar campsite

mozayyaf false

mozAig annoying

mōAzam mostly

mōAzam el wa't most of the time

mōDa adeema old-fashioned, unfashionable

mōt death

mrātak your wife

mrātee my wife

mrāt ibn daughter-in-law

n

naAam yes

naAam? pardon (me)?, sorry?

naAl sole (of shoe)

nabāt plant

nabātee/nabātaya vegetarian (man/woman)

nadah call

naDDāra glasses, spectacles, (US) eyeglasses

naDDāra shamsaya sunglasses

nafa' underground, (US) subway; tunnel

nafoora fountain

nahr river

nahr en-neel Nile

naHt carving

nak-ha delicacy

nakhla palm tree

namoosa mosquito

namoozag form (document)

nasa forget

nasayt I forget, I've forgotten

nasheeT lively

nashra brochure

naTara rain

nazal get off; get out; go down

nāAim soft

nādee coffee and gaming house

nādir rare; hardly ever

nām sleep

nār (f) fire

nās people

nāshif dry (adj)

nebeet wine

neDeef clean

nehāya end

neHās aSfar brass

neseeb son-in-law; brother-in-law

neseeba daughter-in-law; sister-in-law

netlā'a baAdayn! see you later!

nimra number, figure

nimrit el kōd dialling code

nisma breeze

nī not cooked, raw

nokta joke

noor light

noS half

fee noS el-balad in town

noS ellayl midnight

fee noS ellayl in the middle of the night

noS eQāma half board

noS et-taman half-price

noS sāAa half an hour

noS tazkara half fare

nozha picnic

nōA quality; type

nōm wefTār bed and breakfast

o

oddām in front

oghnaya song

ogra fare

okht sister
oktobar October
olā (f) first
omāsh material, cloth
omm mother of
ordon: el ordon Jordan
orīyib recent
  min orīyib recently
  orīyib awee nearby
orobba Europe
orobbee European
osra malakaya dynasty
ostāz Mr
osīyar short
otobees bus
otobees el maτār airport bus
otobees safar long-distance bus
oτn cotton
oττa cat
ow or
owalan at first
owil embāriн the day before
  yesterday
owwil (m) first

Ō

ōda room
ōda lewāhid single room
ōda litnayn twin room; double
  room
ōdit es-sofra dining room

Q

Qahira: el Qahira Cairo
Qanāl canal
Qanāl es-sways Suez Canal
Qar-rar decide

Qarya village
Qānoon law
Qism department
Qīma menu
Qods: el Qods Jerusalem
Qonsolaya consulate

r

ra'aba neck
ra'aς dance
ra'āςa belly-dancer
raAee gemāl camel driver
rabb god
ra'eesee main, central
raff shelf; bunk
ragaA go back; get back;
  come back, return; give
  back
raggaA vomit
rakab get on
rakan park
ramla sand
ramz bareedee postcode, zip
  code
raQam number
raQam er-rīhla flight number
raQam telefōn phone number
rasm drawing; charge
rasm eddokhool admission
  charge
rasmee formal
rasm iʀāfee supplement
ra'ς dance
raseef platform, (US) track;
  pavement, sidewalk; jetty
ra'ς shaAbee folk dancing
ra'ς shar'ee belly-dance; belly-
  dancing

rattib arrange, fix
raTeb damp; cool
rayāDa sport
rā'eA wonderful
rāgil man
rāgil bolees policeman
rāH go; go back
rākib/rākba passenger (man/woman)
rās (f) head
reef countryside, country
reeH (f) wind
reggāla men
reHla journey; excursion, trip
reHla beg-gemāl camel trip
reHla dākhilaya domestic flight
reHla gowaya flight
reHla osīyara excursion
reHla saAeeda! have a good journey!
reHla shamla package holiday
reHla yōmaya scheduled flight; day trip
rekheeS cheap, inexpensive; low
resāla message
ri'atayn lungs
rigl (f) leg; foot
rikoob el khayl horse riding
robA quarter
robAomaya four hundred
rofiyaA thin
rokba knee
rokhSa licence
rokhSit sewā'a driving licence
rokoob eg-gimāl camel ride
romādee grey
roshetta prescription

S

sa'Aa chilled
saAeeda greetings
saAet HayT clock
sabaAtāshar seventeen
sabat basket
sabAa seven
sabAeen seventy
sa'f ceiling
safar travel; departure; journey
safar bel gimāl camel trek
safāra embassy
safeena ship (large)
sahl simple, easy
sakan live; accommodation
sakheef silly
sakrān drunk
salālim (f) stairs
sama sky
samak fish
sameen valuable
sana year
sanya second (in time)
sara' steal
saradeeb catacombs
sareeA quick, fast
satāyer blinds; curtains
sayeH tourist (man)
sā' drive
sāAa hour; wristwatch
sāAid help
sāda plain
sāHil coast
sāyib loose
seAr rate
seAr et-taHweel exchange rate
sha'a flat, apartment

shaAr hair

shabakit namosaya mosquito net

shabboora mist; fog

shad pull

shafāyef lips

shafsha' jug

shagara tree

shagh-ghal work

shahr month

shaHāt beggar

shamāl north

shamāl gharb northwest

shamāl shar' northeast

shamAa candle

shams (f) sun

shamsaya umbrella

shamsayit blāj beach umbrella

shamwā suede

shanab moustache

shanTa bag; hand luggage; briefcase

shanTit Dahr rucksack

shanTit eed handbag, (US) purse

shanTit safar suitcase

shanTit wesT money belt

shar' east

fee esh-shar' in the east

sharāb drink

shar'ee eastern

shaT shore

shaT el baHr coast

shāb young

shāf see

shākhs person

shāl carry

shāriA street

shāriA gānaybee side street

shāTer clever

shāz unusual

shebbāk window

shebbāk tazākir box office

shebsee® crisps

shedeed strong

sheek cheque, (US) check

sheek sayāHee traveller's cheque

sheesh shutter (on window)

sheta winter

fesh-sheta in the winter

shimāl left

shirāA sail

shirka company (business)

shita shower (of rain)

shī tea (drink)

shīyāl porter (in hotel)

shoAāA esh-shams sunshine

shoft/shoftee ...? have you seen ...? (to man/woman)

shoghl work ; job; business

shokran thanks, thank you

shokran gazeelan, shokran giddan thank you very much

la', shokran no, thanks

shonaT luggage, baggage

shōka fork

shwīya (a) few; a bit

shwīya shwīya gradually

sibā' gimāl camel racing

sigār cigar

sigāra cigarette

siggāda carpet

sikka alley

sikkeena knife

silmee peaceful

simeA hear

sinna tooth
sireer bed; couchette; berth
sireerayn twin beds
sireer faraDānee single bed
sireer litnayn double bed
sirg saddle (for horse)
sit woman
sitta six
sittāshar sixteen
sitteen sixty
sittoomaya six hundred
sīHa tourist (woman)
so'āl question
sobʌomaya seven hundred
sokhn hot
sokkar sugar
soo' market, bazaar
soor fence
sorya Syria
sosta zip
sowā' driver (man)
sowā'a driver (woman)
sowā' taksee taxi-driver
stella® lager

S

Saʌb hard, difficult
SabāH el khayr, SabāH en-noor
 good morning
Saboon soap
Sadafa shellfish; shell
SafeeHa can; large tin
SafeeHit ... a can of ...
SafHa page
SaH right, correct
SaHara desert; Sahara
SaHā get up
SaHba friend; girlfriend;

owner
SaHeeH? really?
SalHa valid
SallaH mend, repair
Salōn compartment (on train)
Sanaya tray
Sandoo' box
Sandoo' el bosTa letterbox,
 mailbox
Saraf spend; cash; change
Sarf change
SaT-H roof
SaTr line
Sayd samak fishing
Sayf summer
 feS-Sayf in the summer
SāHib friend; boyfriend;
 owner
Sāla lounge; foyer
Sālit el akl dining room
Sālit es-safar departure
 lounge
Sedr chest
SeHHee healthy
Sifr zero
SobaʌA finger
SobaʌA rigl toe
SobH morning
SodāʌA headache
Soghīyar small, little
Soof wool
Soora poster; painting;
 photo; picture

t

taAbān tired
ta'geer Aarabayyāt car rental
taHseen improve
taHt below; down; under
taHweed turning
taksee khidma service taxi
takyeef (howa) air-
   conditioning
talateen thirty
talat talāf three thousand
talattāshar thirteen
talāta three
ta'leed fake; imitation
talfeeAa scarf
talg ice
tallāga fridge
taman price; charge
tamaneen eighty
tamania eight
tamantāshar eighteen
tamām perfect; completely
tanda sunshade
tanee more; another; other
taQāTOA Toro' junction;
   crossroads, intersection
tarabayza table
ta'reeban almost, nearly;
   quite; approximately
tawalet ladies' (toilets),
   ladies' room
tawalet rigālee gents (toilet),
   men's room
tazkara ticket; single ticket
tazkara maftooHa open ticket
tazkara waHda single ticket
tazkarit Aowda return ticket,
   round-trip ticket

teAbān snake
teAbān kobra cobra
tebeA follow
tegāh towards
tekheen fat
temsāl statue
ti'eel heavy
timsāH alligator
tisaAtāshar nineteen
tisAa nine
tisAeen ninety
tisAomaya nine hundred
tisbaH/tisbaHee Aala khayr
   good night (to man/woman)
tizkār souvenir
toHaf antiquities
toHfa antique
toltomaya three hundred
tomnomaya eight hundred
torāb dust
tormī tram
towSeel delivery (of mail)
tsharrafna nice to meet you

T

Ta'aya hat
TaAm taste; flavour
Taba' plate; dish, bowl
Tabakh cook
TabAan certainly, of course;
   definitely
   la' TabAan certainly not; of
   course not
TabeeAee natural
Taboor queue
Taf-fa switch off
Tafīya ashtray

Talaa go up
Talab ask
TamaA greedy
Tar fly
Tard package, parcel
Taree' road; avenue; route
Tawāri' emergency
Taweel long; tall
Tayr bird
Tābea stamp
Tālib/Tāliba student (male/female)
Tāza fresh
Teaem nice
Teen mud
Teez back part; bottom (of person)
Tefl child
Tekheen thick
Tīyāra plane, airplane
Tīyib OK
Tool height; length
Tool ellayl overnight
Tool el yōm all day
Tor'a corridor
Torab cemetery
Toro' map
Towālee straightaway

W

wa and
wa'af stop
wadee valley
wadee el mlook Valley of the Kings
wadee en-neel Nile Valley
wagaA hurt; pain; ache
wagba meal

wag-ha front
wagh eblee Upper Egypt
wag-hit el baHr seafront
waHda (f) one
waHda waHda gradually
waHeed alone
wala ana nor do I
wala Haga none
wala wāHid/waHda nobody
walad boy
walla otherwise
wallaA turn on, switch on
wallāaa, wallāaet sagāyer lighter
wana? and me?, what about me?
wara behind
wara' leaf; paper; banknote
wara' el bardee papyrus
wara' Ha'iT mural
wara' tawalet toilet paper
warda flower
warshit Aarabayyāt garage (for repairs)
wasākha dirt
waSal come; arrive, get in
waSl receipt
waSla connection
waSSal deliver
wa't time
wa't Taweel a long time
wazn weight
wāDiH clear
wāHa oasis
wāHid (m) one
wāTee low
we Alaykom es-salām reply to es-salāmoo Alaykom (lit: and peace be upon you too)

we baAdayn then, after that
weddee friendly
weHesh bad; ugly; not nice; badly
  mish weHesh awee not so bad
weHesh awee ugly
wesikh filthy
wesT waist; centre
wesT el balad town centre; city centre
weSool arrival
widān ear
wikālit safar travel agent's
winta/winti? how about you?
  (to man/woman)
wish face

y

yaAnee so-so
yahoodee Jewish
yalla ... let's ...
  yalla besoraa! hurry up!
  yalla nimshee! let's go!
yanāyer January
yarHamkom allāh! bless you!
ye'khar delay
yemeen right (not left)
yeshmal include
yesmaH let (allow)
yetAash-sha have dinner
yimkin maybe; it depends
yolyo July
yonān: el yonān Greece
yonānee Greek
yonyo June
yowmayan daily
yōm day

el yōm ellee ablo the day before
el yōm ellee baAdo the day after
el yōm et-tanee the other day
yōm eg-gomAa at the weekend
yōm el arbaA Wednesday
yōm el Had Sunday
yōm el itnayn Monday
yōm el khamees Thursday
yōm es-sabt Saturday
yōm et-talāt Tuesday

z

za' push
zaAlān angry
zaHma crowded
zakee intelligent
zamān a long time ago
zamb fault
zayt oil
zāhee bright (light etc)
zār visit
zibāla bin; dustbin, trashcan; rubbish, trash
zī the same; similar
zo'a' cul-de-sac
zokām cold (illness)
zōga wife
zōr throat

Z

Zarf envelope
ZābiT bolees police officer

Arabic-English:

Signs and Notices

Contents

GENERAL SIGNS

خطر khaTar danger

خطر ممنوع اللمس khaTar mamnooA ellams dangerous, do not touch

... ممنوع mamnooA ... ... forbidden

إستعلامات isteAlamāt information

المفقودات el mafQoodāt lost property, lost and found

منطقة عسكريّة ممنوع الإقتراب أو التصوير manTe'a Aaskarayya mamnooA el eQtirāb wat-taSweer military zone, keep clear, no photography

ممنوع الإستحمام mamnooA el estiHmām no bathing

ممنوع التخييم mamnooA et-takhyeem no camping

ممنوع الدخول mamnooA ed-dekhool no entry, no admittance

ممنوع التصوير mamnooA et-taSweer no photographs

ممنوع التدخين mamnooA et-tadkheen no smoking

ممنوع السباحة mamnooA es-sibāHa no swimming

ممنوع المرور mamnooA el moroor no trespassing

ABBREVIATIONS

سم centimetres

جم grams

س hours

كجم kilograms

كم kilometres

ل litres

م metres

ملجم milligrams

ملل millitres

دق minutes

ق piastres

ج Egyptian pounds

AIRPORT, PLANES

مطار maTār airport

أوتوبيس المطار otobees el maTār airport bus

وصول wesool arrivals

مغادرة moghādara departures

رحلات دوليّة reHalāt dowlayya international departures

رحلات داخليّة reHalāt dākhilayya domestic departures

صالة الوصول Sālit el wesool arrivals hall

صالة السفر sālit es-safar
departure lounge

محطة الوصول maHaTTit el
weSool destination

الرحلة تأخرت er-reHla
ta'akharit delayed

رقم الرحلة raQam er-reHla
flight number

تفتيش الحقائب tafteesh el
HaQā'ib baggage check

أخذ الحقائب akhd el HaQā'ib
baggage claim

التسجيل والدخول
et-tasgeel wed-dokhool
check-in

بوّابة bawwāba gate

إستعلامات isteAlamāt
information

BANKS, MONEY

بنك 'bank' bank

بنك إسكندريّة 'bank'
iskinderaya Bank of
Alexandria

بنك القاهرة 'bank' el Qahira
Cairo Bank

بنك مصر 'bank' maSr Masr
Bank

البنك الأهلي المصري el
'bank' el ahlee el maSree
National Bank of Egypt

الخزينة el khazeena cashier

قسم العملة الأجنبيّة qism el
Aomla el agnabaya foreign
exchange

ثمن الشرا taman esh-sherā'
buying rate

ثمن البيع taman elbayA
selling rate

نسبة التحويل nesbit
et-taHweel exchange rate

جنيه مصري geneeh maSree
Egyptian pound

قرش irsh piastre

جنيه إسترليني geneeh
esterleenee pound sterling

دولار أمريكي dolār
amreekee US dollar

دولار كندي dolār kanadee
Canadian dollar

دولار أسترالي dolār ostrālee
Australian dollar

كريدت كارد 'credit card'
credit card

بنقبل الكريدت كارد
bne'bal el 'credit cards' we
accept credit cards

مابنقبلش الكريدت كارد
ma bne'balsh el 'credit cards'
credit cards not accepted

شيك سياحي sheek sayāHee
traveller's cheque

BUS, TRAM AND METRO TRAVEL

أوتوبيس otobees bus

باص ميني menibos minibus

موقف أوتوبيس mow'af otobees bus station

محطّة أوتوبيس maнaттit otobees bus stop

محطة maнaтta terminal

رصيف raseef ... bay no. ..., lane no. ...

وصول wesool arrivals

مغادرة moghādara departures

مخصّص لكبار السن mokhassas le kebār es-sin reserved for the elderly

مكيف mokayaf air-conditioned

تكييف takyeef air-conditioning

كشك تذاكر koshk tazākir ticket kiosk

رقم الكرسي raqam el korsee seat number

ترام 'tram' tram

تورماي toromāī tram

محطة ترام maнaттit 'tram' tram stop

مترو metroo underground, (US) subway

COUNTRIES

الجزائر el gazayir Algeria

أمريكا amreeka America

أستراليا ostrālia Australia

كندا 'Canada' Canada

مصر masr Egypt

إنجلترا ingiltera England

فرنسا faransa France

ألمانيا almāniya Germany

العراق el Arā' Iraq

إسرائيل isrā'eel Israel

الأردن el ordon Jordan

لبنان libnān Lebanon

ليبيا libya Libya

عمان Aomān Oman

فلسطين falasTeen Palestine

قطر Qatar Qatar

السعوديّة es-soaodayya Saudi Arabia

السودان es-soodān Sudan

سوريا sorya Syria

تونس toonis Tunisia

تركيا torkaya Turkey

CUSTOMS

جمارك gamārik Customs

للأجانب فقط lil agānib faQaT non-Egyptian passport holders only

للمصريين فقط lil maSrayeen faQaT Egyptian passport holders only

فى حدود المسموح fee Hodood el masmooH nothing to declare

زيادة عن المسموح zayāda Aan el masmooH something to declare

جوازات gawazāt passports

مكتب النقد الأجنبى maktab en-naQd el agnabee currency declaration office

سوق حرّة soo' Horra duty-free

EGYPTIAN HISTORY

برج القاهرة borg el Qahira Cairo Tower

القلعة el alAa Citadel

المماليك el mamaleek City of the Dead (Tombs of the Mamelukes)

كليوباترا kelobatra Cleopatra

الدير البحرى ed-dayr el baHree Hatshepsut's temple

إيزيس izees Isis

نفرتارى Nefertari Nefertari

نفرتيتى Nefertiti Nefertiti

الأهرام el ahrām The Pyramids

رمسيس ramsees Rameses

أبو الهول aboo el hōl The Sphinx

معبد أبو سمبل maAbad aboo simbil Temple of Abu Simbel

مدينة هابو madeenit haboo Temples of Rameses

وادى الملوك wadee el mlook Valley of the Kings

وادى الملكات wadee el malekāt Valley of the Queens

EMERGENCIES

إسعاف isAāf ambulance

مطافىٔ maTāfee fire brigade

بوليس bolees police

مديرية أمن moderayit amn police headquarters

قسم ... ism ... ... Police Station

بوليس المطار bolees el maTār Airport Police

شرطة السكة الحديد shorTit es-sikka el Hadeed Railway Police

البوليس النهرى el bolees en-nahree River Police

شرطة السياحة shorTit es-sayāHa Tourist Police

بوليس المرور bolees el mroor Traffic Police

محطّة إسعاف maHaTTit isAāf
first-aid post

FORMS

عنوان Ainwān address

العنوان فى مصر el Ainwān
fee maSr address in Egypt

التاريخ et-tareekh date

تاريخ الميلاد tareekh el milād
date of birth

تاريخ الصدور tareekh
eSSodoor date of issue

مدّة الإقامة moddit el iqāma
duration of stay

الإسم بالكامل el esm bil
kāmil full name

الجنسيّة el ginsaya
nationality

الوظيفة el waZeefa
occupation

رقم الباسبور raQam el basbōr
passport number

محل الميلاد maHal el milād
place of birth

جهة الصدور gehit el eSdār
place of issue

الديانة el dayāna religion

التوقيع el towQeeA signature

رقم الفيزا raQam el veeza
visa number

رقم التأشيرة raQam el
ta'sheera visa number

GEOGRAPHICAL TERMS

حدود Hedood border

قناة Qanāl canal

دلتا delta delta

صحرا saHara desert

مركز markaz district

شرق shar' east

محافظة moHafZa
adminstrative district

خليج khaleeg gulf

جزيرة gezeera island

بركة birka lake

جبل gabal mountain

شمال shimāl north

واحة wāHa oasis

راس ras point, head

مديرية moderayya province

نهر nahr river

ملاحة mallāHa salt lake

جنوب ganoob south

عين Aayn spring

وادى wadee valley

غرب gharb west

HEALTH

عيادة Aayāda clinic

دكتور/دكتورة doktōr/
doktōra doctor (m/f)

جرّاح/جرّاحة أسنان garrāH/
garrāHit asnān dentist (m/f)

مستشفى mostashfa hospital

قسم العيادة الخارجيّة Qism
el Aīyāda el khārigayya
outpatients' clinic

أجزاخانة agzakhāna
pharmacy, chemist's

صيدليّة sīdalayya pharmacy,
chemist's

HIRING, RENTING

للإيجار lil egār for hire, to
rent

عجل للإيجار Aagal lil eegār
bicycles for hire

تأجير عربيّات ta'geer
Aarabayyāt car rental

HOTELS

فندق fondo' hotel

لوكاندة lokanda small hotel

بنسيون banseeyōn boarding
house

بيت شباب bayt shabāb
youth hostel

مساكن الطلبة masākin
eT-Talaba hostel

إستراحة istirāHa resthouse

إوض فاضية ewaD faDiya
rooms to let

أوضة ōDa room

أوضة بالتكييف ōDa bil
takyeef room with
air-conditioning

أوضة لتنين ōDa litnayn
double room/twin room

أوضة لتنين ōDa litnayn
double room

أوضة لواحد ōDa le wāhid
single room

دورة الميّه dort el mīya toilet,
rest room

تكييف takyeef air-condi-
tioned; air-conditioning

حمّام Ham-mām bathroom

حمّام داخل الغرفة Ham-mām
dākhil el ghorfa en-suite
bathroom

حمّام خاص Hammām khās
private bathroom

دوش dosh shower

حوض سباحة HōD sebāHa
swimming pool

NOTICES ON DOORS

مفتوح maftooH open

مغلق moghlaQ closed

دخول dekhool entrance

خروج khoroog exit

مخرج makhrag exit

باب الطوارئ bab eT-Tawāri'
emergency exit

إسحب esHab pull

إدفع edfaA push

العطلة الأسبوعيّة el AoTla el
isbooAayya closing days

من ... إلى ... min ... ila ...
from ... to ...

مواعيد العمل mowAaeed el
Aamal opening hours

ممنوع الدخول mamnooA
ed-dikhool no entry

خاص khās private

PLACE NAMES

العبّاسية el Aabbāsayya
Abbasiya

أبو سمبل aboo simbil Abu
Simbel

إسكندريّة iskinderaya
Alexandria

أسيوط asyooT Assyut

أسوان aswān Aswan

باب زويلة bab zwayla Bab
Zuwaila

القاهرة el Qahira Cairo

دهب dahab Dahab

الفيّوم el fayyoom El Faiyum

الخارجة el kharga El Khargs

الموسكي el mooskee El

Muski

السيّدة زينب es-sayyida
zaynab El Saiyida Zeinab

إسنا esna Esna

الجيزة el geeza Giza

حلوان Helwān Helwan

الإسماعيليّة el ismaAelayya
Ismailia

الكرنك el karnak Karnak

خان الخليلي khān el
khaleelee Khan el Khalili

الأقصر loo'Sor Luxor

المنيل el manyal Manial

مرسى مطروح marsa
maTrooH Marsa Matra

المقطم el me'aTTam Mokattam

الجرنة الجديدة el gorna
e-gedeeda New Gurna

مصر القديمة maSr el adeema
Old Cairo

الجرنة القديمة el gorna el
adeema Old Gurna

بورسعيد bor saAeed Port
Said

سقّارة sa-āra Sakkara

شرم الشيخ sharm
esh-shaykh Sharm el Sheikh

سينا seena Sinai

سيوة seewa Siwa

السويس es-sways Suez

وادى حلفا wadee Halfa Wadi
Halfa

POST OFFICE

مكتب بريد maktab bareed
post office

مكتب البوسطة الرئيسى
maktab elbosTa elra'eesee
main post office

خطابات khiTābāt letters,
mail

بريد جوّى bareed gowee
airmail

مستعجل mistaAgil express

عادى Aadee ordinary

خطابات داخليّة khiTābāt
dakhilayya inland mail

خطابات خارجيّة khiTābāt
khārigayya overseas mail

بيع الطوابع bayA eT-TawābeA
stamps

RELIGION

الله allāh Allah

الله أكبر allāhoo akbar Allah
is almighty

بسم الله الرحمن الرحيم
besmillāh er-raHmān
er-raHeem in the name of
Allah most kind most
merciful

الصبر جميل es-Sabr gameel
patience is beautiful

لا إله إلا الله la ilāh illa allāh
there is no God but Allah

قبلة ibla facing Mecca

جماعة الإخوان المسلمين
gamāAit el ekhwān el
moslimeen The Muslim
Brotherhood

محمّد moHammad
Muhammad

القرآن el Qor'ān The Quran

رمضان ramaDān Ramadan

ذكر zikr religious ritual

جامع gāmiA mosque

جامع الأزهر gāmiA el az-har
Al-Azhar Mosque

مسجد الحسين mazgid el
Hosayn Al-Hussein Mosque

جامع إبن طولون gāmiA ibn
Tolōn Ibn Tulun Mosque

المتحف الإسلامى el mat-Haf
el eslāmee Islamic Museum

جامع محمّد على gāmiA
moHammad Aalee
Muhammad Ali Mosque

جامع السلطان حسن gāmiA
es-sooltān Hasan Sultan
Hasan Mosque

RESTAURANTS, CAFÉS, BARS

مطعم maTAam restaurant

حاتى Hātee kebab house

قهوة ahwa traditional coffee
house, tearoom

نادى nādee coffee and
gaming house

فطاطرى faTāTree pastry
shop

حلوانى Halawanee patisserie

كافيتيريا 'cafeteria' snack
bar

كشرى kosharee snack bar
selling kosharee, an
Egyptian rice speciality

بار 'bar' bar

كازينو kāzeno bar and tea
room, usually along the Nile

محل عصير maHal Aaseer
juice bar

STREETS AND ROADS

سكّة sikka alley

كورنيش kornaysh corniche,
coastal road

زقاق zo'ā' cul-de-sac

عطفة AaTfa lane

حارة Hāra lane, alley

طريق Taree' road

ميدان medān square

شارع shāriA street

TIMETABLES

جدول المواعيد gadwal el
mowaAeed timetable,
schedule

ميعاد الوصول meAād el
wesool arrival time

وقت القيام wa't el Qayām
departure time

ميعاد القيام meAād el Qayām
departure time

درجة daraga class

نوع القطر nōA el aTr class of
train

إكسبريس 'express' express
train

سياحى sayāHee fast train
with limited stops

مجرى magaree fast train with
limited stops

درجة أولى daraga oola first
class

درجة تانية daraga tania
second class

جهة الوصول gehat el wesool
terminates at ...

رقم القطر raQam el aTr train
number

TOILETS

للرجال lil rigāl gents' toilets, mens' rest rooms

للسيّدات lil siyedāt ladies' toilets, ladies' rest rooms

دورة الميّة dowrit el miya toilet, rest room

دورات الميّة dawrāt el miya toilets, rest rooms

حمّامات عامّة Hammāmāt Aamma public toilets

TOURIST INFORMATION

حجز تذاكر طيران وبواخر Hagz tazākir Tīyarān we bawākhir advance booking for air and sea travel

تأجير سيّارات وأوتوبيسات ta'geer siyarāt we otobeesāt car and bus rental service

رحلات يوميّة reHalat yowmayya day trips

حجز فنادق Hagz fanādi' hotel reservations

رحلات نيليّة reHalāt neelayya Nile Cruises

رحلات سياحيّة reHalāt sayaHayya package tours

TRAIN TRAVEL

محطّة قطر maHaTTit aTr railway station

حجز تذاكر ... Hagz tazākir ... advance booking for ...

إستراحة istirāHa buffet

بوفيه bofayeeh buffet

محطّة مصر maHaTTit masr Cairo Main Railway Station

هيئة سكك حديد مصر hī'it sekkak Hadeed masr Egypt Railways

درجة أولى daraga oola first class

معلومات maAloomāt information

أمانات amanāt left luggage, baggage checkroom

رصيف ... raseef ... platform no. ..., track no. ...

درجة تانية daraga tania second class

درجة تانية ممتازة daraga tania momtāza second class superior

درجة تالتة daraga talta third class

شبّاك تذاكر shebbāk tazākir ticket office

تذاكر tazākir tickets

Menu Reader:

Food

ESSENTIAL TERMS

bread Aaysh

عيش

cup fongān

فنجان

dessert Helw

حلو

excuse me (to get attention) min faDlak

من فضلك

fish (noun) samak

سمك

fork shōka

شوكة

glass (tumbler) kobbāya

كوبّاية

(wine glass) kās

كاس

knife sikkeena

سكينة

meat laHma

لحمه

menu elmenew

المنيو

pepper (spice) felfil eswid

فلفل إسود

plate Taba'

طبق

salt malH

ملح

soup shorba

شوربة

spoon maAla'a

معلقة

starter (food) fateH lil shahaya

فاتح للشهيّة

table tarabayza

ترابيزة

excuse me! (to man) low samaHt!

لو سمحت!

excuse me! (to woman) low samaHtee!

جرسونة! لو سمحتى!

could I have the bill, please? (to man/woman) momkin el fatoora, low samaHt/ samaHtee?

ممكن الفاتورةلو سمحت/ سمحتى؟

BASICS

زبدة zebda butter

سمنة samna clarified butter

قشطة ishTa cream

دقيق di'ee' flour

عسل نحل Aasal naHl honey

مربى miraba jam

لبن laban milk

عسل إسود Aasal eswid
molasses

زيت zayt oil

زيت زيتون zayt zatoon
olive oil

سكر sookkar sugar

خل khall vinegar

زبادى zabādee yoghurt

BREAD

عيش Aaysh bread

عيش فينو Aaysh feeno
baguette

صميت Simeet bread rings
covered with sesame seeds

فينو مدور feeno medowar
bread rolls

ساندوتش 'sandwich'
sandwich

عيش شامى Aaysh shāmee
white pitta bread

عيش بلدى Aaysh baladee
wholemeal pitta bread

CHEESE

جبنة gibna cheese

جبنة فلاحى gibna fallāHee
cottage cheese

جبنة رومى gibna roomee
hard, yellow, mature cheese

جبنة قديمة gibna adeema
mature gibna fallāHee

جبنة تلاجة gibna talaga
mild white cheese

جبنة مطبوخة gibna
maTbookha processed
cheese wedges

جبنة بيضة gibna bayDa
salty white cheese, similar
to feta

CONDIMENTS, HERBS, SPICES

ينسون yansoon anise

فلفل أسود filfil eswid black
pepper

حبهان Habahān cardamom

شطة shaTTa chilli

قرفة erfa cinnamon

قرنفل oronfil cloves

كزبرة kozbara coriander

كمون kamoon cumin

حلبة Helba fenugreek

كزبرة خضرة kozbara khaDra
fresh coriander

زنجبيل zangabeel ginger

نعناع neAnāA mint

بهارات boharāt mixed spice

جوزة الطيب gōzit eTTeeb nutmeg

بقدونس ba'doonis parsley

زعتر zaAter oregano

فلفل أحمر filfil aHmar paprika

زعفران zaAfaran saffron

ملح malH salt

سمسم simsim sesame seeds

تمر هندى tamr hindee tamarind

كركم korkom turmeric

COOKING METHODS

فى الفرن fel forn baked

مسلوق masloo' boiled

ديب فراى 'deep fry' deep-fried

مقلى ma'lee fried

مشوى mashwee grilled

بالزيت bi zayt in oil

مسبك mesabek simmered

بالبخار bil bokhar steamed

محشى maHshee stuffed (usually with minced meat and/or rice, herbs and pine nuts)

DESSERTS, CAKES AND BISCUITS (COOKIES)

حلويات Halawayāt sweets, desserts

كيكة keeka cake

بسكوت baskōt biscuits, cookies

بقلاوة be'lāwa baklava – layers of flaky filo pastry and nuts, soaked in syrup

جلاش goolāsh baklava

كحك kaHk biscuits made with flour and butter and covered in icing sugar

خشاف khoshaf dried fruit soaked in milk or syrup (eaten during Ramadan)

زلابية zalabya fritters soaked in syrup

سلطة فواكه salaTit fowākih fruit salad

أم على oom Aali hot pudding made from filo pastry soaked in milk with raisins, sugar, coconut, nuts and cinnamon

أيس كريم 'ice cream' ice cream

جيلاتى Jelāti ice cream

بليلة bleela milk pudding with nuts, raisins and wheat

مهلبية mahalabaya milk pudding with rice, cornflour and rosewater, topped with pistachios

بالوظة balōza pudding made from cornflour, ground rice and sugar

مشمشية meshmeshia pudding made from cooked dried apricots and cornflour

ارز باللبن roz bil laban rice pudding

بسبوسة basboosa semolina cake with nuts, soaked in syrup

كنافة konāfa sticky noodle-like pastry with nuts and syrup

قطايف aTayef thick pancake filled with nuts and coconut and soaked in syrup

فطير feTeer type of pancake made from layers of flaky pastry with sweet or savoury fillings

EGGS AND EGG DISHES

بيض bayD eggs

أطباق البيض aTbā' el bayD egg dishes

عجّة ʌega baked omelette with onions, parsley and flour

بيض مسلوق bayD masloo' boiled eggs

بيض مقلى bayD ma'lee fried eggs

أومليت 'omelette' omelette

بيض بكبدة فراخ bayD bi kibdit frākh scrambled eggs with chopped chicken liver

شكشوكة shakshooka scrambled eggs with minced beef

بيض ببسطرمة bayD bi basTerma scrambled eggs with spicy cold meat

FISH AND FISH DISHES

سمك samak fish

طاجن سمك Tāgin samak baked fish with rice or cracked wheat

كابوريا kaboria crab

قراميط arameeT eel

ثعابين taʌabeen eel

ترانشات taranshāt fillets

سمك مقلى samak ma'lee fish fried in oil

سمك مشوى samak mashwi grilled fish

إستاكوزا stakosa lobsters

بوری boree mullet

إخطبوط ekhTaboot octopus

طاجن جمبری Tāgin gambaree potted shrimps

جمبری gambaree prawns; shrimps

رز بالجمبری roz bi gambaree prawns and rice

فسيخ feseekh salted fish

سردين 'sardine' sardines

رنجة ringa smoked herring

كلماري kalamari squid

سبيط Sobayt squid

مرجان morgan type of flat fish

بلطی bolTee type of freshwater fish similar to bream

FRUIT

فواكه fowākih fruit

تفاح toffāH apples

مشمش mishmish apricots

موز mōz bananas

قشطة eshTa custard apple

بلح balaH dates

تين teen figs

تين شوكی teen shōki Indian fig

عنب Aenab large, sweet grapes

عنب بناتی Aenab banātee

small, seedless grapes

جوافة gawāfa guava

ليمون lamoon lemons; limes

منجة manga mango

شمام shammām melon

توت toot mulberries

برتقال بصرة borto'ān biSora navel oranges

برتقال borto'ān oranges

خوخ khōkh peaches

كمثری komitra pears

أناناس ananās pineapple

برقوق bar'oo' plums

رمان rommān pomegran-ates

سفندی safandee satsumas

فراولة farowla strawberries

بطيخ baTeekh watermelon

MEAT AND MEAT DISHES

لحمة laHma meat

لحمة بقری laHma ba'aree beef

لحمة بقری كندوز laHma kandooz braised beef

فراخ frākh chicken; grilled or stewed chicken, served with vegetables

شكشوكة shakshooka chopped meat and tomato sauce with an egg on top

كباب kabab chunks of

meat, usually lamb, grilled with onions and tomatoes

بط baT duck

وز wizz goose

حمام مشوى Hamām mashwi grilled pigeon

نص فرخة مشوية nos farkha mashwaya half a grilled chicken

كلاوى kalāwi kidney

لحمة ضانى laHma Dānee lamb; mutton

كبدة kibda liver

كفتة kofta minced meat flavoured with spices and onions, grilled on a skewer

شيش كباب وكفتة sheesh kabab wi kofta minced meat flavoured with spices and onions, grilled on a skewer

طرلى Torlee mixed vegetable casserole with chunks of lamb or beef

حمام Hamām pigeon

طاجن حمام Tāgin Hamām pigeon in a Tāgin, stewed with onions, tomatoes and rice in an earthenware pot

أرانب arānib rabbit

مخ mokh brains

سحق sogo' sausages

لحم فيليه laHma felay

sirloin steak

شاورما showerma slices of spit-roast lamb, served in pitta bread

بتللو laHma btelloo veal

كوارع kawareA sheep's trotters

لحمة قوزى laHma oozee spring lamb

رياش rayash T-bone steak

حمام محشى Hamām maHshee stuffed pigeon

ديك رومى deek roomee turkey

إسكالوب بتللو 'escalope' bi telloo veal escalope

MENU TERMS

منيو 'menu' menu

لستة lista menu

مشروبات mashrobat drinks

أطباق البيض aTbā'el bayD egg dishes

مشويات mashwayat grills

أطباق شرقية aTbā' shar'aya oriental dishes

نشويات nashowayat rice, pasta and potatoes

أنواع الشورية anwaA e-shorba soups

حلويات Halawayat sweets, desserts

مقبلات moqabbilāt starter

مشهيات moshahyāt side
dishes

NUTS, SEEDS ETC

لوز lōz almonds

جوزهند gōz hind coconut

بندق bondo' hazelnuts

فول سوداني fool soodanee
peanuts

فزدق fozdo' pistachio nuts

حمص Hommos roasted
chickpeas, sugar-coated or
dried and salted

لب lib roasted seeds
(melon, sunflower etc)

عين جمل Aayn gamal
walnuts

PULSES, GRAINS AND
PASTA

لوبيا lobia black-eyed
beans

فول مدمس fool midamis
brown Egyptian beans,
similar to broad/fava beans

فول fool brown Egyptian
beans, usually served with
oil and lemon, sometimes
also with onions, meat, eggs
or tomato sauce

حمص Hommos chickpeas;

houmous

فلافل falāfel deep-fried
balls of spicy brown bean
purée

طعمية TaAmaya deep-fried
balls of spicy brown bean
purée

عدس بجبة Aads bigebba
green lentils

فاصوليا faSolia haricot
beans

عدس Aads lentils

عدس أصفر Aads aSfar red
lentils

فريك freek cracked wheat,
bulgur wheat

أرز roz rice

كشرى kosharee rice,
lentils, noodles and onions
with a spicy tomato sauce

أرز بشعرية roz be sheAraya
rice with noodles

مكرونة makarōna macaroni

مكرونة بالبشامل
makarōna bel bashamil pasta
baked in bechamel sauce,
similar to lasagne

مكرونة عيدان makarōna
Aīdan spaghetti

شعرية shaAraya vermicelli

SOUPS

شوربة shorba soup

أنواع الشورية anwāa
e-shorba soups

شوربة فراخ shorbit frākh
chicken soup

شوربة عدس shorbit Aads
lentil soup

شوربة لحمة shorbit laHma
meat soup

ملوخية molokhaya soup
made from Jew's mallow
(similar to spinach) with
meat or chicken broth and
garlic

فتة fatta soup made from
meat stock with bread, rice
and tomato, sometimes with
fried garlic and vinegar

شوربة طماطم shorbit
TamaTem tomato soup

شوربة خضار shorbit khoDār
vegetable soup

STARTERS (APPETIZERS), SNACKS, SIDE DISHES AND SALADS

بابا غنوج baba ghan-noog
aubergine/eggplant purée
with sesame-seed paste

حمص Hommos chickpeas;
houmous

تبولة taboola cracked
wheat and tomato salad with
onion and parsley

سلاطة زبادى salaTit zabādi
cucumber and yogurt salad

طعمية TaAmaya deep-fried
balls of spicy bean purée

فول مدمس fool midamis
Egyptian brown bean purée

سلاطة خضرة salāTa khaDra
green salad

بدنجان مخلل bidingān
mikhallil marinated
aubergine/eggplant

سلاطة شرقى salāTa shar'ee
mixed vegetable and onion
salad

سلاطة salāTa salad

طحينة TeHeena sesame-
seed paste mixed with
spices, garlic and lemon,
eaten with pitta bread

سلاطة بيضة salāTa bayDa
spiced yoghurt with herbs

سلاطة طماطم salaTit
TamāTim tomato salad

جبنة بيضة بالطماطم
gibna bayDa bi TamāTim
white cheese and tomato
salad

ورق عنب wara' Aenab vine
leaves stuffed with minced
meat and/or rice, herbs and

pine nuts and flavoured with
lemon juice

طرشى Torshi pickles

VEGETABLE DISHES

بدنجان محشى bidingān
maHshee stuffed aubergine/
eggplant

كرنب محشى koromb
maHshee stuffed cabbage

كوسة محشية kosa
maHshaya stuffed cour-
gettes/zucchinis

فلفل محشى filfil maHshee
stuffed peppers

بطاطس محشية baTāTis
maHshaya stuffed potatoes

طاجن خضار Tāgin khoDār
vegetables baked with
tomatoes

VEGETABLES

خضار khoDār vegetables

خرشوف kharshoof
artichokes

بدنجان bidingān auber-
gines, eggplants

فول حراتى fool Herātee
broad beans

كرنب koromb cabbage

جزر gazar carrots

قرنبيط arnabeeT cauli-
flower

فلفل حامى filfil Hāmee
chillies

كوسة kosa courgettes,
zucchinis

قتة atta large cucumber

خيار khiyār small cucumber

ثوم tōm garlic

فاصوليا faSolia green
beans

فلفل أخضر filfil akhDar
green peppers

فلفل أحمر filfil aHmar
paprika; red peppers

خس khass lettuce

بامية bamya okra

بصل baSal onions

بسلة bisilla peas

بطاطس baTāTis potatoes

سبانخ sabānekh spinach
beet

بصل أخضر baSal akhDar
spring onions, scallions

ذرة dora sweet corn, maize

بطاطا baTāTā sweet
potatoes

طماطم Tamātim tomatoes

لفت lift turnips

ورق عنب wara' Aenab vine
leaves

جرجير gargir watercress

فجل figl white radish